Missouri Harvest

Missouri Harvest

A Guide to Growers and Producers in the Show-Me State

Maddie Earnest & Liz Fathman

REEDY PRESS
St. Louis, Missouri

Webster
UNIVERSITY
Press

Published by

Webster University Press
c/o Webster University Library
470 East Lockwood Avenue
St. Louis, MO 63119-3194

Reedy Press
PO Box 5131
St. Louis, MO 63139
www.reedypress.com

Library of Congress Control Number: 2012933957

ISBN: 978-1-935806-25-7

Please visit our website at www.Missouri-Harvest.com.

Photographs and recipes in this book are used with permission by the credited farms and companies.

Design and cover photography by Alvin Zamudio

Printed in the United States of America
12 13 14 15 16   5 4 3 2 1

Contents

Acknowledgments — vii

Map of Missouri's Regions — ix

Foreword, by Joel Salatin — xi

Introduction — xv

Veggies, Grains, & Beans — 3

Fruits — 59

Meats — 95

Dairy — 147

Nuts & Honey — 167

Recipes & Tips — 197

Finding Missouri Products — 221

Afterword, by Lori Diefenbacher — 267

Index — 270

Acknowledgments

As the co-founder and co-owner of Local Harvest Grocery and Café, Maddie's interest in local foods stems back to the family gardens of her youth and courses at Hendrix College which sparked an interest in farming and knowing your food. While she loves to eat goat cheese, sheep cheese, grass-fed beef, organic popcorn, and occasionally grows her own food, she doesn't consider herself a foodie. She would love to thank her parents, Hugh and Susan, for making her pick okra and haul railroad ties and loads of dirt. Much gratitude to all the farmers in Missouri and especially for the time they gave to provide answers and information for the book. And of course many thanks to her patient husband, Jason, her son, Beck, and friends who listened to her rattle on endlessly about topics like no-till farming and chestnuts. Lastly, Maddie thanks her understanding staff who picked up the slack while she worked on the book.

A food enthusiast and anthropologist, Liz has an interest in local food systems and all they imply. From the sustainability of growing and buying locally raised food, to the difference in the flavor and quality, to the act of supporting the local economy, Liz's interest in the Farm-to-Table Movement has, like that of many others, developed along the way. She has learned a lot about the importance of local foods and food growing methods from authors Michael Pollan and Mark Bittman and farmer and author Joel Salatin, and sends thanks to the farmers of Missouri for growing all this good stuff, the store owners for stocking it, and the chefs for preparing it. She owes a debt of gratitude to her parents, Melanie and Tony, who cultivated her love of nature, and her husband, Paul, her gardening, foraging, cooking, and eating partner. A special thanks goes out to Jon Andelson at Grinnell College, whose course on human adaptation and ecology was Liz's first encounter with a serious study of the ways humans eat.

Map of Missouri's regions

Map

ix

Tower Grove Farmer's Market, photo by Sara A. Finke

Foreword

"What can I do to change America's food and farming system?"
The question pops up nearly every time I present a talk. Whether the venue is a
university campus, urban foodie group, or sustainable agriculture gathering, it's a
universal request.

I'm fascinated by the apparent stranglehold that the current industrial-
mechanical system has on people. Even those who know something is wrong with
factory farming and shipping food an average 1,500 miles from field to fork seem
stymied about actually changing things. It's such an entrenched, monstrous system,
after all. How do you change such a thing?

Unfortunately, human nature tends to thrive on self-pity and victimhood.
People generally feel powerless to change the agri-industrial complex, global food
processors, and aggregators. They are too big. They control the politicians. They own
the banks. Oh, what are we to do?

Into that hand-wringing steps *Missouri Harvest*, an ultimately empowering and enlightening guide to facilitate action from eaters who want to change things. The sheer variety of locally available products shows that participating in the local healing food system is not arduous. Missouri, like most areas, can and does produce a cornucopia of raw and processed foods.

Participating in the local food economy does not require a life of ascetic sacrifice. It is, instead, like a grand treasure hunt, finding the food and farming gems imbedded in every region. Anyone who thinks the pleasure of meeting Mickey Mouse at Disney is better than discovering succulent juicy apples has never visited the farm and enjoyed the romance of discovering this dinner dance partner.

Most Americans have not courted their dinner dance partners for a long time. Accustomed to a supermarket box of processed microwave-ready material containing unpronounceable ingredients, most eaters' visceral food relationship perished with TV dinners. More and more people realize that an integrity food system requires dancing, courting, flirting with dinner. But they don't know where this food partner lives.

Thanks to Maddie Earnest and Liz Fathman's work, Missourians now have the address book for their dinner dance partners. The food and farmers are waiting for people who care about their health, their local economies, humane animal treatment, and landscape healing to show up for the dance.

Is it too much trouble? Not at all. The kind of food and farming system Missouri has today is the result of decisions people have made for several decades. What's on our plates is a painting, or sculpture, visibly representing what we value. Take a look at it. Does it represent healthy earthworms? Healthy rural economies? Thriving diversified decentralized family farms?

Or does this dance partner on our plate represent factory farming, routine drugging, and food foreign to our bodies? *Missouri Harvest* is full of food possibilities that offer an antidote to the fears and shortfalls of industrial fare. I wish every state had one of these guides.

As a farmer, I'm struck by how many of these entries indicate a fledgling enterprise desperate for customers. Many of the farmers listed in this book yearn to leave their "town jobs" and focus full time on their farms. A few more customers can make that possible. Although each of these listings is necessarily short and pithy, I assure you that a whole book could be written about each one. These farms and the people who run them are fascinating.

Patronizing them instead of the faceless global-industrial system yields rich information and historical-geographic identity. Some of these farms have been around a long time and are now into their second generation of patrons. Others are just entering the exciting world of direct marketing and value adding. You, as reader, will help write their stories. Your participation in their landscapes, the work of their hands, the vision of their souls, will ultimately create their success and struggles.

Enjoying the earth's bounty, coaxed by their gifts from soil, air, and water, does not require a government policy change, a tax incentive, or a new bureaucracy. We can all participate in this food relationship every time we eat.

What can I do? What can you do? We can join these integrity food producers who massage the Missouri landscape. In doing so, we can participate in an historic dinner dance, building a relationship with our food and the precious resources—both human and ecological—that build flesh of our flesh and bone of our bone. Herein lie some wonderful partners. Let the dance begin.

Joel Salatin
Polyface Farm
February 2012

Tower Grove Farmer's Market, photo by Sara A. Finke

SUPPORT YOUR FARMERS' MARKET
Become a _____ Today

CHOCOLATE
HONEY STIX
25¢
5 for $1.00

Eggplant
3.00 lb.

Introduction

From Local to Global: How Did We Get Here?

How many times have you walked into a supermarket? Countless. And when you do, it is easy to take for granted the vast quantity and variety of foods available there, in some cases twenty-four hours a day. Pull out a shopping cart and begin wheeling it down the aisles of produce, piled high with lettuce, tomatoes, onions, peppers, potatoes, corn, bananas, mangoes, and dozens of varieties of citrus fruit, berries, apples, pears, and more. We take it as a given that there are deep red tomatoes stacked like billiard balls in November and ignore the irony that there are only a handful of fruits and vegetables many people even associate with a season, like asparagus, corn on the cob, and watermelon (even though they are all available year-round).

We fail to consider that mangoes, avocados, bananas, and many other fruits and vegetables would or could never be grown in Missouri. Instead, we check our list, choose the best-looking bunch of radishes, broccoli, scallions, and carrots (possibly even choosing organic, if available), and head to the meat department. There we find ground turkey, chicken tenders, pork steaks, and a rump roast, all neatly packaged and ready to cook—sometimes with helpful recipes or, in the case of some Thanksgiving turkeys, with a built-in thermometer! After we put our meat in our cart, we head to the dairy section, where milk, eggs, cheese, butter, yogurt, and sour cream are stocked like building blocks.

Feeling pretty proud that we have shopped the perimeter, where the "healthy" foods are, we venture into the interior for staples like rice, peanut butter, cereal, coffee, and tea, and maybe some snacks like cookies, crackers, and chips. Every trip to the supermarket is different yet similar: different in that the vast array of choices excites us into trying new products; similar in that the supermarket is never out of what we are looking for, be it watermelon in winter or apple cider in the spring.

The modern supermarket has taken much of the seasonality out of shopping and eating. Once, not that long ago, people ate fresh what was in season and ate canned what was not. Maybe they did the canning themselves, or maybe they bought canned goods at the store. But with the growth of the supermarket and agricultural practices that went along with it, distribution chains and long growing periods in warmer climates have given the United States year-round access to any and all kinds of foods that a generation ago was unheard of.

How did we get to the point of expecting all our favorite foods to be available 24/7, 365 days a year? When did we find ourselves with so much inexpensive and plentiful food? What happened to our relationship with the food growers and producers? People have always had to eat, but what changes have led us from our origins as nomadic scavenger-hunter-gatherers eating what was available to us then and there to modern supermarket trollers looking for the next new food trend?

The Journey from There to Here: A Brief History of Agriculture

Agriculture, as it relates to food, has been around for a long, long time (since the Neolithic revolution, approximately 10,000 years ago), and for much of that time it consisted mostly of cereal/grain crops with other indigenous fruits, vegetables, and tubers. Agriculture is commonly defined as the deliberate cultivation and breeding of crops and livestock to produce more or bigger yields, and it uses methods and techniques that extend beyond the individual's capacity or ability, such as irrigation, assisted labor as in draft animals and (later) tractors, and plows. Over time, the techniques improved, crops yielded more, and people began specializing in growing single crops (a practice we now refer to as monocropping), sometimes rotating the crops from year to year.

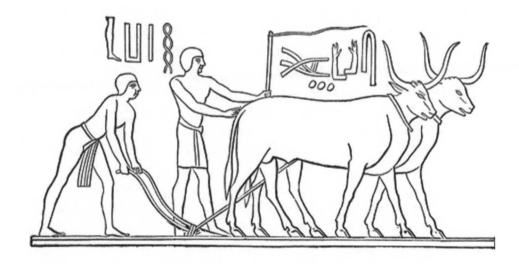

Agriculture also led to the rise of settled human populations (as opposed to nomadic) and increases in population size. But because growing techniques and crop varieties were so productive, fewer people were needed to grow the food for everyone in the settlement. Subsequently, whole classes of non-farming specialists such as the military, clerics, artisans, and others arose. Large crop yields also resulted in surpluses that could not only be stored and later used for future planting, but also could be used for payment to rulers and others as tax or tribute. Surplus crops could be used as trade items or as insurance against future crop failure or other disasters. Although we credit agriculture with giving rise to the development of civilization, much of its history is about subsistence agriculture. People ate what they grew, and although the crop yields were higher, the surpluses were easily used up as seed, tax, or tribute. People usually didn't or couldn't travel far, and trade of surplus crops and livestock was often some form of barter.

The age of European global exploration (starting in the fifteenth century) opened up trade routes for the transportation of non-domestic crops across the seas. New agricultural products were introduced and traded between the Old and New Worlds. Potatoes, tomatoes, tobacco, maize (corn), and cocoa were transported from the New World (Western Hemisphere) to the Old World (Eastern Hemisphere). Wheat, coffee, sugar cane, and other spices were transported from the Old World to the New. Interestingly, a lot of imported crops have become staples in their "new" homes (potatoes in Northern Europe, tomatoes in Southern Europe, manioc in North Africa, sugar in the Caribbean, coffee in South and Central America, etc.). Some of those transitions happened so long ago that it's as if those crops had always been a part of the local food scene.

The Industrial Revolution not only made agricultural practices much easier, but it also opened up many other occupational opportunities to people who otherwise would have farmed. Farming became a specialized occupation, with a middleman added to the "farm-to-table" relationship. Merchants were able to sell the products of the farm in distant markets that were inaccessible to the local farmers. Fewer people working to feed more of the population once again went hand in hand with increased productivity, but at environmental, socio-economic, political, and health/physiological costs.

Partly as a result of these costs, there is a long parallel strand of anti-industrial farming that has co-existed with the rise of large-scale farming. The progression of agricultural practice, described above, has not been linear or without its detractors. Some detractors claim industrial farming harms the earth by disrupting the balance of soils and nutrients. Others contend that monocrops or limited crops are more likely to introduce diseases and contribute to malnutrition because of a lack of variety in the diet. An issue central to farming in the Midwest is that commodity crops (corn, soybeans, and a few others) can have limited value as a food source. Another concern is the perception that we lack a connection between food as it is grown and as it is eaten, that we eat foods out of season, and that there is too much packaging and processing of our foods, sometimes to the point that it no longer looks like food. All of these concerns, alone and together, have led a lot of people to look for alternatives to the supermarket approach to buying and eating food. People are growing more of their own food and are increasingly seeking local sources of food and learning to appreciate the seasons through the different foods that are available over the course of a year. Missouri is as good a place as any— maybe better—to relearn the connection between food and place, food and season, and food and grower. Although it may take more effort than it used to, this book will help you make the most of what Missouri has to offer to anyone interested in eating more locally grown food.

Missouri Agriculture: An Overview

The Midwest is the agricultural center of our country—the nation's breadbasket. The region brings to mind images of cornfields, wheat, and placidly grazing cattle tended to by multigenerational farm families. But what these images evoke is a time and lifestyle that exists now more in the minds of authors, historians, and Hollywood producers. Large agricultural businesses that practice industrial agriculture coupled with farm policies that favor them have left what used to be hundreds of small family farms in the hands of fewer and fewer agribusinesses.

Despite this trend, you might be surprised to learn that Missouri is second only to Texas when it comes to the number of individual farms. In 2010, Missouri had more than 108,000 farms and 29 million acres of farmland. Agriculture is the number-one industry in Missouri, according to the Missouri Department of Economic Development. Missouri employs 298,320 workers in farms and agribusinesses. This is a pretty good number for an industry that has been on the decline since World War II. In the past forty years or so, the numbers have leveled off and have shown a small increase (4 percent) from 2002 to 2007.

The USDA defines a farm as any place from which $1,000 or more of agricultural products were, or normally would be, produced and sold during the census year. The percentage of Missouri farms selling agricultural products valued between $1,000 and $2,499 was 8.2 percent. Small farming operations account for most of the growth in the number of farms in the United States. New farms on average tend to be smaller, and most of their sales do not come from commodity sales. Census data also shows that younger people are responsible for many of the new farms reported.

Farm to Table

Although the small family farm where a farmer can make a living solely from his or her land has become the exception, the growing interest in fresh food and knowledge of the origin of the meal has put the family farm back in the spotlight. This is encouraging in a country where, according to the USDA, large (sales over $250,000) and very large (sales over $500,000) family farms make up only 9 percent of all farms but produce more than 63 percent of the value of all agricultural products sold. As small business is currently seen by many as the future of economic growth, could we tell a similar story about small farms? That remains to be seen.

Like many large and successful corporations in the United States, industrial agriculture is built on a model that maximizes efficiency; centralizes decision making; is profit-driven, modernized, and mechanized; and operates on a massive scale. In the farm business, industrial agriculture has the capacity to feed many people cheaply and independent of some of the factors that might ruin a small farmer. The last fifty years have given us rapid growth in agricultural output. Grocery shoppers in Missouri, as in the rest of the country, have grown accustomed to finding a seemingly endless variety of products at relatively low prices. Despite this explosion in productivity, however, according to the authors of *Hungry for Profit: The Agribusiness Threat to Farmers, Food, and the Environment*, the percentage of money spent on food that goes to farmers in our current system of supermarkets and mega-stores has dropped from around 40 percent in the early twentieth century to less than 10 percent today.

That's a big cut for the middlemen. The food chain has grown in proportion to the agricultural output, adding brokers, distributors, wholesalers, merchandisers, retailers, and others to the equation, so that what used to be a simple trip from farm to table now traverses miles and miles of land and sea and passes through many hands to wind up on your table. Ironically, one of those hardest hit by this change in distribution methods is the one who actually grows the food. One way to reverse that trend is to buy food from someone who grows it close to your home.

Missouri's Farms to Your Table

The products grown in Missouri are quite varied. You won't find orange or lemon groves, but you will find elderberries, peaches, blackberries as big as a half dollar, and some of the best pork in the country. You will find heirloom tomatoes, award-winning cheeses, and trout that is so tender and flavorful it will be your go-to meal again and again. And in the southern regions, you will discover fantastic rice packaged in canvas bags as if ready for the general store. In a state where soybeans and corn are the top commodity crops, you will discover much more, uncovering the bounty of the Missouri Harvest.

Missouri Harvest will take you on a tour of farms throughout the state where the farmers are engaged in a close relationship with the land and with the animals they are raising. You will have a snapshot of the farmers who make up the majority of the 108,000 farms across this state. Some have been farming their land for more than a hundred years and others are new to the industry and are paving a path for other young farmers.

As we take you through the state we want you to be familiar with the terms used to describe the farms and some of the farming methods. Most people are familiar with or have at least heard the term "organic" when referring to food. Other terms, such as "biodynamic farming," may not be as familiar. Throughout the book, we will refer to other terms that may or may not be familiar, but we'd like to start with some of the basics.

Organic food has gained a foothold, and in 2007 the Census of Agriculture, acknowledging this growth, conducted its first in-depth survey of organic farmers in the United States. Many farmers in this book are using organic farming methods but may not be Certified Organic. Around 2 percent of farms in Missouri are considered organic—and growing in number and popularity. The USDA has guidelines for farmers and an application process for organic certification as part of its National Organic Program (NOP). To understand the term "organic," it is easiest to lay out the basic tenets of organic farming and food production.

Organic farmers do not use chemical fertilizers or pesticides and do not use synthetic drugs such as growth hormones and antibiotics with animals (unless the animal is ill); they do not use genetically modified seeds; they use strict practices to build the soil and prevent soil loss and erosion; and they support a range of crops and not one single species when planting and planning. Organic farmers and those using sustainable farming practices often rotate crops from year to year in order to avoid soil depletion. And farmers with animals and vegetable crops will often rotate the crops with the animal grazing and roaming areas to promote natural fertilization of the soil.

The recent designation "Certified Naturally Grown" is an alternative to the USDA's organic certification. It is targeted primarily at small farmers distributing through local channels: farmers' markets, roadside stands, local restaurants, community supported agriculture (CSA) programs, and small local grocery stores. Designation as a Certified Naturally Grown product is comparable to designation as Certified Organic, but at a lower cost to the farmer. The program is run by farmers for farmers; indeed, farmers in the program inspect one another's farms and must agree to perform at least one annual inspection of another participating farm themselves.

"Biodynamic farming" is a newer term to Missouri. Developed in the 1920s by Rudolf Steiner, biodynamic farming shares many of the tenets of organic farming. It differs, however, in that proponents of this method use unique and specific preparations for the compost and soil enhancement. They often involve herbal and mineral additives and sprays. Farmers also plant according to an astronomical sowing and planting calendar. Biodynamic farming was founded on the idea that the farm as a whole is an integrated and self-contained entity with its own unique identity. All parts of the farm are considered in determining and maintaining the health of the farm—even the farmer. Biodynamic practices involve recycling of nutrients, integrating animals and crops, and obviously maintaining the soil.

Many people are confused by the terms "cage-free" and "free-range." These terms are used in reference to egg-laying hens and how they are raised. Cage-free usually means that the chickens are free to roam within a building or large shed. This does not mean they have regular or any access to outdoors, and often they can be tightly packed into a small space. Free-range usually means that hens are able to roam outside. Many farmers who have free-range hens do use some containment to keep them safe. These often involve adjustable fencing, which is moved daily to allow hens to go to new areas. Sometimes the hens are put into barns at night to protect them from coyotes and other predators.

"Pasture-raised" animals graze outdoors in their natural environment, eating grasses and other plants that make up their natural diet. Not only does raising animals in the pasture improve the welfare of farm animals, but it also helps reduce environmental damage by reducing the need to produce feed and to construct the large-scale operations that are home to most grain-fed animals. Finally, studies suggest that pasture-raised meat, eggs, and dairy products are tastier and more nutritious than foods produced on factory farms.

Another familiar expression is "farm-to-table" or "farm-to-fork." These interchangeable expressions are often defined as a movement and are tied to the production and consumption of local foods, although some would reasonably argue that the term has been turned into a marketing phrase meant to capitalize on the increased interest in eating "healthier" food. Another term, "locavore," also describes the practice of buying, cooking, and eating locally raised and produced foods. The terms are most often found in the agriculture, food service, and restaurant communities. As is true of most of the operations described in this book, they are often linked to organic farming, sustainable agriculture, and community-supported agriculture. But is it a movement? Or is it a response? And if so, to what?

The People Involved

The Farm-to-Table Movement consists of three groups of people: food producers, purveyors, and consumers. Food producers include the farmers/growers (plant-based agriculture), the herders/ranchers (animal-based agriculture), community and urban gardeners, and the processors (who do some of the canning, pickling, butchering, etc.). In many cases these roles overlap and/or are performed by the same person, which is not true of large-scale agricultural operations.

The purveyors are the retailers, or places where farm products are sold or distributed, including stores (even some supermarkets have embraced the local food movement), farmers' markets, CSAs and similar subscription services, pick-your-own (commonly called "u-pick") operations, and chefs/restaurants.

Because this book is about the producers and purveyors, their stories are featured throughout. However, without the third group of people—the consumers—this farm-to-table cycle would be incomplete. Consumers are drawn to the Farm-to-Table Movement for different reasons, although in many cases, those reasons converge and overlap, as people who choose to eat locally learn and value more reasons than those that initially drew them in. Some are interested in the health benefits of eating locally sourced foods. They may be vegans, vegetarians, or raw food devotees. Others may be more concerned with food safety, an absence of additives, and so on, believing that food should be in its natural state.

One such person is a recently "converted" vegan named Chris. Chris grew up in Springfield, Missouri, and attended college in St. Louis. Shortly after graduating, he began paying more attention to his diet and the way food made him feel physically. He wanted to lose weight, so he gave up his car and began riding his bike and looked for ways to change his diet. Gradually at first, Chris began eliminating red meat, then poultry, then all meat. Ultimately, he turned to a pure vegan diet that went beyond his physical well-being and grew to encompass a respect for the earth and a desire to live harmoniously with it. When asked about the meaning of farm-to-table, Chris responded that, to him, it is "a local, sustainable, organic movement. None of those words is more important than another, but all three combine to make farm-to-table what it is for me." He sees a correlation between organic growing methods and sustainability both in terms of the careful stewardship of natural resources and our ability to sustain ourselves physically and spiritually. "Through farm-to-table, we allow for both a respect of life and better health for the environment and our bodies."

Chris's experience with the Farm-to-Table Movement is similar to others' in that his initial reason for choosing to eat locally grown food—health—soon transformed into several reasons. What began as a weight-loss diet has become a way of life for him.

Another type of consumer is the "foodie." These folks are passionate about fresh and seasonal foods. They often relish the small batch, the rare, the heirloom, and the exquisite. Some members of Slow Food St. Louis exemplify locavores whose entry into this "movement" was through the stomach. Kimberly, Kelly, and Bill share an interest in the conviviality that sharing a well-prepared meal can inspire. All three have been involved with Slow Food St. Louis for over five years and are now the co-leaders of this chapter of the group. Slow Food is an international organization that promotes fresh, local, and sustainably produced food. It also advocates for the preservation of food traditions and communal dining. Although they all got involved for slightly different reasons, they now share a common commitment to eating locally raised foods for a number of reasons. First, it tastes better and is fresher than food that travels hundreds or thousands of miles. Also, through their small grant programs for local farmers, they can offer financing to encourage farmers to grow heirloom or heritage varieties of produce and livestock. Not only do they enjoy the variety of foods and flavors, but this also preserves older food ways as well as biodiversity, both of which are common goals of the Slow Food Movement.

Another big draw for these three leaders is the chance to get to know the farmers who grow the food, whether at the farmers' market or through the small grant program. As Kelly points out, consumers have become so accustomed to trusting foods in supermarkets because they are produced by corporations, and we trust that those corporations would not harm us. "It's a name brand; we can trust it!" But, she reasons, corporations are not people you see every week, or get to know by doing business with them one-on-one. There are always intermediaries between you and the food in the supermarket model, which is not true when you buy food straight from a local producer. This relationship builds trust. The farmers know they must supply good products or shoppers will not buy them. The shoppers know their purchases support the farmers' efforts to continue to grow good food. The transactions are direct and immediate, and mutual trust to hold up the "bargain" underlies it all. To these Slow Food leaders, this trust is the foundation on which their movement is built. Creating and sustaining community is a core value, whether between buyer and producer, or among members of the organization coming together to eat and share their love of food and good company.

Consumers with political or social reasons for choosing local foods may be protesting agricultural and food policy, or they may oppose land management practices and policies. Some may be protesting agricultural monopolies on crops and/or seed strains or showing opposition to genetically modified foods/crops. Still others may favor supporting the local economy or supporting sustainable economic practices (fair trade). They may train others to farm, promoting urban gardens, for example. Ultimately, they are "voting with the pocketbook." Two examples of food activists are Walker and Sara. As is common among local food advocates, both got involved in less political ways, but once in, they became active in raising awareness of the many social, political, and economic benefits of eating locally sourced foods. An original co-leader of Slow Food St. Louis, Sara is the owner/president of Fair Shares CCSA, a combined CSA featuring locally produced meat, cheese, eggs, produce, bread, pasta, and other items from more than one hundred local producers. Unlike most CSAs that sell products from a single source, Fair Shares works to aggregate products from multiple suppliers, helping get more products to market while providing more variety to the consumer (a lack of which is a common complaint of many CSAs). Sara appreciates knowing how much work is involved in producing the food she eats, knowing that she's voting with her dollar and putting more money in the farmers' pockets, and cooking fantastically fresh, ripe, flavorful, safe, happy food. As one of the original employees of St. Louis Brewery (a.k.a. Schlafly), she has long been an advocate of supporting smaller local businesses. But a trip to the Slow Food Terra Madre event in Torino, Italy, in 2004 raised her awareness of local foods and turned her into a committed locavore.

Walker is the owner of Terra Bella Farms (in operation since 1890, originally as a livestock operation, now as an organic farm). He also started the Root Cellar and is a partner in Broadway Brewery in Columbia, Missouri. Like Sara, Walker also participated in the Terra Madre event in Italy and was drawn to the Slow Food Movement as a way to express a concern for the environment through food choices. He wasn't initially drawn to the movement, seeing it as more social than activist, but through his participation he came to see the organization as allied with his principles about the need for sustainable use of our resources. His life looks exhausting; in addition to the farm and brewery in Columbia, Walker is a perennial presence in Jefferson City, lobbying for farm policies that help small farmers grow food crops. Both Sara and Walker, as well as others, share a commitment to locally produced food as a way of supporting local economies, preserving and managing natural resources, providing local producers with a fair price for their products, and ensuring their ability to continue to grow what they and their local markets want and are able to grow in ways that are less harmful and ultimately more sustainable than large-scale operations.

There are lots of reasons to buy your food locally:

- It's better for the environment because the food travels less distance and uses less fuel for transportation.
- Many Missouri farmers use organic farming methods, which means fewer chemicals are entering the food system.
- It's fresher and more nutritious.
- It tastes better because it's been allowed to ripen naturally.
- More of the money spent at a farmers' market, farm stand, CSA, or farm goes directly to the farmer; there are fewer (if any) distribution points, less advertising, packaging, and other "hidden" costs associated with large-scale food economies.
- When you buy directly from the local farmer, you know exactly where your money is going and that it is staying in your community.[*]
- You are empowering local farmers to make their own decisions about how to manage their farms, when and what to plant, harvest, and process.

But admittedly, it's not always easy. It can be more expensive. It can be hard to find. The natural seasonality of local products means your favorite foods are not available all year long. With a little planning, some flexibility, possibly supplementing your purchases with your own homegrown produce (which, you could argue, is the *ultimate* local food), you too can be a locavore. Nearly everyone who is now a committed locavore began by making gradual, sometimes small changes to the way they bought and ate food. Sometimes this means choosing a restaurant that uses only (or mostly) locally sourced foods. It can mean finding a farmers' market, farm stand, or even a supermarket that sells local products. This book is our contribution to that effort. We hope to make it as easy as possible for you to find local products in all food categories, from fruits and vegetables to meat, dairy, and grains. We'll help you navigate the seasons so you can stock up on fresh favorites and preserve the surplus for enjoying out of season. No matter where you live or travel in Missouri, there are local products waiting for you to discover. Go for it.

---

* According to a 2008 study by the Pew Commission on Industrial Farm Animal Production, large-scale agricultural businesses pay workers less and spend less money in the communities in which they operate than even medium-sized operations.

Missouri Harvest

Veggies, Grains, & Beans

Missouri is often known for corn and soybeans, most of which are raised and sold as commodity crops. Certainly, our climate is not suited to citrus and full-scale year-round growing as is a state like California. But Missouri's small farmers are creative, and through the innovative use of hoop houses and high tunnels they are producing some crops nearly year-round. Additionally, as the state with the second largest number of farms, Missouri is also home to a wide variety of excellent produce.

Missouri farmers raise a host of traditional vegetables and grains, like asparagus, beans, cabbage, sweet corn, cucumbers, greens (collard, kale, chard, etc.), peas, peppers, pumpkins, tomatoes, and wheat. This is by no means an exhaustive list; lots of other vegetables are successfully grown in the state, and new ones are introduced all the time, as the market for them increases. You will read that many farmers are reintroducing old vegetable varieties. These are called heirloom vegetables, and they are enjoying increased popularity as is interest in seed saving.

Climate, soil, water levels, and terrain vary regionally in Missouri, so not all produce is grown in all regions. Rice, for example, is grown exclusively in the southern parts of the state, while mushrooms come mostly from the Ozarks. In each chapter, we divide the growers in the state regionally into northwest, northeast, central, St. Louis, Kansas City, southwest, and southeast (see map on page ix).

Seasonality

Growing and harvesting seasons play a large role in the availability of produce. As such, producers and purveyors plan what and when to grow and market their products. For example, most tomato varieties grown in Missouri do best when the daytime temperatures are in the 80s, and other crops like lettuce are grown in spring and fall (see chart). But many consumers have been trained by supermarket-style shopping to expect products out of season. That said, seasonality can be extended fairly easily by both growers and consumers.

In his new book *Folks, This Ain't Normal* (2011), "celebrity farmer" Joel Salatin recommends some of those ways. The first is directed at the growers and involves the use of hoop houses and/or high tunnels. Many of our farmers do extend their growing seasons this way, which is why you might still find tomatoes in the fall in some parts of the state. The second two—root cellars and canning or preserving—are directed at the consumer. Salatin recommends storing fall crops like sweet potatoes, potatoes, cabbage, and winter-type squashes (acorn squash, butternut squash, and pumpkins) in your basement or a backyard cellar. He also recommends buying in bulk from the farmers during the season and then preserving the extra for later, creating a seasonal larder that is preserved in the summer in anticipation of being able to eat fruit and vegetables throughout the winter. That was a common practice a generation or two ago, but with the convenience of supermarkets, it is no longer a necessity. Salatin would like to see consumers develop a deeper relationship with the farmer that would include "pre-buying" or ordering produce in bulk in order to preserve it for later. It helps the farmer plan how much produce to bring to the market; it builds a lasting relationship between farmer and buyer; and it allows the buyer to enjoy local produce long past its season.

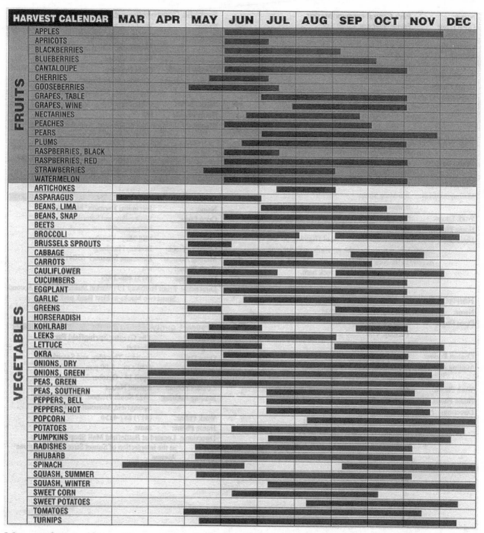

HARVEST CALENDAR		MAR	APR	MAY	JUN	JUL	AUG	SEP	OCT	NOV	DEC
FRUITS	APPLES										
	APRICOTS										
	BLACKBERRIES										
	BLUEBERRIES										
	CANTALOUPE										
	CHERRIES										
	GOOSEBERRIES										
	GRAPES, TABLE										
	GRAPES, WINE										
	NECTARINES										
	PEACHES										
	PEARS										
	PLUMS										
	RASPBERRIES, BLACK										
	RASPBERRIES, RED										
	STRAWBERRIES										
	WATERMELON										
VEGETABLES	ARTICHOKES										
	ASPARAGUS										
	BEANS, LIMA										
	BEANS, SNAP										
	BEETS										
	BROCCOLI										
	BRUSSELS SPROUTS										
	CABBAGE										
	CARROTS										
	CAULIFLOWER										
	CUCUMBERS										
	EGGPLANT										
	GARLIC										
	GREENS										
	HORSERADISH										
	KOHLRABI										
	LEEKS										
	LETTUCE										
	OKRA										
	ONIONS, DRY										
	ONIONS, GREEN										
	PEAS, GREEN										
	PEAS, SOUTHERN										
	PEPPERS, BELL										
	PEPPERS, HOT										
	POPCORN										
	POTATOES										
	PUMPKINS										
	RADISHES										
	RHUBARB										
	SPINACH										
	SQUASH, SUMMER										
	SQUASH, WINTER										
	SWEET CORN										
	SWEET POTATOES										
	TOMATOES										
	TURNIPS										

Missouri fruit and vegetable growing and harvesting seasons, courtesy Missouri Department of Agriculture

Try It Yourself

Of course, a consumer can't get more local than produce grown in their own backyard (or front yard, for that matter!). More and more people are turning to growing their own food, mostly vegetables, but also chickens and other small livestock. This trend seems to be in part a way to offset the higher cost of buying and eating local food, but we also see it as a way for people to connect to the process of growing food and eating what they grow. It gives us a better idea of the hard work involved in producing food and makes us appreciate the time and effort of the farmers we support. Growing one's own food affords us the small pleasure of seeing the spring seedlings transform into towering tomatoes and earthy root vegetables. Putting what we grow ourselves together with what we buy locally from farmers in the market or through a CSA or some other channel results in a veritable community of foods on our tables, each with its own terroir and back-story.

But if growing your own is not your thing, there is a rapidly growing number of stores and restaurants that sell locally grown food. In these chapters we invite you to meet some of the farmers whose products may one day be a guest at your dinner table, and some of the wonderful places you can buy them!

Hoop house, Dry Dock Farms

Northwest Region

Evans' Produce, Burlington Junction

Laura and Paul Evans moved to Burlington Junction in 2008 to start their own farm. Both grew up in farming families. They rent three acres and grow a wide variety of produce. With two high tunnels they are able to extend their growing season.

Products: Tomatoes, sweet corn, cucumbers, eggplant, peppers, pumpkins, sweet potatoes, beets, turnips, radishes, spinach, head lettuce, and leaf lettuce. Laura also makes and sells her own pickles.
Where to buy: Maryville Farmers' Market (Wed. and Sat. morning, 7-noon) and at the farm, but please call first.
Address: 211 Oak Street
Phone: 660-725-4837
Email: evansproduce@gmail.com
Website: N/A
Agritourism: Happy to show the farm, but please call.

Harvest Hills Farms LLC, Mound City

This couple is doing exactly what they want in retirement—farming. Tom and Paula, along with their son, grow on three acres about seven miles outside of Mound City. Both grew up on farms, and even when they were working other full-time jobs they grew corn and soybeans.

Products: Sweet potatoes, tomatoes, green beans, onions, lettuce, sugar snap peas, and some fruits. Paula is passionate about making jams and jellies and uses cherries and berries from their farm along with berries, peaches, and apples from other areas of Missouri and Illinois to make her creations. If you are looking for a unique product, try Paula's crabapple jelly or pear jam.
Where to buy: Maryville Farmers' Market, Mound City Farmers' Market, and they sometimes ship their jellies and jams to individuals who order from their Facebook page.
Address: 13372 Juniper Drive
Phone: 660-442-0124
Email: pkennish@hotmail.com
Website: Harvest Hills Facebook page and Harvesthillfarm.blogspot.com
Agritourism: N/A

The Healing Hearts Farm, Rockport

At Healing Hearts Farm, Charlie Clodfelter and his family (wife, parents, and brother) oversee all parts of their produce production "from seed to shelf." They buy all of their seeds from the Seed Savers Exchange in Iowa and start their own transplants in the basement. They do not use any chemicals or synthetic fertilizers and utilize organic farming methods on the two to three acres they currently have in production. Healing Hearts Farm sells all of their produce within 100 miles of their farm—in 2011, they sold all produce within fifty miles. Check out this new farm.

Products: A wide selection of heirloom vegetables, including broccoli, carrots, and cabbage.
Where to buy: Maryville Farmers' Market, Nebraska City Farmers' Market, Mound City Farmers' Market, Fairfax Community Hospital Farmers' Market, 610 State St., Mound City, and 205 S. Main St., Rockport.
Address: 200 Street in Rockport, half mile west of Hwy. 275 on 200 Street
Phone: 660-744-4975 (cell)
Email: jclodfe@embarqmail.com
Website: Facebook
Agritourism: Call if you would like to set up a visit.

L & R Farm, Rushville

Lanny Frakes has been farming since he graduated from high school in 1967. Most of his farm is in corn and soybeans—1,500 acres—but in 1999 he and his family started doing crop gardens and now have about fifty acres devoted to vegetables. High tunnels and hoop houses help them extend the growing season, and his customers appreciate the fresh food. Lanny will tell you how farming has changed over the years, especially in terms of row crops, but one thing that doesn't change is that "still, everything is controlled by the weather." His son Ryan and Ryan's wife, Amber, along with Lanny's wife, Monie, all live on the farm and work the land together.

Products: Wide variety of produce, cauliflower, broccoli, lettuce, sweet corn, tomatoes, lettuce, and radishes.
Where to buy: Pony Express Farmers' Market, Parkville Missouri Farmers' Market, Zona Rosa Market (shopping area off I-29 in North KC), and wholesale to various grocery stores.
Address: 13371 SW State Rt. KK
Phone: 816-688-7820; 816-390-2760 (cell)
Email: monie.frakes@bbwi.net, lannyfrakes@bbwi.net
Website: N/A
Agritourism: Yes, but please call.

Lesher Family Farm, Westboro

This conventional farmer has about one thousand acres, most of it in corn and soybeans. Each year he grows about eight acres of his farm in pumpkins and has hoop houses for tomatoes, strawberries, and peppers. Terry Lesher has always lived on a farm. When asked why he decided to grow vegetables instead of just row crops, he said they wanted to diversify and to have more contact with people. They use different growing practices for the vegetables in hoop houses, relying more on physical labor instead of tractors, and mulch instead of pesticides for weed control.

> **Products:** Tomatoes, strawberries, peppers, and pumpkins.
> **Where to buy:** Targill, MO (produce stand), Rockport, MO (produce stand), and they have a stand on their farm. If they are around they will wait on the customers at the farm, otherwise it's self-serve and honor system.
> **Address:** From Tarkio, travel north on Hwy. 59 for seven miles, turn west on Route B (look for the sign). Continue for three miles and turn north on Route F. The Lesher Family Farm is located one and a half miles north on Route F on the left-hand side. Look for the signs.
> **Phone:** 660-984-5548
> **Website:** lesherfamilyfarm.com
> **Agritourism:** Products for sale on the farm.

Lost Creek Farm, King City

Darrel was born and raised on farms and has been farming in some capacity most of his life. In 2011 he added two high tunnels to his property to extend his growing season. He and his wife also have a certified kitchen on their property where they prepare an assortment of baked goods for sale at the market.

> **Products:** Darrel says he grows everything—collard and mustard greens, lettuce, spinach, green beans, cucumbers, tomatoes, cabbage, broccoli, potatoes, fall squash, zucchini, and okra, but his biggest seller and what he's known for at the market are his purple hull peas.
> **Where to buy:** Kansas City Market.
> **Address:** 6260 NW Ogle Rd.
> **Phone:** 660-580-0549 (Darrel); 660-580-0574 (Donna)
> **Website:** N/A
> **Agritourism:** N/A

Max & Lula Drydale, Barnard

Max and Lula Drydale have both been farming their whole lives. They currently have five acres in vegetable production and around eighty acres in soybean and corn. As with many small farms, they have a few cows for additional income, and Lula raises chickens for eggs. The chickens live in a pen to protect them from predators.

> **Products:** Eggs and vegetables.
> **Where to buy:** Pony Express Farmers' Market and on the farm.
> **Address:** 39592 State Hwy. H
> **Phone:** 660-939-4173; 816-261-9155 (cell)
> **Website:** N/A
> **Agritourism:** N/A

Muddy Creek Produce, Clearmont

Patty McElroy and her husband have gardens all around town, with about fifteen acres in production and five high tunnels. They've been farming for about fifteen years, and farming income paid for their daughter's college education.

> **Products:** Tomatoes, sweet corn, strawberries, watermelon, cantaloupes, and lots and lots of pumpkins in the fall.
> **Where to buy:** At the farm and Maryville Farmers' Market. They also hope to soon sell to Hy-Vee.
> **Address:** 400 South Sycamore
> **Phone:** 660-729-4672
> **Email:** jpmcelroy@iamotelephone.com
> **Website:** N/A
> **Agritourism:** N/A

Mystic Foods USA, Trenton

This new venture has a big vision. They plan to provide naturally grown tilapia fish and Certified Organic vegetables throughout the state. If all works as planned, Missourians will have access to tilapia year-round as well as year-round tomatoes, lettuces, cucumbers, and squashes. Tilapia will be the main source for most of the plant nutrients, but waste and water will be filtered through four septic tanks to take all the biosolids out. They plan to grow 8,500 head of lettuce at a time using a soil-based hydroponic method. In addition to nutrients from tilapia waste, they will have compost heaps for fertilizer. The eleven greenhouses are to be climate controlled year-round using solar panels and wood stoves. The fish tanks are in place, and fish will be available to the public by summer 2012.

Products: Tilapia, year-round lettuces, four gourmet lettuces, tomatoes, beefsteak tomatoes, cherry tomatoes, colored bell peppers, gourmet squashes, herbs, and blackberries.

Where to buy: They will be selling the produce and fish to stores and chefs. Many of the retailers listed in the shopping section already plan to carry the tilapia.

Address: 1600 Park Lane Dr.

Phone: 660-357-2165; 573-619-9139

Email: suebaird@mysticfoodsusa.com

Website: mysticfoodsusa.com

Agritourism: Call for tours.

Old Ott Farms, Union Star

Penny Dierberger's small farm has been in the family since 1932. In 2004, Penny and her family moved back to help her parents and before she knew it she was farming. Penny uses organic farming methods, and since her child was diagnosed with autism she has investigated the effects of pesticides on her son. Penny somewhat lets the land tell her what to grow—in other words, if a particular plant keeps getting attacked by bugs, she just grows something else.

Products: Cage-free eggs (chickens do get some ground time), kale, chard, spinach, arugula, tomatoes, peppers, green beans, purple beans, edamame, lima beans, yellow-wax beans. She grows what works best without pesticides. She also sells a lot of flower bouquets.
Where to buy: Pony Express Farmers' Market every Saturday.
Address: 12999 NW Pleasant Rd.
Phone: 816-593-2419
Email: pennyjoanne@windstream.net
Website: N/A
Agritourism: Please call or email, she will give tours.

River Bluff Produce, St. Joseph

Mike Black is a conventional farmer and at seventy acres has a "larger" small vegetable farm. He also farms 4,000 acres of row crops—soybeans and corn.

Products: Vegetables, including tomatoes, beets, cucumbers, and pumpkins.
Where to buy: Pony Express Farmers' Market and at Hy-Vee. (He sells directly to Hy-Vee and they distribute produce among their twenty-six stores.)
Address: 12399 SW Bluff Rd.
Phone: 816-646-2344
Website: N/A
Agritourism: No tours.

tland

'er three acres planted in five varieties of garlic at his
wn farm. Along with rich soil and good drainage, Terry says
ect balance of soil nutrients for good garlic. Sho Me Garlic
has been in business since about 2006 and is a perfect resource for garlic seed and
dry garlic. Order early because they sell out quickly.

> **Products:** Five varieties of garlic in 2011: Hardneck (Music, Georgia Fire, Fireball);
> and Softneck (Susanville and Lorz Italian).
> **Where to buy:** The website lists the products for sale, but you must call him to place
> an order. Garlic is harvested around the 4th of July and ships out in mid-August.
> **Address:** 532 Oak St.
> **Phone:** 816-390-2900
> **Website:** shomegarlic.com
> **Agritourism:** N/A

Strawberry Lane Farm, Trenton

Lewis and Marie Kamphefner have been farming since 1993, although the farm
has been in the family since the 1800s. They continue to farm organically on the
three to four acres they have in production, even though they dropped their organic
certification. On their bottom acreage, they grow wheat, soybeans, corn, and alfalfa
on rotation—also with no chemicals or pesticides. The rich, black soil of Muddy
Creek provides a great environment for the host of produce grown here.

> **Products:** Lots of tomatoes (they planted 1,000 plants in 2011), flavorful cantaloupes,
> and musk melons, blackberries, edamame, green beans, and, deer permitting, lots of
> strawberries.
> **Where to buy:** Westport Plaza Farmers' Market in Kansas City.
> **Address:** 510 NE Jade Ln.
> **Phone:** 660-485-6473
> **Email:** kampy@grm.net
> **Website:** strawberrylanefarm.com
> **Agritourism:** N/A

The Veggie Chicks, Parnell

Donna Patton and her daughter have been farming together in Parnell for seven years. They have about one acre in vegetables, and each year they add more fruit trees to their one-acre orchard. They grow as organically as possible and say more and more people want to know how their food is grown. When Donna began vending at the Maryville Farmers' Market three years ago "no one even knew what kale, chard, and greens were—took me awhile to educate our customers. Now they sell."

Products: A wide variety of vegetables, along with blueberries, blackberries, apples, peaches, and soon cherries, pears, and apricots.
Where to buy: Maryville Farmers' Market.
Address: N/A
Phone: 660-986-2300
Email: dspatton37101@live.com
Website: N/A
Agritourism: N/A

Northeast Region

Danjo Farms, Moberly

Dan and Joanne Nelson grew up farming but have had Danjo Farms—a fifteen-acre Certified Naturally Grown farm—for thirteen years. They have created an "All Missouri" Country Store right on their farm where you will find products like BBQ sauce, sorghum, molasses, jams, and hot mustard along with local grass-fed beef and eggs.

> **Products:** Vegetables, heritage turkeys (call to pre-order for Thanksgiving), chicken, pork, baked goods from their Rise 'N Shine Bakery, and other Missouri products at the store. Joanne bakes three times a week. You'll find cookies, breads, and pies, but it is best to pre-order.
> **Where to buy:** Coyote Farm & Home Market (Ashland), MU Farmers' Market, on the farm, and through their CSA.
> **Address:** 1210 Private Rd. 2717
> **Phone:** 660-263-1043 (day); 573-823-5452 (evening)
> **Website:** danjofarms.com
> **Agritourism:** Can do farm tours, but please call to set up.

Green Valley Farm, Kirksville

Steve and Velda Salt are busy people. In addition to a seven-acre vegetable farm on their 146 acres, they also run a small grocery store called Downtown Grocery Store, which specializes in local products. Velda says that Steve has always farmed in some way, and as a kid he peddled the vegetables he grew to the neighbors. They have farmed in Missouri for twenty years.

> **Products:** They specialize in heirloom and ethnic vegetables, herbs, and small fruits. They produce a wide variety of Southeast Asian, Middle Eastern, East European, and Latin American veggies.
> **Where to buy:** Kirksville Farmers' Market.
> **Address:** 28461 Linderville Trail
> **Phone:** 660-332-7217
> **Website:** N/A
> **Agritourism:** N/A

Harvest Pride Farms, Moberly

Robyn and Debbie Lunt are new to farming but are working diligently to expand their gardens. Farmers are nothing if not resourceful, and this duo found a niche by selling to employees at a larger business in their town. They set up a market once a week on-site, and so far it has worked well for everyone. Although not certified, they are using organic growing practices.

> **Products:** Fresh produce and herbs, tomatoes, cucumbers, peppers, Cajun peppers, melons, cabbages, and green beans.
> **Where to buy:** On the farm stand (Thurs., 2-5 p.m.); GE Capital, Moberly, on Hwy. M and Hwy. 63 (Sat., 3-6 p.m.); Ice House, Moberly, at Hwy. M and Morley St.
> **Address:** 1225 South Williams
> **Phone:** 573-722-4792
> **Website:** N/A
> **Agritourism:** Can visit, but call to set up.

Leeside Llamas and Organically Grown Produce, Madison

Judith and Earl Burton stay in farming however they can. In their thirty-plus years in the business they have done it all—raised cattle, sold vegetables to restaurants, and worked full-time jobs off the farm. They now have llamas just as pets and use their two hundred acres to produce hay. They sell about seven hundred hay bales a year, and each bale weighs in at nine hundred to one thousand pounds. This behind-the-scenes farming helps other small farmers in the area keep their animals fed in the winter. The trailer the Burtons use to transport and unload is an added bonus for many farmers who do not have tractors or a way to move a heavy bale of hay. These self-described health nuts believe in taking care of the land. Judith says about organic farming, "It's more work, but work is good for you."

> **Products:** Hay bales.
> **Where to buy:** Call directly.
> **Address:** 25860 Hwy. 151
> **Phone:** 660-295-4824
> **Website:** N/A
> **Agritourism:** N/A

...piary, Louisiana

will see more than two hundred lavender plants and a wide
two acres of their seventeen-acre farm. Peggy Meyer is
e recent addition of a high tunnel with plans to grow lots of
strawberries. The high tunnels will deter deer (who love to feast on the plants), give
protection from the weather, and help prevent erosion. Meyer Farms currently has
three hives for honey production.

> **Products:** Vegetables, berries, flowers, honey, lavender, and lavender honey. Most of
> the lavender is sold fresh.
> **Where to buy:** Louisiana Farmers' Market, once a month to Chandler Hill Farmers'
> Market in Defiance, Eagle's Nest Bed and Breakfast, and the Farm Shed.
> **Address:** 17819 Hwy. UU; adjacent to the Henry Lay Center (sculpture park)
> **Phone:** 573-754-6540
> **Website:** N/A
> **Agritourism:** Yes, but call first.

The Possibility Alliance Farm & Sanctuary, La Plata

Ethan and Sara Hughes are demonstrating to all of us how you can live simply—
for real. They live with no electricity or indoor plumbing on their eighty-acre farm.
They grow their own food, teach others how to live petroleum-free, and how to
be self-sufficient. And they are known for giving out fruit trees. More than 1,200
people visit each year. If you want to see for yourself how to live a simpler life and
witness some people who "walk the walk" when it comes to community service, be
sure to visit. There are some in-depth articles about them on-line.

> **Products:** They don't necessarily sell the food they grow, but they do provide classes
> for folks who want to learn to live more directly from the land. When they do go to
> farmers' markets, they sell their products by donation. You may write or call to request
> a class list or to receive their newsletter.
> **Where to buy:** Classes are on the farm or surrounding farms near La Plata.
> **Address:** 28408 Frontier Ln.
> **Phone:** 660-332-4094
> **Website:** N/A
> **Agritourism:** Yes.

Schmuckers Vegetables, Greentop

Willis Schmucker has forty acres of sweet corn, cantaloupes, and tomatoes. He sells a lot of his vegetables to the Iowa Produce Auction, but you can also buy from the farm stand.

Products: Tomatoes, sweet corn, green beans, cucumbers, eggplant, peppers, cantaloupe, squash, and peaches.
Where to buy: On the farm at the farm stand or Kirksville Farmers' Market.
Address: 25522 Fort Madison Way
Phone: N/A
Website: N/A
Agritourism: N/A

Sunrise Farm, La Plata

Mark Slaughter is making a difference in his community. He currently farms one acre on his 150-acre farm, and donated over 2,000 pounds of food to the food bank. He says there is no reason for people to go hungry with farms all around. He uses organic practices, bat guano, and heirloom seeds, and he's working on value-added products for summer 2012 and an expansion of his farm. His way of farming is dependent on knowing his customers, and he loves farming on the land that belonged to his grandparents.

Products: Heirloom vegetables and herbs.
Where to buy: Kirksville Farmers' Market, Memphis Farmers' Market and Farm Stand (Kirkwood Produce Stand), Hy-Vee, farm stand in La Plata, and Costa Rican Café Company.
Address: N/A
Phone: 660-332-4554
Email: jetboy44@aol.com
Website: N/A
Agritourism: Not yet.

Turkey Run Hostas, Kirksville

Clair Peckosh is known for her hostas, but in 2011 she started growing seedlings, basil, and cherry tomatoes. She wants to grow more vegetables in the future. With twenty years of experience, Clair has the knowledge to succeed.

> **Products:** Tomato plants, tomatoes, basil, and hostas.
> **Where to buy:** Kirksville Farmers' Market, wholesales in Iowa.
> **Address:** N/A
> **Phone:** 660-349-0061
> **Website:** N/A
> **Agritourism:** N/A

Vesterbrook Farms, Clarksville

Carol and Mike Brabo run this recently Certified Naturally Grown farm that has been in their family since 1927. Vesterbrook Farm has twenty-three acres in total—six are used for produce. This farming family of four does get some help during the height of the growing seasons. You will find four high tunnels and a family determined to grow as much of the year as possible.

> **Products:** Mike says they have a 50/50 split with meat and produce. They grow vegetables primarily for their CSA, but also raise free-range eggs, heritage breed bourbon red turkeys, and lamb.
> **Where to buy:** Vesterbrook products can often be found in dishes at the following restaurants in St. Louis: Niche, Sidney Street Café, Acero, The Crossing, Lumina, Scottish Arms, Winslows Home, and Mike Shannon's Steak House.
> **Address:** 16991 Hwy. W
> **Phone:** 573-560-0871
> **Website:** vesterbrookfarm.com/content/5163
> **Agritourism:** Folks are welcome to visit their farm, but call ahead to set up a time.

Central Region

Chert Hollow Farm, Boone County

This small, diversified farm is Certified Organic, and the belief in sustainable farming is obvious in all the choices that they make. Eric and Joanna Reuter started the farm in 2007, and in addition to their beautiful produce, they also use their farm to educate people interested in learning more about organic farming.

Products: Organic produce and fruit.
Where to buy: Columbia Farmers' Market and several restaurants.
Address: N/A
Phone: 573-474-0989
Email: contactus@cherthollowfarm.com
Website: cherthollowfarm.com
Agritourism: Eric and Joanna offer tours. Please email them to arrange a visit. Include the following information: contact name & phone number; number of intended visitors, including children and their ages; proposed date and time of visit (prefer Sundays at 3:00); and any particular interests of the group. Costs for the tours range from $6-$12 a person depending on the size of the group.

Deep Mud Farm, Auxvasse

Jeremy Saurage is young, energetic, and ambitious enough to start his own organic farm. Farm work and training at Claverach Farm, Bellews Creek, and in France and Maine gave Jeremy the knowledge and experience he needed. Visit Jeremy at Maplewood Farmers' Market or Columbia Farmers' Market—you will know it's him by the gregarious shouts announcing his gorgeous vegetables and prices to all passersby.

Products: Organic and heirloom produce.
Where to buy: Maplewood Farmers' Market, Columbia Farmers' Market, various fine dining restaurants in St. Louis including Local Harvest Grocery and Local Harvest Café, in Rocheport at Abigail's and Les Bourgeois Winery and Bistro, in Columbia at the Main Squeeze, Sycamore, Cherry Street Wine Seller and Bistro, and Clovers Market.
Address: 4721 County Road 290
Phone: 573-826-5234
Website: Facebook
Agritourism: N/A

J & T Country Store, Roach

Since 2004, Tanya Apperson has operated the J & T Country Store. You will find produce from their three-acre farm and surrounding farms, as well as items you would find in a traditional store with an emphasis on snack foods for vacationers since many of her customers are visiting the Lake of the Ozarks. Her great grandmother had a store about one hundred years ago, and Tanya is using the same fifteen-foot display counter from that store.

Products: A wide variety of items with an emphasis on produce but also things like pickling spices and chocolate-covered almonds. Cash and check only.
Where to buy: Open Wed.-Sat. 9-5 p.m. Apr.-Nov.
Address: Halfway between Greenview and Climax Springs on Hwy. 7 (west side of the lake—I-44 to Hwy. 5 north by Camdenton) where 5 meets 7 by Climax Springs
Phone: 573-347-3500
Website: N/A
Agritourism: Yes.

Pierpont Farms, Columbia

Pierpont Farms is a thirty-four-acre family farm founded in 2004 by Rob and Angela Hemwall. The Hemwalls promote sustainable agriculture, community involvement, and healthy eating. They are utilizing a high tunnel to help protect crops and extend their growing season.

> **Products:** Wide variety of vegetables and some fruits.
> **Where to buy:** Columbia Farmers' Market, and Farm Stand on Sat. 9-5 or their CSA.
> **Address:** 8810 S. Route N
> **Phone:** 573-499-9851
> **Website:** pierpontfarms.com; Facebook
> **Agritourism:** Farm tours available by appointment.

Red Brick Farm, Sturgeon

Jennifer Holland and her husband wanted a space where their four children could run outside, have easy access to nature, and be surrounded by crickets and cicadas instead of traffic. So, they loaded up the truck and moved to Kansas City. They now make their home on a twelve-acre farm with a 140-year-old house soon to be on the National Register. (The house has its own blog—402Audrain.blogspot.com.) And, Jennifer says, "then came farming." Jennifer tries to grow as naturally as possible but occasionally uses some pesticides. They currently cultivate two acres but have added apple trees, plum trees, and are relocating some of the native blackberry and raspberry bushes to more accessible areas of their farm.

> **Products:** Jams, jellies, fruit syrups, and a wide array of vegetables.
> **Where to buy:** Mexico Farmers' Market.
> **Address:** 402 N. Audrain St.
> **Phone:** 573-687-2105
> **Website:** redbrickfarm.blogspot.com; Facebook
> **Agritourism:** Not at this time, but they are working toward a u-pick spot with apple trees and berries.

The Salad Garden, Ashland

Dan Kuebler has been farming since 1977 and got his first organic certification in 1989. He has held a full-time job throughout his farming tenure but always loved selling at farmers' markets. As he got older he realized he needed some help on the farm in order to continue. So, in 2011, Leslie Touzeau and Liberty Hunter came on as partners in the Salad Garden. These two women came to the farm with several apprenticeships under their belts and an enthusiasm and hunger for farming. Dan is right in saying that many young farmers have the desire, but no land and no cash to buy the equipment to get started. He had the equipment and land, but no other farmers to help. This is a great arrangement for them so far. The farmers try to run the farm as sustainably as possible. They water the garden from pond water and use a solar-powered irrigation system to pump water up the hill.

> **Products:** They grow about everything except sweet corn and start their season early with the use of high tunnels. Enjoy fennel, kohlrabi, radicchio, Asian greens, head lettuces, and nice fall crops into January.
> **Where to buy:** Columbia Farmers' Market, the Root Cellar, Sycamore, and the Main Squeeze in Columbia.
> **Address:** 16471 S. Hawkins Rd.
> **Phone:** 573-657-1125
> **Email:** dlkuebler@yahoo.com
> **Website:** thesaladgarden-mo.com/index.php
> **Agritourism:** Not at this point.

Share-Life Farms, Marshall

Jim and Rose Thomas started farming organically shortly after Rose was diagnosed with environmental sensitivities. They worried that exposure to pesticides and chemicals over her lifetime in farming were causing and had caused harm to her system. Jim says he knew that "there had to be a better way than to poison everything we didn't want to grow what we did want." Both grew up in farming communities and had a lot of exposure to various pesticides through conventional farming. Jim is passionate about the need to farm organically and believes it is important to share their story. He is now the president of the Missouri Organic Growers Association.

Products: Organic produce grown on three to five acres and organic cage-free eggs.
Where to buy: Blue Springs Farmers' Market, Columbia Downtown Farmers' Market, Nature's Pantry, the Main Squeeze, Café Berlin, Door to Door Organics, Missouri Farms for Missouri's People.
Address: 21302 185th Rd.
Phone: 660-886-3936
Website: N/A
Agritourism: Call ahead, but they welcome farm visits and volunteering.

Terra Bella Farms, Columbia

Walker Claridge is well known in the local food movement. He distributes food for other farmers, sells his own produce at farmers' markets, and also is part owner in a local brewery called Broadway Brewery. Walker, who has been a spokesperson for Farm Aid, has done much to advance the local food movement and bring locally grown products to people in the Columbia and St. Louis areas.

Products: Salad mixes, spicy greens, potatoes, arugula, kale, green onions, and onions.
Where to buy: Columbia Farmers' Market, Maplewood Farmers' Market, Local Harvest Grocery and Café, Broadway Brewery, Sycamore, Cherry Street, Uprise Bakery, Niche, Acero, and Yia-Yia's in St. Louis.
Address: 1303 State Rd. M
Phone: 573-387-4881
Website: N/A
Agritourism: N/A

Urban Farm—Columbia Center for Urban Agriculture, Columbia

Located in the heart of Columbia, this urban farm and demonstration garden will give you a peek into the world of farming. You can see moveable chicken pens, beehives, fruit trees, and permanent beds for annual vegetable production. This not-for-profit venture has grown over the last three years to include educational programs, markets on-site, and three full-time staff who work to promote sustainable agriculture.

Products: All types of organic vegetables.
Where to buy: Sycamore, Red and Moe, Cherry Street Wine Seller and Bistro.
Address: 1209 Smith St.
Phone: 573-514-4174
Website: columbiaurbanag.org
Agritourism: Yes.

St. Louis Region

Bellews Creek Farm, Hillsboro

Paul and Nancy Krautmann grow unique produce on their organic (not Certified Organic) farm located about twenty-five miles from St. Louis. Paul is known for helping and inspiring young farmers and has had several interns over the years. Paul has been farming for nineteen years and has seventy-seven acres total with twelve to fifteen acres in production. He grew up on a farm in northwest Missouri, and his grandfather was a well-known farmer in the southwest part of the state who contributed much to farming through his writings and observational skills. His grandfather is the author of *Our Margin of Life*.

> **Products:** His list is long but includes popcorn, pinto beans, black beans, peppers, sweet potatoes, garlic, and a host of delectable greens including spinach, arugula, and mizuna.
> **Where to buy:** Fair Shares, Local Harvest Grocery, Cardwell's in Frontenac, St. Louis University Fresh Gatherings, Todd's Canteen (House Springs), and Sqwires.
> **Address:** 8095 Hwy. BB
> **Phone:** 636-274-7236
> **Website:** N/A
> **Agritourism:** N/A

Berger Bluff, Berger

This small family-run organic farm is situated close to the Missouri River between Jefferson City and St. Louis. Lee and Ingrid Abraham established their forty-acre farm in 1990 and grow seasonal vegetables using organic farming methods. They cultivate two acres each year. This duo has been farming since 1983 when they began as apprentices on Gasconade Farm (no longer in operation).

> **Products:** Asian greens, salad greens, garlic, potatoes, leeks, onions, cabbage, broccoli, and eggplant.
> **Where to buy:** Maplewood Farmers' Market, Fair Shares, Fresh Gatherings at SLU, Stellina Pasta, Truffles, Niche, La Dolce Via, Annie Gunn's, Café Provencal, Local Harvest Grocery, and Salume Beddu.
> **Address:** 4647 Berger Road, 63014
> **Phone:** 573-834-5509
> **Email:** bbfarm@bidnet.com
> **Website:** Facebook
> **Agritourism:** Call to talk with them about this.

City Seeds Urban Farm, St. Louis

This urban agricultural initiative provides job training and therapeutic horticulture to homeless and underserved individuals. The farm has forty-plus raised vegetable beds, a dwarf fruit tree orchard, an outdoor classroom, beehives, and a greenhouse. They use drip irrigation, composting bins, and even a rainwater catch cistern. Produce is donated to local food pantries and sold wholesale to Food Outreach.

> **Products:** Vegetables.
> **Where to buy:** Tower Grove Farmers' Market and Maplewood Farmers' Market.
> **Address:** Located between Market and Pine Sts. at 22nd St.
> **Phone:** 314-588-9600
> **Website:** www.gatewaygreening.org/our-programs/city-seeds-urban-farm/
> **Agritourism:** Call to set up a visit.

Claverach Farms, Eureka

This beautiful farm in Eureka is known for fresh eggs, vegetables, and wines. Joanna and Sam are dedicated to sustainable farming and to keeping their farm and vineyard as natural as possible. Sam grew up on the farm, and the two of them have farmed together for over eight years.

Products: Radish, pea, and sunflower shoots, heirloom vegetables, pasture-raised eggs, and wine from their vineyard.
Where to buy: Maplewood Farmers' Market, Local Harvest Grocery, Local Harvest Café, and other fine eating establishments throughout the St. Louis area.
Address: 570 Lewis Rd.
Phone: 636-938-7353
Website: claverach.com
Agritourism: Joanna and Sam have started hosting farm dinners at their farm. Please check their website for updates on this exciting addition to their business.

Dry Dock Farm, Silex

Dry Dock specializes in heirloom vegetables, flowers, and herbs. They grow their vegetables, herbs, and flowers using bio-intensive methods, no chemicals, no GMO seeds, and the soil is enriched with natural minerals, cover crops, worm castings, and compost. Dry Dock works with other farmers through the River Hills Farmers Alliance and distributes their products through the Dry Dock CSA and to stores in the St. Louis area. River Hills Farmers Alliance has about twenty to twenty-two growers and about 75 percent are Amish. Since their Amish growers do not drive, other farmers in the Alliance, like Dry Dock, act as distributors. Growers agree to not use chemicals on the ground and they are encouraged not to spray. All the chickens are free-range, and they receive no antibiotics or hormones.

Products: Variety of vegetables grown without the use of chemicals and lots of eggs.
Where to buy: Local Harvest Grocery, Dry Dock CSA, Fair Shares, the Racquet Club in St. Louis, City Greens.
Address: 29 Silex Elevator Rd.
Phone: 573-384-5859
Email: drydockfarm@windstream.net
Website: riverhillspoultry.com; be sure to check out the slideshow of photos on their website—very beautiful and great photos of high tunnels.
Agritourism: They do accept visitors, but please call.

Row covers, Dry Dock Farm

Earth Dance Farms, Ferguson

Molly Rockamann founded Earth Dance in 2008 and in 2009 began a farming apprentice program on Mueller Organic Farm in Ferguson. Earth Dance is a non-profit organization, with 501c3 status through a partnership with the Open Space Council. Their mission is to grow and inspire local FARMS—Food, Art, Relationships & Music, Sustainably! Earth Dance operates a season-long educational apprenticeship program whose participants learn about sustainable agriculture from "seed to market." Apprentices are trained in all aspects of small farm management.

Products: Vegetables grown without chemicals or pesticides.
Where to buy: Ferguson Farmers' Market, Maplewood Farmers' Market, and through their CSA. They occasionally sell to restaurants and Local Harvest Grocery.
Address: Mailing address is 302 Thoroughman Ave.
Phone: 314-521-1006
Website: earthdancefarms.org/about-us/
Agritourism: Before planning a visit, be sure to call.

Engelhart Farm, Pacific

Engelhart Farm is the oldest continually running establishment on Old Highway 66. Running since 1922, this on-farm roadside stand is a destination for naturally grown vegetables, bedding plants, and a variety of home décor items. Everything they sell is made or grown on the farm. Although not Certified Organic, the Engelharts are dedicated to crop rotation and the use of cover crops to keep their land healthy. Visit this two-hundred-acre farm and get a glimpse of the past and present existing together comfortably.

> **Products:** Many varieties of tomatoes, squash, pumpkins, turnips, apples, as well as hanging baskets, bedding plants, and potted annuals. You will also find ornamental corn, gourds, natural wreaths, and iron works.
> **Where to buy:** At the farm stand (many of the local farmers buy their starter plants from the Engelharts), which is open April 1-Oct. 31, Mon-Sat. 10:30-5:00 p.m.
> **Address:** 2940 West Osage (Hwy. 66)
> **Phone:** 636-399-3743
> **Website:** N/A
> **Agritourism:** Yes, you will see the farm when you stop in to buy your goods!

ESP (Environmentally Sound Products of Missouri), Wright City

Irvin and Kathleen Huser have their whole business in a two-car garage and four greenhouses. These folks are in the business of worms and starter plants. This is a great place to source worms, worm castings, and super-healthy vegetable starter plants. Worm castings are wonderful to use as food for your garden and plants.

> **Products:** Bedding plants (all vegetables), worms, worm castings (plant food), and worm kits, which include everything you need to make your own "worm farm." They also give classes on vermicomposting.
> **Where to buy:** At the farm in Wright City or the Warren County Farmers' Market, Warrenton Home and Garden Show, and Earth Day in Columbia. You can also call to buy a worm kit directly from them.
> **Address:** 17736 Keller Dr.
> **Phone:** 636-456-3066
> **Website:** espofmo.com
> **Agritourism:** Call for appointment.

International Institute Global Farm Initiative, St. Louis

The International Institute Global Farm Initiative is an agriculture-based career training program for refugees. The job training provides refugees with skills and knowledge that will translate into their own farming endeavors. Current farmers in the program come from Bhutan, Burma, Burundi, Ethiopia, Iraq, Somalia, and Sudan.

> **Products:** Culturally appropriate produce—Asian greens, amaranth, roselle (the Burmese call it sour-sour), sweet potato leaves, fava beans, and produce that is common to Americans.
> **Where to buy:** Tower Grove Farmers' Market.
> **Address:** Two farming sites in the city
> **Phone:** Global Farms Coordinator, Whitney Sewell 314-773-9090 x 134
> **Website:** www.iistl.org/globalfarm.html
> **Agritourism:** Contact the Global Farms coordinator.

Ivan's Fig Farm, Dittmer

Ivan Stoilov loves figs and started growing them because he couldn't find good fresh figs in his area. Fig trees need warm conditions for growth, and Ivan creates that with a combination of high tunnels and geothermal energy.

> **Products:** Several varieties of figs (some with seeds sourced from friends in other countries) and heirloom peppers and tomatoes. Also fig preserves, roasted peppers, and tomatoes.
> **Where to buy:** Tower Grove Farmers' Market, Maplewood Farmers' Market.
> **Address:** 8517 Dittmer Catawissa Rd.
> **Phone:** 636-285-0420
> **Website:** N/A
> **Agritourism:** N/A

Liberty Farm, Affton

Chris Clark grows using organic practices on a quarter acre he leases in Affton. Chris started farming in 2010, but he credits his mom with his green thumb. He sees a lot of potential in urban areas for more growing and is demonstrating efficient use of space.

> **Products:** Tomatoes, peppers, onions, eggplant, and some strawberries and fruits.
> **Where to buy:** Tower Grove Farmers' Market, and he is looking into an on-site basket-style delivery service for people in his area.
> **Address:** N/A
> **Phone:** 314-651-5137
> **Email:** chris.n.clark@gmail.com
> **Website:** Not yet
> **Agritourism:** Can call him to do u-pick.

Nature's Bounty Farm, St. Charles

Charlie always dreamed of moving to the 145-acre farm that has been in their family since the 1850s. After he retired in 2005, he and his wife built a house and moved to the farm where he now has realized his dream to be a Certified Organic farmer. Charlie and his brother also raise a few head of cattle along with the two acres in vegetables and berries. The recent addition of a high tunnel will extend the growing season.

> **Products:** Lots of varieties of heirloom tomatoes, potatoes, zucchini, green beans, blackberries and raspberries, greens, turnips, sugar snap peas, hybrid white turnips. Charlie is known for his tomatoes.
> **Where to buy:** Ferguson Farmers' Market.
> **Address:** N/A
> **Phone:** 636-887-3229
> **Website:** N/A
> **Agritourism:** N/A

Strumpler Farms, Pacific

Julia Strumpler considers her farm a hobby farm. She raises eggs and produce on about an acre of land in Eureka. She also has boer goats and sheep at her mom's farm in Warrenton. The goats are sold for meat and are raised for show. The sheeps' wool is used for spinning and felting. Julia has also started doing natural wool-dying workshops.

> **Products:** Eggs, produce, goats, and wool products.
> **Where to buy:** Year-round produce stand on the honor system; you can buy her wool at her mother's store Bittersweet Baskets and Basket Supply in Warrenton.
> **Address:** 6444 Riverview Dr.
> **Phone:** 636-432-4008
> **Website:** www.strumplerfarms.com, bittersweetbasketsandsupply.com
> **Agritourism:** Can visit.

Sunflower Savannah, Beaufort

Sam and Bill Wieseman run these twenty-two acres as a Certified Naturally Grown farm. Sam explains that "Everything on the farm has a purpose—sheep on the farm for manure and meat, chickens and ducks for manure and eggs, plus they eat a lot of bugs. Geese help with the grass, cats for vermin . . . everything has a job. And our Great Pyrenees is a guard dog, not a pet." Sam is known for her delicious granola, flavorful salsa, and her beautiful flowers. She also sells a refreshing lemonade at her Farmers' Market stalls.

> **Products:** Fresh cut flowers, produce, salsas, and granola.
> **Where to buy:** In St. Louis at Tower Grove Farmers' Market, Maplewood Farmers' Market, Local Havest Grocery. In Columbia at the Root Cellar. You can also buy at the farm and her flowers can often be found at Flowers at Four Seasons in Washington, Oakland Florist in Union, and Belvia's Blooms in Union.
> **Address:** 6290 Hwy. 185
> **Phone:** 573-259-1533
> **Website:** www.sunflowersavannah.com, sunflowersavannah.blogspot.com
> **Agritourism:** Call if you want to visit or to purchase products.

St. Isidore Farm, Moscow Mills

Bob Lober and his family have farmed St. Isidore for fifteen years. They have thirteen acres and cultivate a little over one acre a year in produce. St. Isidore Farm is not Certified Organic, but they do use organic practices for growing their produce and no feed supplements are fed to the hogs.

> **Products:** Organic produce, pork products, and raw goat's milk.
> **Where to buy:** Annie Gunn's, Cardwells, BC's Kitchen, Harvest, Yia-Yia's, and Fair Shares.
> **Address:** 459 S. Ethlyn Rd.
> **Phone:** 636-661-5956
> **Website:** N/A
> **Agritourism:** N/A

Thies Farm, St. Louis

Thies Farm and Greenhouses is a fifth-generation farm that has been in business at the same location on North Hanley Road since 1885. What started as a truck

farm has grown into a St. Louis institution. Thies also operates a second location in Maryland Heights. With over 120 acres in total, you'll find a wide variety of produce. And don't miss "Pumpkinland," a festival that runs the entire month of October.

> **Products:** Find a great range of fresh produce, plants, jams, jellies, gardening supplies, dressings, and seeds. They have a wide assortment of annuals, perennials, herbs, vegetable plants, and hanging baskets in 45,000 square feet of greenhouse space. Christmas trees available at the Hanley location.
> **Where to buy:** At the farm.
> **Address:** 3120 Maryland Heights Expressway and 4215 N. Hanley Rd.
> **Phone:** 314-469-7559 (Maryland Heights); 314-428-9878 (Hanley Road)
> **Website:** thiesfarm.com
> **Agritourism:** Yes

Three Girls and a Tractor, Marthasville

John and Shari Kopmann (and their girls) have twenty-plus acres of produce. This includes eight acres in sweet corn, twelve acres in melons, squash, and watermelon and a couple acres in tomatoes and peppers. They are not organic but really try to not spray because as Shari says, her daughters eat produce right out of the gardens. They handpick all of their produce. When asked how they avoid spraying their corn, Shari says they grow their corn in shifts and pick at first ripening to avoid worms. Both Shari and John have full-time jobs off the farm. Please notice that they sell a lot of their produce to school districts who are active in the farm-to-table movement.

> **Products:** Corn, tomatoes, peppers, melons, and squash.
> **Where to buy:** Washington Farmers' Market, Rockwood School District, Wright City School District, Washington High School, and Wright City Farmers' Market.
> **Address:** 17234 Bouef Island Rd.
> **Phone:** 636-433-2121; 636-357-8075
> **Email:** girlsandatractor@aol.com
> **Website:** N/A
> **Agritourism:** N/A

Windy Hill Farm, St. Louis

Elva Seifert specializes in bedding and starter plants and has been growing plants for eight years. She credits her son with engineering her greenhouse watering system and with growing the vegetable starters.

> **Products:** Spring bedding plants like begonias, petunias, marigolds, and dianthus along with tomato and pepper vegetable starters.
> **Where to buy:** Ferguson Farmers' Market from April-May.
> **Address:** 12260 Larimore
> **Phone:** 314-583-1567 (cell phone for Elva)
> **Website:** N/A
> **Agritourism:** Call to buy directly from her farm/greenhouses.

YellowTree Farm, Affton

Justin Lesczc saw the movie *Home Grown* in 2007 and thought, "I can do that." So he did. He and his wife, Danielle, started raising produce at their home and added in a few rabbits and chickens for meat. Justin also started foraging and learning about all that is already naturally available to anyone. When they needed more land, they found a spot to rent in Fenton from folks who have a five-hundred-acre farm.

> **Products:** They grow a lot of heirloom and unusual vegetables to sell to restaurants. High volume doesn't work on the small amount of land that they have.
> **Where to buy:** Farmhaus, Sydney Street, Niche, Stellina Pasta, Truffles, and Perennial Artisan Ales.
> **Address:** N/A
> **Phone:** 314-482-9203
> **Email:** justin@yellowtreefarm.com
> **Website:** yellowtreefarm.com; Facebook
> **Agritourism:** N/A

Kansas City Region

Bear Creek Farms, Osceola

Robbins and Jim Hail run this fourteen-acre farm that houses Certified Organic growing fields, cattle, and some horses. The couple has farmed in some capacity since 1979. In 2000 they became Certified Organic. When asked why they decided to grow organically, Robbins said, "Because we eat the food."

Products: Although they grow a wide variety of produce, they are known for their 500 varieties of heirloom tomatoes. They sell transplants in spring. In 2012 they plan to sell heirloom apple trees that will survive and thrive in the Midwest. They are also expanding their fig production.

Where to buy: Most of their produce is sold to the Whole Foods Market and at Brookside Farmers' Community Market and Waldo Farmers' Market. You can also find their products in Door to Door Organics.

Address: 12595 Northeast 50 Road (60 miles north of Springfield; 100 miles south of Kansas City)

Phone: 417-282-5894

Website: N/A

Agritourism: Yes, it is an open farm, but please call before you come.

Kansas City Food Circle
(www.KCFoodCircle.org)

The Kansas City Food Circle has an established bulletin board for direct producer-to-consumer networking.

Drumm Farm Garden, Independence

A truly unique marriage of agriculture and social services, East Wind Gardens is a four-acre Certified Organic farm at the Andrew Drumm Institute, an eighty-year-old foster care facility that originally housed an Agriculture Center for Boys. The children participate in garden activities, and 10 percent of the gross revenue supports Andrew Drumm Institute. Soon the Institute will take over the garden and incorporate more farming activities with the youth.

> **Products:** A good mix of vegetables in all season as well as cut flowers.
> **Where to buy:** Farmers' Community Market at Brookside and Westport Plaza Farmers' Market, Door to Door Organics; also available at these local independent restaurants: Room 39, The Farmhouse, Rieger Hotel Grill and Exchange Restaurant, and Bluestem.
> **Address:** 3210 S. Lee's Summit Rd.
> **Phone:** 816-825-3310 (Bruce Branstetter)
> **Website:** drummfarm.org/garden.html
> **Agritourism:** N/A

Fahrmeier Bros. Produce, Lexington

In 2001, this hard-working family transitioned their farm from a row crop and livestock farm to a farm garden and greenhouse business. They use as few chemicals as possible and utilize an Integrated Pest Management Program, which means spraying is fairly infrequent. With three generations involved, they have expanded to include Fahrmeier Family Vineyards with an on-site space for tasting and shopping in their small gift shop featuring local products. At Fahrmeier farm you can pick a pumpkin, purchase flowers, enjoy a hayride, and yes, purchase wine.

> **Products:** Produce and wine.
> **Where to buy:** Kansas City Riverside Market (Wed.), farm stand (Mon.-Sat. 8-6 and Sun 12-5). Farm stand is located off Hwy. 24 between Wellington and Lexington.
> **Address:** 9364 Mitchell Trail
> **Phone:** 816-934-2472
> **Website:** www.fahrmeierfarms.com
> **Agritourism:** Yes.

Haines Farms, Richmond

Doug Haines does a little bit of everything. He's been farming for eight years, but even as a kid he had his own garden. All of his vegetables and fruits are grown organically, and he is Animal-Welfare Approved for his free-range eggs.

> **Products:** Grapes, herbs and vegetables, live bait in the summer, firewood, and free-range eggs that are Animal-Welfare Approved.
> **Where to buy:** Sells at the downtown Farmers' Market in Seltzer Springs (15 miles west of Richmond) and on the farm. He puts up a sign at the end of the driveway that says eggs for sale so folks can just stop in.
> **Address:** 41903 E. 144th
> **Phone:** 816-516-2312
> **Website:** Facebook
> **Agritourism:** Yes, he wants folks to see the farm and while you are there, take a look at the farm animals he's acquired when people no longer wanted them.

Heartland Organic World, Cleveland

This CSA-based farm, with Melanie McIntosh at the helm, plans to double the number of CSA customers next year. They are also talking with several other farms about starting a co-op. Currently they grow on a half acre of their six-acre farm. A high tunnel and heated hoop house will help them extend the growing season.

> **Products:** A wide variety of produce.
> **Where to buy:** CSA. This farm is also interesting because all the extra produce is sold to folks through her daughter's school.
> **Address:** 1800 E. 231 St.
> **Phone:** 913-530-3277
> **Website:** heartlandorganicworld.com
> **Agritourism:** N/A

Karbaumer Farm, Platte City

Klaus and Lee Karbaumer have run this farm since 2005. This farm mainly supports itself by running its own CSA. The Karbaumers use Belgian draft horses, not tractors! And they avoid using chemicals as well.

>**Products:** Organic produce, eggs, and honey.
>**Where to buy:** Sign up for their CSA, stop by and honk to see if they have produce, or find them occasionally at the Platte City Farmers' Market, Eden Alley, Grunauer and Green Acres in Kansas City.
>**Address:** 12200 Missouri 92 Hwy.
>**Phone:** 816-270-2177
>**Website:** www.karbaumerfarm.com
>**Agritourism:** Visitors are welcome but call first. Schedule a horse-drawn wagon or buggy ride.

Nature's Choice Biodynamic Farm, St. Joseph

Fred and Helen Messner started Nature's Choice in 1995 as a Certified Organic farm. Fred even worked as an inspector for organic farms for eight years. In 2001, they decided to become certified as a biodynamic farm as they believe it is a better stewardship practice. Each year they grow twenty-five to thirty different crops on six to seven acres of their thirty-five-acre farm. Buy from Fred and Helen and you're likely to learn the nutritional value of your produce, tips on growing, and information about healthy eating in general.

>**Products:** About twenty-five different produce crops.
>**Where to buy:** City Market in Kansas City, Justus Drug Store—the Restaurant, Blue Bird Bistro in Kansas City, and Sebastienne's at Kemper Art Museum.
>**Address:** 6120 S. Hwy. 169
>**Phone:** 816-596-3936
>**Email:** FGMessner@yahoo.com
>**Website:** Facebook
>**Agritourism:** They can do tours occasionally, but you'll need to call ahead to schedule.

Platte Prairie Farm, Kansas City

Steve Mann uses no-till biodynamic farming methods at this urban farm in Kansas City. Steve offers community classes and is a big proponent of "Food Not Lawns."

> **Products:** A host of vegetables and fruits including broccoli, pak choy, eggplant, sweet potatoes, and wheatgrass.
> **Where to buy:** BADSEED Farmers' Market.
> **Address:** 5223 N. Merrimac Ave.
> **Phone:** 816-746-6595
> **Email:** steve@prairietrading.com
> **Website:** PrairieTrading.com
> **Agritourism:** N/A

Red Ridge Farms, Odessa

Jim and Amy Zumait are working toward organic certification for their farm. They practice no-till farming, on-site composting, and crop rotation. They have a CSA and sell at a local farmers' market. They welcome groups interested in farm tours and like volunteers.

> **Products:** 100-plus varieties of heirloom tomatoes and natural grown flower bouquets.
> **Where to buy:** Farmers' Community Market at Brookside.
> **Address:** 978 NW 1101 Rd.
> **Phone:** 816-690-7161
> **Website:** redridgefarms.wordpress.com
> **Agritourism:** N/A

ban Farm, Kansas City

irted growing in a community garden but soon realized she wanted
he farms about a half acre. For six years Sherri has been farming
the space using organic farming methods, mainly by herself, although she does
occasionally have volunteer help.

Products: Sweet potatoes, greens, kale, Swiss chard, collards, arugula, spinach, herbs,
tomatoes, eggplant, and peppers.
Where to buy: West Port Plaza Farmers' Market.
Address: 3219 East 19th St.
Phone: 816-924-3523
Email: rduf@copper.net
Website: rootdeepurbanfarm.com
Agritourism: N/A

ShroomHeads Organic Farm, Freeman

Tena Bellovich has been growing mushrooms for fifteen years. ShroomHeads is
located outside of Kansas City on twenty-five acres. You'll find organic produce,
mushrooms, and eggs, and they also house a variety of rescue animals.

Products: Tena grows shiitake, oyster, and lion's mane. She forages morels,
chantarelles, porcini, and reishi. Occasionally, she grows maiteke, rameko, and
medicinal mushrooms. She also sells mushroom kits, as well as tomatoes, garlic, and
onions.
Where to buy: Grand Court Farmers' Market, The Farmhouse Restaurant, Renee
Kelly's at Canaan Castle, and Julian.
Address: 12301 E. 264th St.
Phone: 816-966-9446
Website: shroomheads.com
Agritourism: Visitors are welcome, but please bring treats for the rescue animals—
dogs, pigs, horses, llamas, a donkey, and sheep.

URBAVORE Urban Farm (a Project of BADSEED), Kansas City

Check out this unique thirteen-acre urban farm. Brooke Salvaggio and Dan Heryer started BADSEED Farm on a couple of acres in South Kansas City. After four years a zoning issue forced this industrious pair to move their farm and start over. They bought thirteen acres in Kansas City and started URBAVORE. Currently they have two acres in organic vegetable production and have newly planted orchards and livestock.

Brooke and Dan have big dreams for URBAVORE. They are building a homestead on the farm where they will live "off the grid." This means they will not tap into city services like electric and water and will instead rely on solar power, heating, and cooling through passive-solar and innovative design, and water with a rainwater catchment system and cistern. The couple currently teach classes in Urban Homesteading where participants learn how to live an agrarian lifestyle and self-sustainability.

Brooke says of URBAVORE, "We want to be a place where city dwellers can connect with LIFE and experience REAL FOOD. We want to be an example of environmental stewardship and prove that urban agriculture can enhance cities and most importantly, FEED them."

Products: Extensive variety of heirloom vegetables, culinary, and medicinal herbs.
Where to buy: Produce and eggs are available at their farmstand, the BADSEED Farmers' Market, and on Sundays at the City Market in Kansas City.
Farmstand address: 5500 Bennington, Kansas City, every Sat., June-Oct. 2-6 p.m. BADSEED Farmer's Market is at 1900 McGee St., every Friday night during summer and winter market sessions. Check website for dates.
Phone: 816-472-0027
Email: brooke@badseedfarm.com, dan@badseedfarm.com
Website: www.badseedkc.com
Agritourism: Visitors are welcome on the farm and for self-guided tours during the Saturday afternoon farmstand hours.

Wood Mood Farm, Higginsville

Jim will tell you that he has the best soil for growing in the whole state. And it turns out this is almost true. Soil surveys showed that Lafayette County, which is where his farm is located, has the second best soil in the state. You can dig for a couple of feet before you hit clay, and he has never hit a rock. His son has recently joined him in the business, and they grow vegetables on five to six acres with four hoop houses. He also has a few beef cows on the sixty total acres of Wood Mood Farm. When he started growing for restaurants in the early 2000s he heard from chefs that what they really needed was someone to grow staples—potatoes, onions, and greens—that are high quality and local. So he did.

Jim has farmed his whole life. He grew up in a large family and says if you didn't garden you wouldn't eat.

Products: Certified Organic produce from asparagus to zucchini. He grows a lot of root crops, potato varieties, greens, chard, kale, beets, radishes, and turnips.
Where to buy: One Organic Farmers' Market, Brookside Market, Blue Bird Bistro, Room 39, Room 39 Mission Farms, Starker's Reserve on the Plaza, Julian, West Side Community Restaurant.
Address: 20987 Hwy. 20
Phone: 660-584-3552
Email: woodmood@ctcis.net
Website: N/A
Agritourism: Farm tours with extension office; folks can call if they want to visit.

Southwest Region

Campbell's Fresh Market, Clever

In 1995, Mike Campbell changed his life. He left his corporate marketing career behind for the opportunity to work in the soil. The idea had been percolating for years as Mike remembered the eighty-five-year-old farmer he worked for as a teenager. The farmer had been a mentor to Mike, and he always appreciated his love of farming. So, he dove in and hasn't looked back. Mike now has twenty-two acres of produce broken up something like this—two thousand tomato plants, seven to eight acres of sweet corn, four to five acres of green beans, and six or seven acres of pumpkins. In 2001, they added a corn maze and pumpkin patch and found that the entertainment aspect was a fun addition to their business. Mike is a big believer in showing kids where food comes from and in local food production.

> **Products:** Tomatoes, sweet corn, green beans, pumpkins, and some cold crops like cabbages.
> **Where to buy:** At Springfield Farmers' Market (largest growers' only farmers' market) and on the farm.
> **Address:** 177 Carob Rd.
> **Phone:** 417-743-2208
> **Email:** cfm411@aol.com
> **Website:** campbellsmazedaze.com
> **Agritourism:** Pumpkin patch and corn maze called Campbell's Maze Daze in the fall. Also does school tours occasionally called "How Does Your Garden Grow." Call for information on school tours.

Echigo Farms, Seymour

Kumiko and Mark Frank met in Japan while he was teaching at a university. Both shared a passion and love for farming so when they moved to Missouri in 2009, they decided to give it a try. They wanted to bring both the flavors of Japan and Japanese farming methods to the Midwest. Kumiko and Mark believe in no-till farming and seek to farm as close to nature as possible. They have two high tunnels that allow them to farm year-round, and they cultivate two acres a year on their four-acre farm.

Products: You'll find a host of East Asian produce including Japanese tomatoes, eggplants, edamame, and even something called a bitter melon. Used in stir fries and salads, the bitter melon is like a cucumber/melon mix, but you eat it from the outside in. Mark says it looks like a melting candle.
Where to buy: Greater Springfield Farmers' Market, MaMa Jean's, Homegrown Foods.
Address: 3502 Normandy Rd.
Phone: 417-849-4000
Website: echigofarm.blogspot.com
Agritourism: They welcome visitors, but call to set up a tour.

Evening Shade Organics, Milo

Dennis used to be Certified Organic and still farms that way. He grows in large hoop houses and greenhouses in the spring and fall. He likes hoop house growing because he has more control over the water, and the greens stay very tender and do not get dirty during heavy downpours. In the summer he sells vegetables for Mennonite families in his community.

Products: Greens, kale, napa cabbages, cauliflower, onions, garlic, radishes, and strawberries.
Where to buy: Sells to restaurants and stores in the Kansas City area—Whole Foods (two locations) and Nature's Own, Lidia's, Starker's Reserve, Yia-Yia's, Route 39, The Farmhouse, Michael Smith, The American, Mission Hills Country Club, and Carriage Club.
Address: N/A
Phone: 417-684-0405
Website: www.eveningshade.us
Agritourism: Need to call.

Fassnight Creek Farms, Springfield

Dan Bigbee is one of those people who is doing exactly what he wants to do, and what he wants to do is farm. He's been farming at Fassnight for twenty-four years and has about sixteen acres in production. From the time Dan could walk he followed his grandpa around the family garden. Like most farmers, Dan has worked out a number of relationships to help sustain his farm. He allows a tree service to dump all their wood chips on his land. After four to five years, these "useless" chips are wonderful mulch and compost for his produce. He uses drip irrigation, and most of the water comes from his property. While he uses some conventional pesticides, he does that as little as possible and relies on cover crops to enrich his soil. The recent demand for locally grown foods has been wonderful for his business, and Dan has added high tunnels so he can grow year round.

Products: Grows vegetables, some flowers, larkspur, peonies, sunflowers, strawberries, and blackberries.
Where to buy: On the farm 10-6 every day but Sunday. Greater Springfield Farmers' Market and several stores—Homegrown Foods, Down to Earth Foods, and Well-Fed Neighbor. He also sells to the Price Cutters Bistro Market and Restaurant, and Farmers' Gastro Pub restaurant. All the restaurants and stores he sells to are within ten minutes from his farm.
Address: 1366 S. Fort
Phone: 417-818-4417
Website: N/A
Agritourism: Visit the farm to buy produce every day but Sunday.

"People are serious about buying local food. It's a beautiful thing. I've been grubbing around in the dirt for twenty-four years waiting for this to happen."

—Dan Bigbee

Millsap Farms, Springfield

Curtis and Sarah Millsap have been farming for seven years—four years full-time. They have about twenty acres and lease an additional ten. They are dedicated to farming organically and farming year round with the addition of two high tunnels. In the next year they plan to expand their recent foray into no-till farming to cover four acres. A recent visit to the farm found Curtis in the fields with two interns and two WWOOFers (volunteers with World Wide Opportunities on Organic Farms, www.wwoof.org/index2.asp). Every day this extended farm family sits down to a traditional farm lunch signaled by a bell rung at high noon.

Products: A wide variety of crops like arugula, carrots, okra, spinach, cucumbers, and tomatoes, but Curtis experiments to learn what grows best in his area using organic farming methods.
Where to buy: On the farm, MaMa Jean's, Homegrown, the Greater Springfield Farmers' Market, and their own CSA.
Address: 6593 North Emu Ln.
Phone: 417-839-0847
Email: cmillsap1@yahoo.com
Website: www.millsapfarms.com
Agritourism: Call before you visit.

Curtis Millsap showcasing
a lovely white eggplant

Overboe Farm, Springfield

Overboe Farm is also a part of OOVVDA, which is a winery in Sp[...]
raise black and red raspberries and cherries for wine and have some[...]
and unique countertop-height raised beds for produce.

Products: Asparagus, tomatoes, spinach, broccoli, eggplant, sweet potatoes, and lettuces. They also make an assortment of wines including a tomato wine.

Where to buy: Sells on-site and his tomatoes are sold to the Elks Lodge. You'll find their wines at a variety of locations including MaMa Jean's and Heather Hill Farms in Ozark.

Address: 5448 North Berry Ln., five minutes from 44, Exit 80

Phone: 417-833-4896

Website: oovvda.com

Agritourism: Yes, the winery and vegetable beds are open for tourism. Check website for more information.

Seasons Harvest Eco-Farm, Sparta

Larry and Carla Vogel are bringing gardening to the people with workshops on raised-bed gardening and a complete line of organic fertilizers, soil amendments, and pest controls. Oh yeah, and they grow a lot of great produce.

Products: Beets, broccoli, cucumbers, peppers, onions, peas, and tomatoes, to name a few.

Where to buy: CSA and Ozark Farmers' Market. You can also purchase their fertilizers and gardening products on their website.

Address: 315 Diamond View

Phone: 417-634-5414

Website: seasonsharvestecofarm.com

Agritourism: N/A

ine Hollow Ranch, Powell

Gwen and Jerry Schroeder have a diversified farm in Southwest Missouri. This is the kind of farm that could fit in almost any chapter of the book. They raise chickens, rabbits, have a large garden that is grown with organic methods, and a native plant nursery.

> **Products:** Mushrooms, apples, and vegetables.
> **Where to buy:** Neosho Farmers' Market, Webb City Farmers' Market.
> **Address:** 760 Cowan Ridge Rd.
> **Phone:** 417-435-2456
> **Email:** gschroeder@shinehollowranch.com
> **Website:** shinehollowranch.com
> **Agritourism:** N/A

Urban Roots, Springfield

Adam and Melissa Millsap had to do a lot of trash hauling before they could begin farming. The 1.75 acres they bought had eight apartment units and a large lot that previously housed other apartments before a fire destroyed them. That site had become a dumping ground. This industrious couple has transformed the once-barren land with a half acre in vegetable beds and three mobile high tunnels that run on rails. They grow organically and are part of the WWOOF network. Adam tells us that "Generally people in urban farming don't buy property, but with eight apartment units to help pay the mortgage, this is an exception."

> **Products:** Grow everything but corn—beets, radishes, green beans, herbs, watermelon, winter squash, arugula, onions, garlic, carrots, kohlrabi . . . you name it. They plan to offer a CSA in 2012.
> **Where to buy:** Sold at Greater Springfield Farmers' Market, on the farm, and Farmers' Gastropub, MaMa Jean's, and Homegrown Foods.
> **Address:** 831 W. State
> **Phone:** 417-827-7046; 417-597-4858
> **Email:** adam@urbanrootsfarm.com, mel@urbanrootsfarm.com
> **Website:** urbanrootsfarm.com
> **Agritourism:** Yes, please come by and take a look. Their primary motto is "if you know your farmer, you know your food."

Willow Mountain Mushrooms, Tecumseh

Bob and Wendy Semyck run this small family mushroom farm that s[...]
in growing mushrooms and heirloom vegetables. Bob has always been [...]
mushrooms—his first job was picking mushrooms, and he worked for a variety
of growers at large and small farms before moving to Missouri and starting his
own business in 2004. All their produce and mushrooms are grown using organic
methods. If kombucha is your thing, they also sell kombucha "mushrooms" and
provide instructions for brewing your own kombucha tea.

Products: Portobello, crimini, white button oyster, and shiitake mushrooms.
Where to buy: In Ava at Jean's Healthway, in Springfield at MaMa Jean's Market,
Homegrown Food and at Farmer's Gastropub restaurant. Find them also in Tecumseh
at Dawt Mill Restaurant and in West Plains at Howell Valley Grocery and A-La-
Carte restaurant.
Address: P.O. Box 467
Phone: N/A
Email: shroomshack@gmail.com
Website: willowmountainmushrooms.com
Agritourism: N/A

Southeast Region

Aharon's Heirlooms, Cape Girardeau

Aharon could be described as an accidental farmer. He started growing vegetables on a third of an acre that was in his family after he realized they were spending a lot of time just mowing it. Now, eight years later he is growing on close to two acres. He grows using organic methods, except for his sweet corn, and his niche is heirloom vegetables.

Products: A little bit of everything—radishes, mixed lettuces, Swiss chard, onions, leeks, purple long beans, squash, watermelon, winter squash, okra, and lots of sunflowers. He also grows a lot of fingerling potatoes and purple Peruvian potatoes.
Where to buy: Cape Farmers' Market sometimes, but mostly he sells to Molly's Café and Bar (he works there too) and to Celebrations.
Address: 2316 State Hwy. V
Phone: 573-576-8299
Email: aharonsheirlooms@yahoo.com
Website: N/A
Agritourism: Call to arrange a visit.

Blackwell Family Produce, Salem

Lloyd and Josie Blackwell are retired school teachers who have been farming for more than thirty years. They currently have about six acres in production and use cover crops to enrich their soil.

Products: Sweet corn, green beans, tomatoes, broccoli, cauliflower, beets, melons, okra, carrots, and spinach.
Where to buy: Salem Farmers' Market, and their farmstand is open Mon., Wed., Thurs, Fri. from 10-6, June-Aug./Sept. They also sell at the Brick House Restaurant.
Address: 5292 Hwy. CC
Phone: 573-674-2780
Website: N/A
Agritourism: They have a barn with a shed and the shed is the farm stand. Quarter mile off Hwy. CC, look for the sign.

Laughing Stalk Farmstead, Cape Girardeau

Emily and Ross have a small diversified farm on about two acres near Cape Girardeau. They don't use any chemicals or pesticides. Emily and Ross moved to Missouri from Wisconsin because Emily's mom had some land they could use. They love it in the Midwest so far and enjoy the longer growing season.

Products: They grow over forty different vegetables, herbs, and beans with a tremendous number of varieties. They have a CSA and have had a great response to that.
Where to buy: Cape Farmers' Market, Calix Coffee, Celebrations.
Address: 1521 County Road 649
Phone: 573-576-0730
Email: laughingstalkfarmstead@gmail.com
Website: laughingstalkfarmstead.blogspot.com
Agritourism: Can visit the farm, but it is best to call.

Radishes from Dry Dock Farm

Lazy Ox Farm, Alton

Margaret Paskert is in the business of tomatoes—lots of them. For the last five years she's been selling her tomato plants to people all over the country. She no longer has her organic certification, but she still grows that way. With forty acres and a big greenhouse, she still sells out every year. Plants and seeds usually ship to customers between March and June.

Products: Tomato plants including San Marzano and Black Krim, seeds, and other plants including eggplants, basils, culinary herbs, tomatillos, and okras.
Where to buy: On-line and at Baker Creek Festival.
Address: Rt. 2 Box 2749
Phone: 417-778-1677
Website: www.lazyoxfarm.com
Agritourism: N/A

McKaskle Family Farms, Braggadocio

Steve McKaskle has been an organic farmer since the 1970s. He has 1,600 acres currently planted in corn, rice, and soybeans. In the past he has grown organic cotton for Patagonia and has sold his popcorn and rice to companies like Newman's Own. Steve is a big proponent of organic farming and is always searching for ways to grow products more efficiently and to rotate the crops in a way that eradicates as many weeds as possible. His future plans include adding wheat crops, oats, and a mill to make corn meal and flour.

Products: Organic popcorn, organic rice—brown basmati, long-grain brown, and long-grain white—and organic soybeans.
Where to buy: Clovers and MaMa Jean's in Springfield, Local Harvest Grocery and Whole Foods in St. Louis.
Address: P.O. Box 10
Phone: 573-757-6653
Website: mckasklefamilyfarm.com
Agritourism: N/A

Maranatha Farm, Koshkonong

Mary and Skip Badiny have been "gardening" since 1984. She has about five acres of garden and fruit trees that she tends using organic farming practices. She boasts about her amazing "green/hoop house" that can maintain 90-degree inside temps when there is snow on the ground. She says it is tough to find places to sell in her area and that she must match Wal-Mart prices in order to sell her produce. Farmers find a way, though, and Mary's niche has come through—J.B.'s Health Mart. Customers place orders through the store and pick up their produce there.

> **Products:** Produce, perennials, raspberries, dried flowers, and fruit trees.
> **Where to buy:** J.B.'s Health Mart has an email list. You can also go to her beautiful farm.
> **Address:** RR1 Box 119
> **Phone:** 417-764-3698
> **Email:** 7thdaymb@gmail.com (best way to reach her is by emailing)
> **Website:** localharvest.org
> **Agritourism:** Can visit, but call.

Martin Rice, Bernie

Martin Rice was started over 50 years ago on 160 acres in the Missouri bootheel. Now, the same family farms 4,000 acres. In 2000, they constructed their own rice processing facility.

> **Products:** White rice, long- and medium-grain brown rice, and jasmine rice. The rice is packaged in lovely old-timey canvas bags or in bulk to stores and restaurants.
> **Where to buy:** Buy at their on-line store. Also available at Local Harvest Grocery, Sappingtons, through Fair Shares, and many other retail establishments.
> **Address:** 22326 County Road 780
> **Phone:** 573-293-4884
> **Email:** info@martinrice.com
> **Website:** martinrice.com
> **Agritourism:** N/A

On the Wind, Willow Springs

This couple truly goes the extra mile when it comes to healthy growing. They've been farming organically for thirty years and until recently sold to Whole Foods Market. Besides bountiful crops of tomatoes, squash, blueberries, and other seasonal yummies, Ronnie is also known for his eggs. What makes his eggs special is that Ronnie grows sprouts just for the chickens. Fans of his eggs say they have a rich flavor and dark yolk that is unlike any other pasture-raised egg.

> **Products:** Produce, eggs, tomatoes, squash, blueberries, and in 2012 he plans to have grass-fed beef.
> **Where to buy:** Kirkwood Farmers' Market in St. Louis from June-September.
> **Address:** N/A
> **Phone:** 417-469-2616
> **Website:** N/A
> **Agritourism:** N/A

Ozark Forest Mushrooms

Nicola Macpherson has been in the business of mushrooms for twenty-three years. Nicola says the Missouri Ozarks Big Springs region provides the perfect micro-climate for mushrooms and access to a sustainable supply of oak logs. Ozark Forest Mushrooms is a family-owned farm with 18,000 shiitake logs, and the mushrooms are Certified Organic.

> **Products:** Fresh and dried oyster and shiitake mushrooms. Nicola also packages some tantalizing quick meals like Buddhist Delight featuring noodles, dried local mushrooms, and spices.
> **Where to buy:** Local Harvest Grocery, Maplewood Farmers' Market, Tower Grove Farmers' Market, and at the Japanese Festival and Best of Missouri Market at the Missouri Botanical Garden.
> **Address:** N/A
> **Phone:** 314-531-9935
> **Website:** www.ozarkforest.com
> **Agritourism:** Yes, but call to arrange.

Fruits

If you live in or around St. Louis, like we do, it is hard to miss the seasonal pull of the u-pick apple and peach orchards that surround the area. Indeed, fruit operations are probably the most popular and familiar ways that people are connected with farms in Missouri. Many folks have been picking at the same orchard or berry patch for years and know the people who run the orchard/farm. For those who prefer to leave the picking to the professionals, peaches—followed by apples—make their annual appearances at farmers' markets and in stores across the state starting as early as June and extending through December.

Apples are probably the fruit most often associated with u-pick orchards, so their popularity can hardly be disputed. In fact, in the late nineteenth century, Missouri was the leading apple-producing state in the nation (plantsci.missouri.edu/apple/facts.htm). Unfortunately, over the years drought, disease, and the resulting financial hardships have reduced the number of orchards from their heyday in the 1890s. Even so, apples remain a well-loved fruit in Missouri. The most popular apple variety in the Show-Me State is the Jonathan, which has been grown in Missouri for 150 years. Other tried and true varieties include Red and Golden Delicious, Gala, and Fuji. Apples store well when kept cold (30-32°F) with 90 percent relative humidity and some air circulation. Some varieties, including Jonathans, can be kept for several months this way. Of course, if storage space for fruit is at a premium, you can always enjoy fresh apple cider.

Missouri's late summer climate is favorable for apple growing, but the threat of spring freezes can damage both apple and peach trees and affect production, making Missouri among the northernmost states for peach orchards. Some believe that the area around Kansas City on the Missouri River is the best area to grow apples and peaches because of the type of soil and the hilly, terraced landscape. The peach and apple orchards in Missouri grow a wide variety of these fruits, so you are sure to find something you like! Other tree fruits grown in Missouri include pears, apricots, plums, and figs. Many of the state's orchards are not Certified Organic because it is so difficult to prevent pests and diseases in the crops without the use of pesticides. So be sure to use our guide and/or to call ahead to find out what pest management techniques are used.

Berries* are also often featured on u-pick farms and at farmers' markets. The most common to Missouri are blackberries, black raspberries, and strawberries, although many farmers are trying a hand at growing blueberries. Some of the more exotic varieties grown are gooseberries, elderberries, and aronia berries. Red raspberries are harder to find than one would think—for one, because they are difficult to transport—so if that is your favorite berry, we suggest trying to grow some yourself. Berry farmers must take meticulous care of their crops to avoid having to spray them for pests and disease. Again, consult this guide or call about pest management techniques.

For all u-pick farms and farmers' markets, it is a good idea to call ahead to make sure they are open, and be sure to bring cash in case that's the only method of payment. And remember that you can buy a lot and preserve the extra by freezing or canning it or turning it into jams and spreads (see Recipes & Tips).

---

*Although grapes are not berries, we should mention that there is a large and expanding grape-growing business, but because many of the state's grapes are grown for wine production, we limit their inclusion in this guide.

Some interesting native fruits may be easier to find by foraging for them than by looking for them at a market or a u-pick farm. Two notables are the persimmon and the pawpaw. Both are unusual fruits with their own unique tastes and textures—for anyone who has ever eaten an unripe persimmon, the experience may well swear you off the fruit for life because of the alum-like effect. If that has happened to you, we urge you to try again. Ripe persimmon is an excellent ingredient in fall baked goods like breads and traditional puddings (e.g., figgy pudding). Pawpaw is sometimes referred to as the Ozark Banana (among its many nicknames) and tastes like a combination of banana, mango, and pineapple. Because of the difficulty of transporting the fruit, it rarely appears in markets or stores, but we hope to see more commercially available pulp or locally produced ice creams and sorbets, baked goods, or spreads made from this exotic local. But like serious mushroom hunters who fiercely guard the location of their foraging spots, the more well-known pawpaws become, the more we expect people to clam up about where the best groves are found.

Whether your preference is for a crisp red apple in the fall or a perfectly sweet strawberry in the spring, it's easy to get your daily allowance of fruits right here in Missouri.

Pears at Prairie Birthday Farm, photo by Linda Hezel

Northwest Region

Blazerfarmz, Stewartsville

Toby Yager and brothers Chip and Steve Blazer plan to teach us all the wonders of the aronia berry—commonly known as the black chockberry. Native to the Midwest, American Indians used them in pemmican mix, a high-energy paste made up of dried meats, nuts, and berries that provided sustenance on long journeys. The aronia berry has the second-highest ORAC value (oxygen radical absorption capacity), exceeded barely by the goji berry. Although aronias are not inherently sweet, cooking the berries releases the natural sugars. Proponents of the aronia berry say it can help boost energy, has anti-inflammatory properties, and can help regulate high blood pressure and diabetes.

> **Products:** Cold-pressed aronia juice (16 oz.-2 lbs. of berries used for each bottle), fresh-frozen aronia berries, Berryburstz (similar to gummy bears), Aronia Berry Jam, Aronia-Jalapeno Jam, Aronia-Currant Jam, Aronia Berry Jelly, and Aronia Berry Wine (distributed locally by the Windy Wine Co.).
> **Where to buy:** Pony Express Farmers' Market, on-line, and by spring 2012 in many stores across Missouri and the United States, including Hy-Vee.
> **Address:** 6061 SW Rogers Rd.
> **Phone:** 816-294-3343; 816-390-2596
> **Email:** aronia@blazerfarmz.com
> **Website:** blazerfarmz.com
> **Agritourism:** Yes, just call ahead or email Toby.

Schweizer Orchard, St. Joseph

The Schweizer Orchard has a long history of apple farming that began in the 1900s. Steve Schweizer, his wife, Becky, and their sons and daughter-in-law now operate the orchard, market, and Christmas tree farm. The current orchard was planted in 1988 and has u-pick berries, peaches, apples, and pumpkins. They also sell vegetables at their market during the growing season. This orchard and farm has activities from June to December.

Products: U-pick strawberries, blackberries, raspberries, blueberries, peaches, apples, and pumpkins. In 2009 they added a Christmas tree farm. You can select your own, and they will cut it down or you can choose from pre-cut trees. Enjoy hot cider or hot chocolate as you ride through the fields.
Where to buy: At the farm.
Address: 5455 SE State Route FF
Phone: 816-232-3999
Website: schweizerorchards.com
Agritourism: Visit June-December to experience the breadth of products grown at Schweizers.

Northeast Region

Binder's Hilltop Apple and Berry Farm, Mexico

Sandy Binder has a little bit of everything in her three-acre orchard. She is also the sole worker for this orchard, so she stays busy. You will find apple trees, a few peach and plum trees, some vegetable gardens, and a few bee hives for honey. Sandy also keeps a herd of about fifty alpaca and makes hats, socks, and other merchandise from the alpaca fiber. She loves the warmth and versatility of the alpaca fiber.

Products: U-pick apples and pre-picked peaches and plums. At her farm store you can also find apple butter, apple chips, freshly cut and dried flowers, soaps, honey, breads, and even sugar-free jams and jellies. All of the products are made on the farm. The alpaca products are available on the farm or at the Columbia Farmers' Market. She carries a wide variety of alpaca products—sweaters, blankets, hats, socks, gloves, rugs, and even stuffed animals. Alpaca roving and yarn is available to those who want to create their own products.
Where to buy: On the farm at her farm store or Columbia Farmers' Market (check her website for farmers' market dates).
Address: 24688 Audrain Road 820 (go to website for directions)
Phone: 573-721-1415
Email: applesandalpacas@ktis.net
Website: applesandalpacas.com
Agritourism: Open July to the end of October (or until last fruit is picked!). Binder's has a picnic area. Sandy offers educational tours and soap-making classes. Call Sandy or check the website for information on classes and tours.

Blue Heron Orchard, Canton

Dan Kelly planted Blue Heron Orchard in 1990. The orchard is unique in Missouri because it is a Certified Organic Orchard and farm. When asked about the challenges of keeping the orchard organic, Dan says that a lot of the work happens during the planning and planting phase. You need to make sure you have the correct soil and balance of nutrients. Secondly, you must maintain the orchard. Dan and his wife and partner, Cherie Sampson, spend a lot of time cleaning the orchard—picking up rotting apples, dropped limbs, etc. This helps with disease and insect control. Pruning also is crucial to make sure light reaches the inside of the tree. This continual upkeep makes it harder for insects and diseases to flourish. Dan also grows a host of organic annual produce.

Products: Winesaps, Pristine, Gala, Jonathan, Courtland, Golden Delicious, Red Delicious, Empires, Freedom, and a smattering of antique apples from August-October along with Certified Organic vegetables like greens, peppers, and squash. They offer a variety of value-added products including applesauce, apple butters, smoked jalapenos, apple syrup (Pomona's Ambrosia), fresh apple cider, and apple cider vinegars.

Where to buy: Clovers in Columbia, and in St. Louis at Local Harvest Grocery, Maplewood Farmers' Market, the Garden Gate Shop at Missouri Botanical Garden, Sappington Farmers' Market, Maude's Market, and Fair Shares.

Address: 32974 220th St.

Phone: 573-655-4291

Email: blueheronrchard@centurytel.net

Website: blueheronorchard.com

Agritourism: U-pick is by appointment only.

Reaping the bounty at Blue Heron Orchard

Lost Branch Blueberry Farm, Brashear

Robert Price and his wife had twenty-seven acres and a desire to grow food—they just didn't know what to grow. When inspiration struck to grow blueberries, Robert ignored the naysayers who said it was too hard to grow blueberries in Missouri. He loves growing blueberries and says the blueberry farm has brought out each family member's particular gifts as they work the land together—granted he said that he and his son have spent a lot of time on their knees praying and patching the soil. He realizes now that spending a little more time on the soil beforehand would have prevented some of the problems he had with the blueberries. Despite those issues and bad weather in 2011, the bushes still produced 4,500 pounds. He is hoping for 6,000 to 7,000 pounds in 2012. Robert does not use sprays on the bushes and swears by clean pruning techniques. He has learned a lot since the first planting in 2006. He looks forward to growing more blueberries, is waiting on the asparagus to reach full production, and hopes to add peach trees.

Products: U-pick blueberries and some pre-pick. They also raise grass-fed sheep that he sells through Vesterbrook Farm.
Where to buy: At the farm, and Truman State buys some blueberries for use at the school.
Address: 21507 Lost Branch Way
Phone: 660-342-1771
Email: pricefamilylbdf@gmail.com
Website: lostbranchblueberries.com
Agritourism: Enjoy the on-site picnic area and check out the donkeys and lambs when you go to pick. Call the farm or check the website for picking updates.

> "A garden is like hosting visitors, and an orchard is like family."
>
> —Dan Kelly, Blue Heron Orchard

West Orchards, Macon

Dan and Mary West planted this ten-acre orchard in 1995 as a small family venture. What started as a three hundred-tree hobby farm is now a thirteen hundred-tree full-fledged business. They grow seventeen varieties of apples as well as some peach, pear, and apricot trees. They describe themselves as a low-spray operation, and some years they do not spray at all. Dan and Mary also keep bees, and their honey can often be found at the farm store. This u-pick operation is great for families and offers restrooms, picnic areas, and a refreshment stand.

> **Products:** Honey and seventeen varieties of apples including Pristine, Arkansas Black, Honeycrisp, Rome Beauty, Jonafree, Senshu, Redfree, Gala, and Liberty. You can also find fresh pressed cider in September and a variety of pies, jams, and jellies.
> **Where to buy:** U-pick and pre-picked at the farm.
> **Address:** 25875 Jewell Ave.
> **Phone:** 660-651-7582
> **Email:** sales@west-orchards.com
> **Website:** west-orchards.com
> **Agritourism:** Call or check the website for ripening dates.

Wilsdorf Berry Patch, Madison

Debbie Wilsdorf opened the berry patch in 2006. Her daughter is now in college, so Debbie keeps things going on her own. She says she spends a lot of time hand-weeding in March-October to keep rows tidy and to minimize pests. She uses a few herbicides, but as little as possible. Debbie is serious about her berries and has even written a book called *Fruits of the Midwest—A Cookbook and Guide from Harvest to Table*. Look for it on-line or buy from Debbie.

> **Products:** Blackberries, strawberries, and daylily plants.
> **Where to buy:** On the farm.
> **Address:** 14976 Monroe Road 1039
> **Phone:** 660-651-0378
> **Website:** wilsdorfberrypatch.com
> **Agritourism:** U-pick farm.

Central Region

Anne's Acres, Lincoln

Leslie and Rob Exendine began planting about eleven years ago and have no plans to stop. They started with blueberry bushes, which are not easy to grow in Missouri. About three hundred of their two thousand bushes (planted over time) are at full production. A recent property expansion has them dreaming of grapes and even almond trees. You will also find some pecan and black walnut trees on the property.

Products: Blueberries.
Where to buy: On the farm.
Address: 20521 Fordney Rd.
Phone: 660-221-5906
Email: annesacres@embarkmail.com
Website: N/A
Agritourism: Call in advance for a picking report and picking hours. They sell out every year.

Elderberry Life, Hartsburg

Terry Durham has been farming since 1978, when he put in his first big organic "market" garden. During the 1980s they ran a CSA and started doing some wholesale. And then they began gearing up for elderberries. He now has thirty-two acres in elderberries, and they are all grown without the use of pesticides. This native Missouri berry has not been grown commercially in the state until now, although there is a lot of potential. Terry says that 95 percent of the elderberry products sold in the country are imported. Elderberry Life has been working with the state and with researchers to promote and increase elderberry production. The elderberry boasts proven antioxidant and immunity properties. Many folks use it often during cold and flu season for prevention or to decrease the duration of symptoms. Farmers interested in growing elderberries can attend workshops with Terry in the summer. Elderberry bushes can take up to five years to reach full production, and while they can be a profitable berry, they are also highly perishable and must be processed almost immediately after harvest.

> **Products:** Elderberry Throat Coat and Health Cordial, Elderberry Juice, Elderberry Jelly, and frozen elderberries. Terry also sells elderberry plants. (The products are sold under the River Hills Harvest label.)
> **Where to buy:** Buy on-line or at the following: in St. Louis at Sappington Farmers' Market, Maude's Market, Local Harvest Grocery; in Columbia at Hy-Vee Stores, Clovers, Moser's, and World Harvest; in Jefferson City at Jefferson City Health Center; and at Laughing Ladies in Rolla.
> **Address:** N/A
> **Phone:** Terry 573-999-3034; Deni 573-424-9693; Roger 919-602-2082
> **Email:** info@elderberrylife.com; elderberrylife@gmail.com
> **Website:** elderberrylife.com
> **Agritourism:** Give farm tours by appointment.

Missouri Highland Farm, Jamestown

Mary Brauch started the farm in 1986 partly because she wanted to be in the country. She had seen a berry farm outside of Kansas City and thought it looked like something she could do. Growing berries is not for the impatient, as it takes up to three to five years (sometimes longer) to produce a good yield and fully establish the bushes. Now more than twenty-five years later, she has two acres in blueberries along with blackberries, gooseberries, and asparagus. She does not spray her berries.

Products: U-pick or pre-picked blueberries, blackberries, gooseberries, and asparagus.
Where to buy: On the farm and at Columbia Farmers' Market.
Address: 17071 Garrett Rd.
Phone: 660-849-2544
Website: missourihighlandfarm.com (get picking info from website)
Agritourism: Open Thurs.-Sun. only, June and first half of July.

The Peach Tree Farm, Boonville

The Arnetts bought Peach Tree Farm in the early 1990s, and Bruce said they might have gotten one crop off the trees before they completely replanted it. Peach trees will produce for about twenty-five years. Since they started, they have expanded and now have about 2,400 trees as well as some vegetable crops, which they also sell on the farm. Bruce says their farm is different because they never refrigerate their peaches—they pick what is ready, sell them, and when they sell out they are done for the day. The Arnetts relocated a log cabin built in 1818 to their farm. They also have an oak wood peg barn built in the 1800s on their property. These beautiful old buildings look lovely set among the trees and provide a perfect spot for purchasing juicy peaches. About seventeen years ago they started a pumpkin patch, which allowed them to diversify their offerings.

Products: Find peaches from mid-June through mid-Sept. and pumpkins Sept.-Oct.
Where to buy: Usually only on the farm, but in 2011 he had so many peaches that he sold them at farmers' markets throughout the area in order to sell them all. He has never sold them wholesale.
Address: 24863 Hwy. 98
Phone: 660-882-8009
Email: arnettspeachtreefarm@gmail.com
Website: thepeachfarm.com
Agritourism: Lots of family activities in the fall, including a hay bale maze, barnyard animals, and pumpkin patch. Pumpkin is u-pick, but peaches are not.

Pick and Pick, Columbia

Sam and Deanna began farming in 2004 after they retired. Their son and his wife are moving back to Missouri from California and plan to take over most of the farm labor, leaving Sam and Deanna (hopefully, she says) more in the role of consultants and participants. Pick and Pick is a unique farm because everything is u-pick, not just the fruits. It is a great place to show your kids and your friends where your food comes from and a wonderful place to learn how to pick produce of all kinds. They focus on strawberries, asparagus, and blackberries but have other seasonal vegetables like pumpkins, tomatoes, and peppers. They use as few sprays as possible because, as she says, "We eat it too."

> **Products:** Tomatoes, peppers, raspberries, strawberries, blackberries, and pumpkins.
> **Where to buy:** On the farm and sometimes at the Columbia Farmers' Market when they have extra produce.
> **Address:** 5910 South Rangeline Rd.
> **Phone:** 573-999-4036 (farm); 573-449-8031 (business)
> **Email:** pickandpick@centurytel.net
> **Website:** pickandpick.com
> **Agritourism:** U-pick farm.

St. Louis Region

Centennial Farms, Augusta

Centennial Farms is what the name says—a centennial farm. They received their official designation in 1976, recognizing that this farm had been operated by the same family for more than one hundred years. Ellen and Bob Knoernschild are the fourth generation to run the farm, which was first established in 1854. The sixth generation, their grandchildren, live on the farm. In 1967 they planted their first orchards and vineyards. There are now more than one thousand apple trees, four hundred peach trees, vineyards, berries, and vegetables on seventy-five acres.

Products: Twelve varieties of peaches (not u-pick), blackberries (u-pick by appointment only), vegetables, twenty-four apple varietals available as u-pick or already picked. Find apple butter, preserves, peach butter, blackberry syrup, and honey from their farm in the market at Centennial Farms.

Where to buy: Maplewood Farmers' Market and on the farm. Their apple butter is available at Dierberg's Market and Local Harvest Grocery (jams also) in St. Louis, at Olde Town Spice Shop in St. Charles, and at Missouri Mercantile.

Address: 199 Jackson St.

Phone: 636-228-4338

Website: centennialfarms.biz

Agritourism: The on-site market is open July-early November. Centennial Farms hosts u-pick apples in the fall, u-pick blackberries by appointment, and in September they turn their farmstead into a "Pumpkin Fantasyland" with a play area, fort, play tractor, and hay rides.

Heritage Valley Tree Farm, Washington

Vernon and Bee Spaunhorst started the Tree Farm twenty-five years ago on land that has been in Vernon's family since the 1850s. Their children are the seventh generation on the farm. As Bee tells it, they decided to plant trees instead of corn, which is what a lot of folks grow on acreage such as theirs. As you can imagine, it takes a lot of patience when your crops are pecans (about twenty-five years to production), Christmas trees, and apple trees. Today, they have twenty acres in Christmas trees, six acres in apples, and ten acres in pecans. They also operate a lovely bed and breakfast in a 150-year-old log house with modern updates.

Products: U-pick apples (Gala, Enterprise, and Gold Rush), Christmas trees, and pecans in the shell.

Where to buy: On the farm.

Address: 1668 Four Mile Rd. (four miles from the Missouri River)

Phone: 636-239-7479

Email: hv@yhti.net

Website: heritagevalleytreefarm.com/treefarm1.htm

Agritourism: Their u-pick apples available on the honor system (so bring cash), together with the "choose and cut" Christmas tree farm make the trip an event for the family. Hot cider, hot chocolate, and freshly baked cookies make Christmas tree hunting extra tasty.

Huckleberry Hollow, St. Clair

At Huckleberry Hollow you will find two and a half acres of delicious blueberries. Don Dauster has had this operation for fifteen years and grows his blueberries with no sprays or insecticides. You will find clean-mulched rows with four varieties of blueberries on bushes that reach up to seven feet high. He loves his u-pick operation and jokes that on the first days of blueberry season each year his main job is to park cars for the rush of folks who have waited patiently all year for more berries. Don says he grows as organically as possible, because you should not wash blueberries. He says when you wash them the "fuzz" comes off, and that is the part that contains the antioxidants.

> **Products:** Blueberries and some blackberries (about 5 percent of the farm is blackberries).
> **Where to buy:** On the farm, from about the second week of June to the second week of August. He is open seven days a week during picking season. Check his website or look for his ad in the local papers announcing opening day.
> **Address:** 1712 Sycamore Ln.
> **Phone:** 636-629-0668
> **Website:** www.h-hollow.com
> **Agritourism:** This u-pick operation provides buckets and has a small play yard for the kids. You will find chairs in the shade for relaxing and some roving chickens and peacocks.

Hart Apiaries, Lonedell

Troy Hart grew up on a ranch with cattle and horses, and he will tell you he doesn't care if he ever drives another fence post again. Luckily for berry and honey lovers he did not abandon farming altogether. Hart Apiaries boasts six hundred blueberry bushes bursting with berries as well as honey from his twenty to twenty-five hives. Troy started his blueberry farm with the help of a grant program called SARE (Sustainable Agriculture Research and Education). Customers bought shares of his farm years in advance of the product (blueberries take five to seven years to reach u-pick production). Almost like an extreme CSA, this up-front support allowed him to start his blueberry business and gave the initial investors delicious blueberries in return. He mulches his bushes by hand with sawdust from a local sawmill and doesn't use pesticides or insecticides. Troy has an off-farm job, and his wife, kids, and mother-in-law help out when he has to leave town for business.

Products: U-pick blueberries, honey, beeswax, and candles. Some years he even has pawpaws.
Where to buy: On the farm, CDR Naturals in Bourbon, and Natural Health and Home in Hillsboro.
Address: 3738 Hwy. 47
Phone: 636-629-5814
Email: berries@hartapiaries.com
Website: hartapiaries.com
Agritourism: Farm tours upon request.

Liberty Blueberry Farms, Farmington

Joy and Mark Boyer bought Liberty Farms in 2008 for an extra project. And this is one big extra project. With help from their two sons, they run this eight-acre blueberry and three-acre blackberry farm. The bushes are quite established, as this farm has been around since the 1980s. At one time, it was the largest blueberry farm in Missouri. Joy says they don't spray their berries because they haven't had to. Japanese beetles and late freezes have been tough on their blackberry crops the past couple of years, but they hope for a better yield next season.

Products: U-pick and pre-picked blackberries and blueberries.
Where to buy: On the farm.
Address: 1450 Hwy. OO
Phone: 573-701-0281
Email: info@libertyblueberryfarms.com
Website: libertyblueberryfarms.com
Agritourism: U-pick operation.

Thierbach Orchards & Berry Farm, Marthasville

Thierbach Orchards offers lots of activities for the whole family, including u-pick apples, peaches, cherries, and berries along with a petting zoo, on-site market, hay rides, and even a straw tunnel.

Products: Apples, blackberries, blueberries, peaches, pumpkins, strawberries, and tart cherries; u-pick—berries, peaches, and apples.
Where to buy: Crops usually available May-October; please call for ripening and picking details.
Address: 85 Town Branch Rd.
Phone: 636-433-2299; 636-433-2757
Website: thierbachorchards.com
Agritourism: There is a market along with the orchard. From July-Oct., the market is open daily, Mon.-Sat. 9-6 and Sun. 11-6. In the fall be sure to walk the corn and honeysuckle mazes.

T.L. Baumann, Foristell

Tammy and John Baumann planted their orchard ten years ago on this family farm. They have twenty-one total acres and cultivate about five to six of those. They have 120 fruit trees and a new high tunnel to increase produce production. John says they are in the process of gaining their organic certification. This innovative farm is investigating the use of geese, guineas, and chickens for weed and bug control through a research grant with Lincoln University.

Products: Eggs, plums, apples, apricots, plumcots, apriums, peaches, pears, vegetables, and herbs. Apriums are complex plum-apricot hybrids with more apricot characteristics, with a light fuzz and the appearance of an apricot. Plumcots are a simple plum and apricot cross.
Where to buy: Wright City and Foristell farmers' markets, and Mannino's Market in Flint Hill.
Address: N/A
Phone: 314-952-7041
Email: john@tlbaumann.com
Website: tlbaumann.com
Agritourism: Visit by appointment.

Wind Ridge Farm, New Melle

Wind Ridge is a family-owned and managed fruit farm in business since 1991. You will find four different varieties of peaches, including Redhaven, Cresthaven, Canadian Harmony, and Encore, as well as four varieties of blueberries. And you can see for yourself if there is a flavor difference between thorny and thornless blackberry bushes, because they have them both. They minimize their use of sprays by utilizing pheromone traps and crop scouting.

Products: U-pick blueberries and blackberries. Peaches and produce are pre-picked.
Where to buy: On the farm.
Address: 3511 Hwy. F
Phone: 636-828-5900
Website: windridgefarm.net
Agritourism: Vegetables and peaches are pre-picked, but berries are u-pick. Call or check updates on the website before visiting.

Kansas City Region

The Berry Patch, Cleveland

Tom Willis and his wife, Penny, have had the Berry Patch since 1975, and it opened as a u-pick in 1980. The Berry Patch minimizes the use of chemicals and pesticides. Tom says they don't make a pledge never to use them, but they just haven't had to use them much. He says the business suffers a little because of that, but he thinks it is worth it. With about twenty acres in blueberries, they are probably the largest blueberry farm in Missouri. You will find a couple of acres in blackberries as well.

> **Products:** Blackberries, blueberries, jams, and jellies. Blackberries are strictly u-pick, while blueberries are both pre-picked and u-pick. Be sure to check out their country store, where you will find jams and jellies, local honey, and other novelties.
> **Where to buy:** On the farm.
> **Address:** 22509 State Line Rd.
> **Phone:** 816-618-3771
> **Email:** tomwillis@theberrypatchonline.com
> **Website:** theberrypatchonline.com
> **Agritourism:** U-pick farm with gift shop, refreshment stand, and restrooms. They can host birthday parties and school tours. Enjoy tractor "train rides" for kids, a nature trail, and hay bale climbs. In the off-season they are open a couple of half days a week for frozen blueberries and store items.

Duncan's Berry Farm, Smithville

The berry bushes and rhubarb patch are the newest inhabitants of this farm, which houses a one-hundred-year-old house and barn. The bushes were planted in 2009 and are starting to produce in larger amounts. Blackberry bushes are u-pick, but not yet for blueberry bushes. Keep an eye on this newer farm!

Products: Blackberries, blueberries, rhubarb, and jams.
Where to buy: On the farm and at Briarcliff Farmers' Market.
Address: 908 County Road F
Phone: 816-873-3053
Email: duncansberryfarm@live.com
Website: duncansberryfarm.com
Agritourism: You can buy from the farm. Call or email for a picking appointment.

First Fruits Orchard, Drexel

First Fruits Orchard is located on land that has been in Randy Rash's family since the 1880s. When he and his wife inherited their fifty-three acres, they decided to make use of it. So far that has meant one thousand fruit trees, seven hundred blueberry bushes, a quarter acre in strawberries, and a quarter-acre vegetable garden. Randy and his wife are dedicated to using organic growing practices and plan to become Certified Organic. There are a lot of drawbacks to organic farming, according to Randy, like lots of hand-weeding, but they want folks to be able to pop fruit into their mouths without worry. Bee hives on the property help with pollination, and pond water is used for watering.

Products: Organic blueberries, strawberries (Ozark Beauties and Red Giants), and pumpkins. The fruit trees (pears, apples, plums, and peaches) should be producing by 2013.
Where to buy: On the farm.
Address: 9100E State Route A
Phone: 816-674-7579
Email: info@1stfruitsorchard.com
Website: 1stfruitsorchard.com
Agritourism: U-pick blueberries and hayrides in the fall in their pumpkin patch.

John & Linda's Fruit and Berry Farm, Bates City

John grew up on a dairy farm, so he is familiar with hard work. He and his wife, Linda, both work full time and own and operate the berry farm. They have had the farm since early 2000 and make the most of their five acres. The orchard and berry patches are u-pick and pre-picked. You will find a spectrum of fruits here that last from June to October. They have about 50 apple trees, 250 peach trees, and lots of berry plants.

> **Products:** Strawberries (June), blackberries (July), peaches and nectarines (July-August), and apples (October). They also grow some summer crops that you can pick up while you are there.
> **Where to buy:** Buy pre-picked at the farm or pick your own. It is always good to call first to make sure they have product available, either picked or on the trees/bushes. Open daylight to dark during picking season.
> **Address:** 2428 Texas Prairie Rd.
> **Phone:** 816-690-6293
> **Email:** johnj45@hotmail.com
> **Website:** www.localharvest.org/john-linda-fruit-and-berry-farm-M21257
> **Agritourism:** U-pick and pre-pick operation. See the farm when you buy products.

Prairie Birthday Farm LLC, Kearney

In 1995, Linda Hezel and her family purchased a small farm near Kansas City where Linda could return to her roots as a farm girl. It did not take long for them to realize that intense row cropping had left the soil on their farm extremely depleted. Linda and her family have worked hard to rebuild their soil and have created a beautiful and productive organic food farm interspersed with native prairie. By removing non-native grasses (horses helped by over-grazing) and planting native wild flowers and grasses, they are beginning to return the land to its former more fertile and diverse state. Linda will tell you that "American agriculture was built on the back of prairie soil," and their farm showcases what is possible when you mix annual vegetable crops with perennial plantings and native prairie. At her farm you will find meandering plants and vines instead of rows and tidy gardens. Linda is willing to experiment and learn from her plants. "Plants tend to find places they like to grow and companions they want to grow with—who would have thought you could grow a tomato under a pine tree." Not us, Linda, not us!

Products: Heirloom vegetables, berries, edible wild fruits (pawpaws, wild black cherries, elderberries), Concord grapes, mixed heirloom tr[...] peaches, plums, quince, apricots), as well as pecan, hazelnut, and hick[...]
Where to buy: Linda sells to a variety of fine restaurants in the Kansa[...] including The Farmhouse, Bluestem, Room 39, and Café Sebastienne i.. ..ie Kemper Museum of Contemporary Art.
Address: Clay County
Phone: 816-781-9654
Email: flavor@prairiebirthdayfarm.com
Website: prairiebirthdayfarm.com
Agritourism: Linda does farm tours, hosts volunteer apprentices, and offers some classes, but please call to arrange.

Schreiman Orchards, Waverly

This eighty-year-old, three-generation orchard was originally known as Kapelman & Willer-Old Bachelor Orchard. These two men planted the orchard themselves, and it stayed in the family until 2009 when the Christopherson family bought the operation. This family remains dedicated to being a "mom and pop" orchard and business. They replanted the entire orchard three years ago and are now literally seeing the fruits of their labor. This area of the state is wonderful for growing fruit, mainly because of the rich loess soil that runs along the Missouri River. John Christopherson says the good drainage helps and that the trees just thrive in the soil.

Products: Apples and peaches are sold at the original road stand built in 1928. Find peaches the second week of June through mid-September and apples August-November. They have planted a lot of antique varieties like Arkansas Black, Grimmes Golden, Northern Spy, Strawberry Chengo (an older variety that has a hint of strawberry to the apple when ripe), and Cinnamon Spice. They also grow strawberries and blackberries. At the produce stand, which is more like a small store, you can purchase homemade breads, candies, and apple butter.
Where to buy: On the farm.
Address: 29032 Hwy. 24
Phone: 660-493-2477
Email: schreimanorchards@hotmail.com
Website: schreimanorchards.com
Agritourism: You will see the orchard when you stop to buy their pre-picked fruit. Be sure to sign up for their weekly email with picking updates.

Sibley Orchards & Cider Mill, Buckner

Rita and Patrick Farrell have been the guardians of this orchard since they purchased it in the 1990s. Sibley Orchard was started in the 1950s. You will find more than apples here. They have blackberries, peaches, a selection of produce, and also a pumpkin patch with hayrides. Pack a lunch and enjoy a picnic around the lake with some fresh-pressed cider.

Products: U-pick blackberries, apples, peaches, summer and fall vegetables, and pumpkins. Apple wood for smoking is also available in the fall.
Where to buy: Visit the farm to buy products.
Address: 3717 N. Buckner-Tarsney Rd.
Phone: 816-650-5535
Email: sibleyorchards@hotmail.com
Website: sibleyorchards.com
Agritourism: Hayrides year-round. Cider press demonstrations and picnic areas enhance your u-pick experience.

Timberland Westside Community Orchard, Kansas City

This ambitious community orchard is *free*. Still in its infancy, the founders want to make fruit available to everyone and make food more readily available in areas of Kansas City where there is little access to healthy food and produce. The planting kicked off in late spring 2011, and the trees should be producing by 2013 or 2014. Timberland and Skills USA planted the orchard at their conference, and other area groups are maintaining the grounds. This orchard is the first of several that are planned for the Kansas City area. Be sure to check it out—it is one of the largest, if not the largest, community orchard in the country.

Products: Blueberries, nectarines, pears, and peaches. Twenty different varieties of apple trees, plum, peach, apricot, cherry, and forty blueberry bushes.
Where to buy: *Free* orchard and berries. Visit to pick.
Address: 21st St. and Belleview Ave. (Tony Aguirre Community Center)
Phone: 816-200-6557
Email: etapper@kcdesignbuild.com
Website: N/A
Agritourism: The city is working on a program that will locate the type and species of each tree available for free picking using your GPS or the city website.

Uncle Will's Blackberry Farm, Windsor

Denzil and Ellen Cooper grow 10,000 blackberry bushes on land that has been in their family since 1832. They started planting in 2004 and now have about two miles of plants if you walked every row—this means lots of berries. Denzil said he is going to let a lot of the bushes "start over" (he mows them down so they can regrow) so 2012 could bring fewer berries than usual. He does not use chemical sprays or fertilizers. Uncle Will's is named after Denzil's great-great-uncle who died in 1936. Apparently the farm was always known as "Will's Place."

> **Products:** U-pick blackberries and a small amount of apples, peaches, and nectarines. He said he often just gives the tree fruit away. They will pre-pick blackberries for large orders.
> **Where to buy:** On the farm.
> **Address:** 953 SE Hwy. 23
> **Phone:** 660-647-3390
> **Website:** N/A
> **Agritourism:** U-pick.

Weston Red Barn Farm, Weston

This beautiful farm outside of Kansas City is a great place to visit. Opened in 1990, Weston Red Barn Farm is the realization of Steve Frey's dream. He and his wife, Cindy, operate the business and have created a place where children and families can enjoy an authentic farm setting. There are activities nearly year-round, including u-pick, a pumpkin patch, and school tours, and you can even rent the farm for weddings and events. Please check the website for updates and current events.

> **Products:** U-pick blackberries and pesticide-free apples. Low-spray u-pick orchard, pumpkins, and peaches; no spray on the blackberries and strawberries; local produce, relishes, salsas, jams, jellies, and even soaps, linens, and vintage children's games at their country store.
> **Where to buy:** On the farm.
> **Address:** 16300 Wilkerson Rd.
> **Phone:** 816-386-5437
> **Email:** westonredbarnfarm@gmail.com
> **Website:** westonredbarnfarm.com
> **Agritourism:** Visit this working farm and farm store. They have produce, locally raised meats, and farm-fresh eggs at an on-site farmers' market. Each year more than 14,000 kids visit the farm.

Southwest Region

Auglaize Berry Patch, Montreal

Jerry and Jeannette George are no strangers to farming. They have had their farm since 1970 and have always had cattle. In 2005 they decided to try their hand at blueberries and harvested their first crop in 2008. They now have about an acre in u-pick blueberries. Jeanette was excited to talk about a new venture on their farm—Lucybelle Cakes. Their daughter started this specialty cake business and sources local ingredients as much as possible, including berries, honey, and eggs from Auglaize Berry Patch. These beautiful cakes are a wonderful addition to the area.

> **Products:** U-pick blueberries, garden-fresh vegetables in season, and sometimes honey.
> **Where to buy:** On the farm and at Camden County Farmers' Market.
> **Address:** 9507 St. Rd. A
> **Phone:** 573-346-5775
> **Email:** jgeorge@zigs.net
> **Website:** No website for berry patch, but check out lucybellecakes.com for pastry shop
> **Agritourism:** U-pick June 7-July 3 for blueberries. Produce throughout the summer is available at the house.

Berry King Farm, Joplin

Neil and Ruth Gilstrap have gardened and grown produce since the early 1970s. A few years ago they planted a test crop of berries and loved it. They are now both retired and focus on growing the best berries possible. They do not use any herbicides, pesticides, or fungicides, and they love that people can just eat the berries off the vine.

> **Products:** Blackberries.
> **Where to buy:** On the farm, u-pick, and pre-picked.
> **Address:** 6832 Eland Rd.
> **Phone:** 417-624-1539
> **Email:** berrykingfarm@hotmail.com
> **Website:** berrykingfarm.com
> **Agritourism:** U-pick berries.

The Berry Patch, Bolivar

Jim and C. C. Gulick developed the Berry Patch themselves twelve years ago. They have about 150 blueberry bushes and quite a few blackberry bushes on their fifteen-acre farm.

> **Products:** Blackberries and blueberries available as u-pick and pre-pick. They also grow strawberries and vegetables but use those mainly for their value-added products like jams, jellies, salsas, pickles, and apple butter.
> **Where to buy:** They have an on-farm store where you can buy year-round, and you can buy seasonally at the Bolivar Farmers' Market.
> **Address:** 1014 East 394th Rd.
> **Phone:** 417-777-4586; 800-983-9021
> **Website:** N/A
> **Agritourism:** Visit the on-farm store year-round. They are open every day 7-7.

Blackberry Lane Gardens, Crane

Mike and Paula Sherwood have been farming for a long time but started selling to the public in the early 2000s. They began with bedding plants, and three years ago when they decided to grow vegetables and blackberries they also received organic certification. Paula knew that they had never used pesticides or chemical fertilizers, nor had her grandparents, and that made the certification process easier. All of the edibles they grow are organic. They plan to triple their blackberry production and add a u-pick component by 2013.

> **Products:** Blackberries, broccoli, and other veggies.
> **Where to buy:** In the summer they sell to MaMa Jean's and Homegrown Food, but most folks buy directly from the farm.
> **Address:** 1172 Blackberry Ln.
> **Phone:** 417-818-8264; 417-818-8520
> **Email:** psherwood@blackberrylanegardens.com
> **Website:** blackberrylanegardens.com; Facebook
> **Agritourism:** A farm stand is open six days a week, April 1-August 1; after that, call for produce availability. And if you are interested in learning to pick or helping with farm chores, please ask. They welcome the opportunity to teach and to have help.

Braker Berry Farm, Oronogo

Wendy and Greg Braker have two acres in blueberries, some blackberry bushes, and a total of about five acres with produce. As with most farms, the acreage in production varies each year. The land was all pasture when they purchased it. They have high tunnels and use those to increase their pepper and tomato production. Wendy says that they want to expand into pumpkins and melons over the next couple of years. They use water from their own pond for irrigation, have not needed to spray anything on the berries, and have used both organic and conventional sprays for produce.

> **Products:** U-pick blueberries and blackberries as well as pre-picked. They sell the tomatoes, peppers, and sweet corn at farmers' markets.
> **Where to buy:** On the farm and at Webb City Farmers' Market and a farmers' market at Freeman Hospital in Joplin. A hospital in town and several nursing homes also buy their tomatoes, peppers, and other produce.
> **Address:** 941 SW 90th Ln.
> **Phone:** 417-842-3609
> **Website:** N/A
> **Agritourism:** June and July for u-pick operation. Call to visit or buy from the farm.

Delp Blackberry Farm, Richland

Bob Delp always loved being outside and loved growing. Lillian Delp said that when they first had the fifty-four acres, they planted and ran a Christmas tree operation that put their boys through college. Once the boys graduated, the trees were too much work, but Bob "had to be growing something." Bob did a lot of research and decided to plant blackberries on the hilltops where folks told him nothing would grow. That was at least fifteen years ago, and now there are three acres of robust blackberries. Bob passed away in 2009, and Lillian found it too hard to manage the blackberry farm herself. Enter Bill and Suzy Aistrope, who had moved to a small neighboring farm in the early 2000s and helped Bob and Lillian in past years. Lillian says they are like her own kids, and she loves having them and their children so close. Her own sons live in Rolla and California. Bill and Suzy wanted to help, and they now lease and manage the blackberry farm with guidance from Lillian. Lillian still gives the picking report and continues to work with customers, many of whom she has known for years.

Products: U-pick blackberries and pre-picked large special orders.
Where to buy: At the u-pick farm.
Address: 32825 Holiday Hills Rd.
Phone: 573-765-4465 (Lillian runs the picking report); 573-855-7359 (Bill and Suzy)
Email: billaistrope@yahoo.com
Website: N/A
Agritourism: U-pick farm.

G's Orchard, Verona

Mark Graves has had the berry and fruit farm for eight years and has about ten acres in production. He has a wide variety of fruits and garden produce available, including three hundred blueberry bushes, with more coming into production soon. In 2005, he added a farm store that is open seasonally.

Products: Blueberries and blackberries (u-pick and pre-picked), peaches, cantaloupe, apples, pears, pumpkins, and a variety of vegetables.
Where to buy: U-pick berries or at the farm store, Wed.-Sat. 10-5, from the end of June through the beginning of November.
Address: 2096 Farm Rd. 1130
Phone: 417-669-4583
Email: peachman8@yahoo.com
Website: N/A
Agritourism: If you are coming during business hours, you don't need to call. Check for berry availability before going.

Ozark Mountain Orchard, Highlandville

Ozark Mountain Orchard, located just south of Springfield, produces fruits from May to October on trees, bushes, and vines. Starting with strawberries and ending with apples, you will find blueberries, blackberries, peaches, pears, and melons in between. They sell at a variety of locations, including Soulard Farmers' Market in St. Louis. This farm has an active Facebook presence.

> **Products:** Strawberries, blueberries, blackberries, peaches, apples, pears, raspberries, watermelon, cantaloupe, honeydew melons, and some tomatoes and corn.
> **Where to buy:** Soulard Farmers' Market in St. Louis, Greater Springfield Farmers' Market in Springfield, Christian County Farmers' Market and Ozark Farmers' Market Downtown. They have a big produce stand in Springfield at 4564 Campbell.
> **Address:** 2949 Pleasant View Rd.
> **Phone:** 417-443-3343
> **Website:** ozarkmountainorchard.com
> **Agritourism:** N/A

Persimmon Hill Berry Farm, Lampe

In 1982 Earnie and Martha Bohner converted vacant fields into two acres of blue-berries, blackberries, raspberries, gooseberries, and plums. The original concept was a farm where families could have an enjoyable u-pick experience. And it worked. Since then, they have added log-grown shiitake mushrooms and a line of gourmet foods that includes jams, jellies, BBQ sauces, syrups, and even shiitake mushroom sauces.

> **Products:** Blueberries, raspberries, gooseberries, and a diverse array of sauces and jams. Check the website for a full list, but here's a short list to get you excited: Gooseberry Walnut Jam, Blueberry Syrup, Blackberry Glaze, Blueberry Barbecue Sauce, Persimmon Butter, and even sugar-free spreads.
> **Where to buy:** You can order their gourmet products, including their blueberry muffins, on-line or by phone. The berries are u-pick.
> **Address:** 367 Persimmon Hill Ln.
> **Phone:** 800-333-4159 (order line)
> **Email:** earnie@persimmonhill.com
> **Website:** persimmonhill.com
> **Agritourism:** Visit the farm for u-pick or stop by their store for homemade goodies.

Rocky Top Berry Farm, Verona

Andrew Akin said his grandfather planted the blueberry plants the year Andrew was born—1982. His grandpa then added strawberries and in the early 1990s started blackberry bushes. Andrew and his two brothers were put in charge of the blackberries and for awhile became well known after an article was written detailing the young boys' blackberry business. Their grandfather died in 2009, and the family is working to restore the berry patches. Andrew says they don't use any pesticides or sprays and try to grow as naturally as possible. Rocky Top Berry Farm has many loyal customers but also has its fair share of one-time visitors, since many people pass the farm on the way to Branson. Andrew believes they have had visitors from nearly every state in the United States.

Products: U-pick and pre-pick blackberries and blueberries. They hope to have strawberries again in the near future.
Where to buy: On the farm.
Address: 23286 Lawrence 1140
Phone: 417-498-6574
Email: rockytopbb@gmail.com
Website: N/A
Agritourism: Picnic area at the farm and a gazebo with shade and cold water for guests.

Roger's Blueberry, Lebanon

Roger Harwell had in mind a small farm where he could be close to family and enjoy the outdoors. This retired Baptist preacher is really enjoying his retirement occupation. He has six hundred blueberry plants that he has been cultivating for eleven years, and he says the farm is so well tended that walking between the rows is like walking on carpet. The six-foot-tall plants are pruned for easy picking. As with many blueberry growers, he usually has more customers than he has blueberries.

> **Products:** U-pick and pre-picked blueberries.
> **Where to buy:** On the farm.
> **Address:** 21988 Rice Dr.
> **Phone:** 417-533-5797
> **Email:** rharwell@embarqmail.com
> **Website:** N/A
> **Agritourism:** U-pick operation.

Sunshine Valley Farms Orchards, Rogersville

For more than twenty years people have enjoyed picking berries and apples at Sunshine Valley Farms. Jan and Michael Wooten started the farm from scratch after looking for property for about ten years. According to Jan, they got "carried away." They have 2,000 apple trees, 350 peach trees, some plums and Asian pears, along with 3½ acres of blueberries and an acre of blackberries. In addition to berries and apples, they grow a large garden that provides food for the on-site café opened in 1996. Jan confesses that she never did a formal business plan but just knew there was a market for fresh-baked pies and a light menu. After lots of readjusting and adapting to customer requests, they now offer lunch, lots of baked goods, and once a month they host a farm dinner. One thing that farmers who sell directly to customers learn is to listen to what consumers want. Jan gives a great example. She is originally from the East Coast and loved red raspberries. No one wanted those, so she relented and planted black raspberries and blackberries. Now she is a convert—especially to blackberries. This multifaceted business is, as Jan says, "a three legged stool"—the fruit, the bakery, and the café.

Products: They grow blueberries, blackberries, raspberries, apples (Pink Lady and Arkansas Black are two of the unusual varieties, but they grow twenty varieties), peaches, and pears. The apples are pre-picked and the berries are u-pick. Ninety-five percent of the fruit they use in their café and bakery is grown on-site.

Where to buy: On the farm, at Springfield Farmers' Market, and sometimes at Homegrown Foods.
Address: 8125 A.D. Highway
Phone: 417-753-2698
Email: jan@sunshinevalleyfarm.com
Website: sunshinevalleyfarm.com
Agritourism: U-pick farm with market and café, open May 1-Thanksgiving. The market and café hours change seasonally. Check website for hours.

U-pickers at Sunshine Valley Farms Orchards

Thompson Bees & Berries, Joplin

Howard Thompson planted a wide array of crops when he started and says that by a process of elimination he ended up with peaches and blueberries. He has been farming since about 2002 and believed this would be a good activity for retirement, although he hasn't yet retired from his career as a physician. Thompson has also raised bees for about six years and is the president of the Missouri Blueberry Council.

Products: U-pick blueberries, some blueberries are sold at Webb City Farmers' Market, and the honey is sold at the Freeman Hospital Farmers' Market. The peaches are pre-picked, but according to Howard they are so temperamental that he has only had one good crop in the ten years he has had the trees. He is also establishing some blackberry bushes.
Where to buy: At the farm, at Webb City Farmers' Market, and at the Farmers' Market at Freeman Hospital.
Address: 707 Saginaw Rd.
Phone: 417-781-0648
Website: N/A
Agritourism: U-pick the last week of May to mid-July, 5:30 p.m. to dusk.

Southeast Region

Brandywine Farms, Rolla

Dave and Mary Hinze started their blueberry farm in 1982. Before they picked up their first blueberry bushes from Arkansas they had never even seen one. Many years and much experience later, they have about three acres in production. Read their website for a great description of blueberry bush maintenance.

> **Products:** Blueberries.
> **Where to buy:** U-pick operation on the farm.
> **Address:** Highway 63 as it heads south from Rolla. See website.
> **Phone:** 573-364-8032
> **Website:** rollanet.org/~hinze/index2.html
> **Agritourism:** U-pick.

Cardoza Blueberry Farm, Alton

Roxana Cardoza says that when they first started their blueberry farm in the mid-1990s they didn't have enough customers. Now they have the opposite problem. They have 2,400 blueberry plants over three acres, and Roxana is committed to growing organically. She has never sprayed, she handpicks lots of caterpillars when necessary, and she uses organic fertilizers. One interesting product she uses is feather meal. It is high in nitrogen and blueberries love it. Plenty of pruning keeps the bushes healthy, and as Roxana tells it, the hardest part is getting the bushes established.

Products: Blueberries.
Where to buy: On the farm. She takes phone orders for pre-pick berries and says people begin placing orders in January and February. Customers pick up their orders at the farm.
Address: Outside of West Plains. Contact for directions.
Phone: 417-764-3792
Email: roxanacardoza@gmail.com
Website: N/A
Agritourism: See the farm when you pick up.

Greenhill Vineyard and Farm, Hartville

Joan and Ed Barry bought their farm in 2003 and weren't sure what they were going to do with it, but they were toying with the idea of blueberries. A soil test told a different story, with results that showed soil perfectly suited for grapes. They thought this seemed easy but soon learned that it is a lot of work. For three years, while the vines grew (1,000 vines), they didn't worry much about the grapes. Well, they didn't worry until they realized they would have 9,000 pounds of them. They quickly peddled them to friends and neighbors, bought a listing on a u-pick site, and advertised on Craig's List. And the rest is history. People now come from all over Missouri for their grapes. Although they have been approached by local vineyards, they are dedicated to selling to individuals and home wine makers. They are considering wholesaling to small local grocery stores in the area because they believe in access to local foods.

Product: Chambourcin, Seyvals, and Concords. This year they have seedless grapes coming into maturity. Canadice and Mars Seedless should be mature in 2012.
Where to buy: On the farm as u-pick. They occasionally will do pre-picked grapes.
Address: 4905 Hwy. 5
Phone: 417-741-7396
Email: greenhillfarm@hotmail.com
Website: www.greenhillgrapes.com
Agritourism: U-pick is mid-August to mid-September.

Scenery Hill Farm, Bucyrus

Linda and Phil Bailey, along with four of their children, live on this farm nestled in the Missouri Ozarks. They bought this established farm—around since the 1970s—and grow three acres of blueberries and chestnut trees. Linda said she has started getting calls from folks out of state who want to buy the chestnuts.

Product: Blueberries are u-pick and pre-picked, and chestnuts are pre-picked.
Where to buy: On the farm for blueberries, and pre-picked are available at Old #1 General Store in Huggins—a little country store with a bit of everything, including sandwiches and gas. The store has been in operation since the 1940s and is now run by the Baileys. Chestnuts are available on-line or at the farm.
Address: 11400 Rocky Ridge Rd.
Phone: 417-926-3148
Email: sceneryhills@yahoo.com
Website: N/A
Agritourism: Crops are usually available in June and July. Hours are Mon.-Sat., 7:30 a.m. to 8:00 p.m. Call for picking availability. Chestnuts are available in October.

Simpsons Family Farm, Mountain Grove

The Simpson family started in commercial grape production in the early 1970s and was one of the first commercial strawberry operations in Missouri to convert to plasticulture growing.

Products: Strawberries, blackberries, honey, vegetables, mums, and bedding plants.
Where to buy: U-pick and pre-picked at the farm, Cabool Farmers' Market, Mountain Grove Farmers' Market, and Ava Farmers' Market.
Address: 8748 Simpson Rd.
Phone: 417-926-5308
Email: manager@simpsonsfamilyfarm.com
Website: simpsonsfamilyfarm.com
Agritourism: U-pick farm.

Trace Creek Blues, Glen Allen

It took a couple of years of prep that included adding an irrigation pond before Linda and Henry Whitener could open their u-pick blueberry farm in 1988. At the time they opened they had two thousand bushes. Henry grew up on a farm and was a hog and cattle farmer but had a hankering for an operation like they have now. This talented couple offers more than blueberries. Linda makes stained glass, which you can see by appointment. Some pieces hang in the cabin, where you weigh and pay for your blueberries. Henry built the log cabin over three years completely by hand and using "old fashioned ways." He also has a one-man sawmill used mainly by locals.

Products: U-pick blueberries.
Where to buy: On the farm.
Address: RR1 Box 1685
Phone: 573-238-2878
Email: l.whitener@yahoo.com
Website: tracecreekblues.com
Agritourism: Open June (around the 15th) into July. Open a couple of days a week and by appointments. Always call before coming to pick and for directions.

The cabin at Trace Creek Blues

U-Pick Berry Patch, Mountain Grove

Michael Matthews has been growing blackberries for about four years. He works at a fruit experiment station in Mountain Grove and says it helps to have experts around for growing advice. You will find about six hundred plants at his u-pick farm and a house that dates back to 1900.

Products: U-pick blackberries, or call ahead for picked berries.
Where to buy: On the farm.
Address: 9292 Wheeler Arch
Phone: 417-926-3566
Email: michaelmatthews@missouristate.edu
Website: N/A
Agritourism: U-pick, open 7-7 Mon.-Sat. during blackberry season.

Southeast Region

Meats

Livestock in Missouri consists mostly of beef, pork, and chicken, with heritage and other specialized breeds becoming increasingly popular. In addition, there are several other varieties of livestock raised for meat, including lamb, bison, elk, turkey, goose and duck, trout, and rabbit. The farmers featured in this chapter usually raise several different types of animals.

Grass-Fed Versus Grain-Fed

Cattle, bison, and other herd animals like lamb raised for consumption can be fed one of two ways: exclusively on grass, or on a combination of grass and grain. Grass-fed/grass-finished livestock eat nothing but fresh forage (grass and other small wild plants) and dried hay and silage from birth to slaughter. Among the benefits touted of grass-fed meat are its higher levels of omega-3 fats, conjugated linoleic acids (CLA), and its lower fat content. Grass-fed meat requires careful cooking because it is leaner (some folks like to add butter to finish grass-fed steaks), and the fat sometimes has a yellow tint to it. Grass-fed animals have less environmental impact because they graze where they live and do not require additional fodder. To raise grass-fed livestock one must have enough year-round forage for animals, and because some claim the type of forage can affect the taste of the meat (some think it tastes stronger and beefier), the grass should be a variety that is palatable to the consumer. Grass-fed meat versus a traditional cattle operation (where cattle eat *only* grain the last few months and typically on a feed lot) can be more expensive because the animal takes longer to grow to slaughter size.

Grass-fed/grain-finished animals listed in this book start out eating exclusively forage, but are then "finished" on grain on the farm while also still eating grass. The farmer adds corn and soy and other grains to their diet during the last months before slaughter. Many people, including some of the farmers we talked to, prefer the flavor of grain-finished meat. There is more fat, more marbling, and the fat is usually whiter and "cleaner-looking" than grass-fed meat.

Although hogs may eat forage (grass, alfalfa, acorns, etc.), their diets are almost always supplemented with grain and silage.

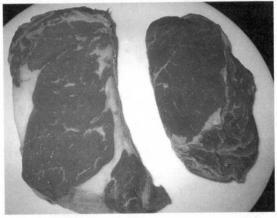

grain-finished   grass-fed and finished

Pasture-Raised, Free-Range, and Cage-Free

Poultry and other meat animals can be pasture-raised, free-range, and cage-free. Pasture-raised animals include cattle, swine, other herd animals, and poultry. They live their entire lives on family farms eating fresh grass in the pasture during the warmer months and hay and silage during the winter months or when fresh grass is not available, such as during a drought.

Many animal farmers raise several species of animals, and "rotational grazing" has become popularized, in part through the efforts of Joel Salatin of Polyface Farm.

Many farmers featured in this chapter cite him as the inspiration for their own operations. Rotational grazing can be especially beneficial when farmers have a mixed-species operation. Each animal herd grazes the fields in succession, and as they do, what they leave behind benefits the next herd. For example, cows eat grass nearly down to the ground, and as they do, they leave behind dung that hosts insect larvae that become food for the chickens grazing the fields after the cows. The chicken guano has high levels of nitrogen that fertilizes the grass, allowing it to once again become lush fodder for the cattle. Rotational grazing is an elegant system, and farmers find that with it they have far fewer problems with pests and diseases.

"Free-range" is virtually the same thing as pasture-raised but generally refers to poultry and means the chickens are allowed to roam in a large expanse (such as a field) during the day and are moved inside at night for protection. "Cage-free" generally refers to poultry, and means the animals are not caged up, but they usually have a smaller area to roam. Often the chickens are kept in large chicken houses. Their roaming is likely limited to the hen house. The farmers in this chapter use one or more of these methods, and they avoid using hormones and antibiotics (unless the animal is ill), in compliance with USDA/NOP organic guidelines.

Meat Processing

Farmers can have their meat processed at USDA-inspected or state-inspected facilities or facilities that do both. Farmers who want to sell in a retail facility must have their animals processed at a USDA-inspected facility. USDA processing plants can be far away from individual farms, and some farmers believe off-site processing affects the flavor of the meat because the animals become stressed during the trip. Because of this, some farmers slaughter on-site, sometimes with the help of a local meat locker, and then sell on-site. One of the farmers featured in this chapter is developing a Mobile Meat Processing Unit (MMPU), which is another USDA-approved method for animal slaughter and processing. Of the farmers who sell directly, most sell whole or half beeves or hogs that they can process into smaller cuts, and some sell smaller cuts directly. If you decide to buy this way, consider getting a large freezer and/or share with friends and family.

So get out the grill and sharpen up your knife! This chapter introduces you to the mouth-watering array of locally raised Missouri meats.

Northwest Region

Boondocks Farm, Mound City

Eldon and Sue Roseman have a diversified farm on their 120 acres. They have half an acre in flowers, some row crops, a cold frame, fruit, and they raise hogs on the land.

> **Products:** Pork, cut flowers, vegetables, and berries.
> **Where to buy:** Pony Express Farmers' Market and The Club in Mound City buys their pork and flowers.
> **Address:** 15376 Memphis Rd.
> **Phone:** 660-442-3978
> **Email:** swissy@socket.net
> **Website:** N/A
> **Agritourism:** N/A

Clover Hill, Linneus

Brad and Jane Whitaker moved to Linneus in 2001 to get away from the chemical spraying that was all around their previous farm. Their 150 acres are used for growing non-GMO grain, and pastures for hogs, cattle, and chickens. The cattle are 100 percent grass-fed/grass-finished, and they grow and grind their own grain to feed the chickens and hogs. The farm was Certified Organic until 2011 when they decided they no longer wanted to pay the certification fees.

> **Products:** Pasture-raised beef, pork, and chicken.
> **Where to buy:** They sell products through a private buyers' club in Kansas City and Columbia (sign a membership agreement with Clover Hill, and order from the farm).
> **Address:** 19075 Island Dr.
> **Phone:** 660-258-7093
> **Email:** cloverhillmilk@yahoo.com
> **Website:** N/A
> **Agritourism:** N/A

MSF Farm, Linneus

Mike Fries (pronounced Freeze) is a sixth-generation farmer, and his son, Jeff, who works with him, is the seventh. Mike said his great-great-great-grandfather died while moving cattle across the U.S. in the 1850s. The son bought a farm in Missouri, and Mike's parents live there still. Throughout all these years, the family has raised cattle. The cattle raised today eat primarily grass, but are fed some grain and hay that Mike grows on the farm. The herd of about one hundred mama cows receives no antibiotics or hormones. Mike and his family are in partnerships with two other farmers to produce the beef. On MSF Farm you will also find Berkshire hogs that are also raised with no hormones or antibiotics.

They sell as much as possible to individual consumers, but their location in North Central Missouri makes it challenging to reach as many customers as they would like. Mike, his wife, Sharon, and Jeff also run a fencing business and have developed products that meet the fencing needs of many farmers. They also have solar panel options for use with electric fencing. These are invaluable to farmers who are raising their animals on the land and not in confinement. Their website details the wide array of products—fencing, brackets, solar panels, wood garden boxes, and, of course, their meat products.

Products: Quarter, half, and whole beeves. Cuts and ground are for sale at the farmers' market. Berkshire pork products are also available at farmer's market or on the farm.
Where to buy: Chillicothe Farmers' Market, spring-fall; buy from them directly.
Address: 22538 Hwy. Y
Phone: 660-895-5258
Email: msffarm@grm.net
Website: msffarm.com
Agritourism: Contact Mike or Sharon if you want a tour.

Rains Natural Meats, Gallatin

This retail butcher shop, slaughterhouse, and farm is a wonderful find for fans of pasture-raised, hormone- and antibiotic-free meats. David and Steve Rains raise hogs, beef, and lamb on pasture. And, since their USDA-inspected slaughterhouse is right on their farm, the animals don't need to be transported. They used to ship a lot of their meat to high-end stores in California, but it was hard to keep up with the large orders. Increased demand in Missouri has been integral to their success. Rains also processes meats for other farmers in the area and is an important resource for farmers.

> **Products:** Pasture-raised, hormone- and antibiotic-free meats (pork, beef, lamb) from their farm. Their meat is sold under the "Rains" label. You will also find meat for sale from other farmers under the "D&S" label.
> **Where to buy:** At their retail store, on-line, and they sell to Blue Bird Bistro in Kansas City.
> **Address:** Three miles east of Gallatin on Hwy. 6 at 23795 260th Rd.
> **Phone:** 660-663-3674
> **Website:** rainsnaturalmeats.com
> **Agritourism:** Store hours, Mon.-Fri. 9-5:30 and Sat. 9-12.

Sunrise Pastures Farm, Laclede

Tauna Powell and her family maintain a herd of about seven hundred cows. They have enough acreage to breed on-site and then sell the calves and yearlings to other grass-finishing producers. Every year they sell ten to fifteen whole beeves directly to consumers, and some of their cows are sold at sale barns—as with many farmers, market conditions shape their decisions about where to sell their products.

> **Products:** Beef.
> **Where to buy:** Email for direct purchase of whole beeves.
> **Address:** 19554 Fort Rd.
> **Phone:** 660-963-2685
> **Email:** atpowell@windstream.net
> **Website:** mastersranch.com
> **Agritourism:** N/A

Wells Family Farm, King City

Kim and Steve Wells raise Certified Organic cattle. Steve is a fourth-generation farmer, and in 2002, he and his wife, Kim, decided it was time to make a change. They obtained organic certification for their land and cattle and became a Certified Humane Family farm. On Wells Family Farm you will find 100 percent grass-fed/grass-finished cattle, a closed herd, and a couple who make the most of their nine hundred-plus acres by selling from plants and trees already on the farm—think hickory nuts, black walnuts, and brambleberries like black raspberries and blackberries. Kim and Steve have big goals. By spring 2012 they plan to have their own Certified Organic processing plant and butcher shop. This will allow them to put Certified Organic on all of their products and offer this option for other Certified Organic beef farmers in the area.

> **Products:** Beef products, tree nuts, horse manure, bug repellent, walking sticks, berries, and even some horseradish. They also process the older cows and sell one-pound packages of ground beef for pet food.
> **Where to buy:** Wed. evenings at Westport Plaza Farmers' Market in K.C., Sat. at Farmers' Community Market at Brookside, and BADSEED Farmers' Market in the winter. The Barkery, a pet store, sells one-pound ground beef for pet food.
> **Address:** N/A
> **Phone:** 660-783-2930; 660-562-7892
> **Email:** info@wfforganicbeef.com
> **Website:** wellsfamilyfarms.com
> **Agritourism:** Please call if you'd like to visit.

Northeast Region

Bountiful Acres, Madison

Cyril Penner and his family have been farming on forty acres in Madison for five years. They are not Certified Organic, but they use sustainable and humane farming methods for their birds. Mostly, they raise goats, ducks, turkeys, and Cornish chickens. They are all free-range with no hormones, and their diet is supplemented with non-GMO grains. Bountiful Acres also boasts a natural water supply without fluoride or chlorine.

> **Products**: Goats, chickens, turkeys, eggs, and ducks.
> **Where to buy:** Mainly word of mouth—they take orders.
> **Address:** 13217 Monroe Rd. 1050
> **Phone:** 800-847-5490
> **Website:** Bountifulacres.org
> **Agritourism:** Visitors are welcome but should call ahead.

Bowood Farms, Clarksville

The McPheeters' farm has been in the family for four generations. Since 1989 they have grown native perennials as well as ground covers and annuals, and they are now also known for their bison. Their herd ranges from 130 to 150 animals raised on 300 acres. The McPheeters practice a very hands-off approach with their herd. They are raised in their natural family groups and are allowed to establish their own social order. Their animals are strictly foragers with no grains, and they are never given steroids or antibiotics. In 2006, the McPheeters opened a retail facility, restaurant (Café Osage), and a small produce farm in the middle of St. Louis City. This beautiful urban oasis boasts a large vegetable garden, nursery, rooftop garden, and a gift shop featuring local artisans, seeds, and eco-friendly products.

Products: Bison: cuts, ground, filets, jerky, summer sausage, and meat sticks.
Where to buy: Bowood Farms, in shares of Fair Shares and Local Harvest Grocery. The bison is also served at Café Osage (the restaurant at Bowood Farms) and Sub Zero.
Address: 1245 Little Missouri Rd.
Urban Address:
Bowood Farms retail operation and Café Osage is at 4605 Olive St., St. Louis
Phone: 419-226-4540
Phone for St. Louis: 314-454-6868
Website: bowoodfarms.com
Agritourism: N/A

Davis Farm, Paris

Charles Davis has been farming for more than fifty years. He has been Certified Organic since 1997 for his beef and grains. He has 230 acres and raises about 20 head of cattle at a time along with organic corn, soybeans, wheat, and red clover. Charlie wants his cows stress free, so they eat only grass and hay, and he has them butchered on the farm by a local locker to reduce or eliminate agitation and stress at slaughter. (Most cattle are transported from the farm to another site to be slaughtered.) He says that stress at the end makes the meat tough. He sells his organic Angus beef directly to consumers. Charlie's wife says that the secret to cooking grass-fed beef is to cook it slowly. They cook roasts and steaks in the crockpot and say the meat is so tender you don't need a knife to cut it.

Products: Organic beef by the half and whole. (He has great prices by the way.) He does sell his wheat and corn, but mainly to wholesalers and to other animal farmers who want organic grain for their animals.
Where to buy: Directly from Charlie.
Address: 13948 Hwy. 15
Phone: 660-327-4792
Website: N/A
Agritourism: N/A

Lazy L. Elk Ranch, Unionville

Joyce and Lloyd LaRue are crazy about elk. They keep a herd of about one hundred elk on fifty acres, and in the winter they are fed a good grade of hay. In order to work in their pastures safely, Joyce and Lloyd feed the elk some grain by hand to "keep them docile." It takes eighteen months to raise an elk for meat.

Products: Cuts of elk, snack sticks, and summer sausage, retail and wholesale. They ship worldwide and have a webpage that lists their products.
Where to buy: On-line or call Joyce to place the order. Most of the stores that sell their products for retail are in Iowa, but you can find a few of their products at Local Harvest Grocery in St. Louis.
Address: 10713 State Hwy. 149
Phone: 660-933-4682; 660-341-7992 (cell)
Website: premiumelks.com
Agritourism: Call to set up a farm tour.

Primmer Pasture Pork, Brashear

Tom Primmer and his wife, Colleen, have been farming for a little over thirty years, but have only been selling meat for three years. The Primmers raise heritage hogs, including Hereford, and sell breeding stock to other farmers as well as for retail. The hogs are raised on pasture and are not given growth hormones. Check out their website for more information.

Products: Whole or half hogs along with retail cuts at farmers' markets.
Where to buy: The Downtown Grocery, Pickler's Famous (in Kirksville), Kirksville Kiwanis Farmers' Market, and throughout the year you can contact Tom to buy directly.
Address: 16519 Hazel Green Way
Phone: 660-323-5548 (farm); 660-342-4327
Email: primmer@marktwain.net
Website: primmerpasturepork.webs.com
Agritourism: N/A

A Primmer pig

Singing Prairie Farm, La Plata

Singing Prairie is an organic family farm run by John Arbuckle, a ninth-generation American farmer, his wife, Holly, and their two children. Singing Prairie is an experiment in low-input sustainable agriculture. They utilize a pasture-based system of multi-species grazing and are implementing permaculture principles. The Arbuckles moved to Missouri in 2010 from Maryland, where they farmed and had a CSA. Encouraged by their friends at The Possibility Alliance to relocate, the Arbuckles are happy with their decision to make Missouri their home. This is a farm to watch for ideas in simple living and innovative ways to grow crops, raise animals, and make it all work together sustainably.

> **Products:** Eggs and chickens directly from the Arbuckles.
> **Where to buy:** Three Hy-Vee stores in Columbia, both Clover locations in Columbia, Hy-Vee in Kirksville, Café Co (Costa Rican Café), and meat birds for sale on the farm.
> **Address:** N/A
> **Phone:** 660-332-4020
> **Website:** N/A
> **Agritourism:** This is a teaching farm. Call for information about internships and classes.

Sugar Creek Piedmontese, Elsberry

All cattle farmers will tell you that a cow is not just a cow—there are lots of different breeds and crossbreeds, and genetics matter. So, when Beth Lavy and her family decided to raise cattle sixteen years ago they chose the Piedmontese because it is a breed known to produce a lean yet tender meat. Beth says they "haven't had a bad cross yet." Their cattle are raised on grass but receive a grain ration two times a day. Their diet is 80 to 85 percent grass and hay, and the remainder is grain. This family farm does not use hormones or steroids and uses antibiotics only if necessary.

> **Products:** Cuts of beef as well as quarter, half, and whole beeves with deposit. Most of what they sell is in individual cuts.
> **Where to buy:** Clayton Farmers' Market, Ferguson Farmers' Market. Please check website for updated locations.
> **Address:** 343 Barrett Rd.
> **Phone:** 636-734-6620 (Beth); 636-734-6638 (Mary); 573-384-5946
> **Email:** sugar_creek_pied@yahoo.com
> **Website:** sugarcreekpiedmontese.com
> **Agritourism:** N/A

Terry Spence, Unionville

Terry has farmed for sixty-two years—pretty much since birth—with the exception of a two-year stint in the city. Farming is in his blood, and the city life was easy to leave. Although he has raised a lot of animals in his time, he now raises only cattle using rotational grazing. His animals are antibiotic- and hormone-free. Additionally, Terry ensures that his cows have little stress at harvest. Terry will tell you that you undo all the hard work of raising healthy and tender meat by stressing the cow in the last hours of life—the increased adrenalin leads to tough meat.

Terry spends a lot of time thinking about how to make processing easier for farmers and how to increase access to local food for all people. He has been involved in developing and promoting a Mobile Meat Processing Unit (MMPU). The MMPU (picture a semi-trailer) is a traveling meat locker and has everything needed for slaughter. This is revolutionary to farmers in rural areas who often must truck their animals for two or more hours just to reach a processing facility. With animals like bison, this is even harder due to their temperament and size.

Ideally, a region would also develop a cut-and-package facility, which would provide an aging facility and easy custom packaging. The USDA approved the MMPU, and it is now being used in several states, including Colorado and Nebraska. Imagine a world where school systems could use meat right from their area! Imagine a world where farmers could process right on their farms more easily and with less stress to the animal! This is what Terry and the people he works with want you to consider. Terry's group offers free consulting to communities who are interested in MMPUs and is compiling information about regulations, etc., to make it easy for communities in various states to obtain them. Terry does not profit from the sale of MMPUs except to say we all profit when we find ways to keep meat local.

Products: Quarter, half, and whole beeves.
Where to buy: Call Terry to order, but you have to book in advance. He books his slot at the processing plant six months to a year in advance.
Address: 32672 115th St.
Phone: 660-947-3873
Email: tespence@nemr.net
Website: N/A
Agritourism: N/A

Quality Over Quantity

Terry Spence hears from folks that locally raised meat is too expensive. Terry suggests: "Instead of eating meat five times a week—eat it two to three times a week." This sounds radical to many of us, but improving the quality of the meat you eat does not need to cost more if you decrease consumption. Buying locally from farmers with high-quality, sustainable farming operations keeps money in the region and, in terms of rural areas, can bring money to areas of economic deprivation.

Thompson Premium Beef, Kirksville

Tony Thompson says that you can make as much money if not more by "not working your beef." This means taking a more hands-off approach—letting them forage on grasses and hay and not giving vaccinations. He's been running his operation this way since 2005. His hay pastures are also all-natural (no synthetic fertilizers). When Tony decided to farm in this manner he researched various breeds that were known to be good raised solely on grass. He decided on the Ronagnola—an Italian breed with a long history—who are naturally heat-, cold-, and fly-resistant. This extraordinarily muscled breed has small muscle fibers that Tony says create a better product. Many of Tony's cows end up going to the sale barn, but he would love to increase his direct-to-consumer market.

> **Products:** 100 percent grass-fed/grass-finished beef, quarter, half, and whole beeves.
> **Where to buy:** Directly from Tony.
> **Address:** N/A
> **Phone:** 660-341-8150
> **Email:** tony.thompson@mo.usda.gov
> **Website:** N/A
> **Agritourism:** N/A

U.S. Wellness Meats, Monticello

In the late 1990s, John Wood set out to raise 100 percent grass-fed/grass-finished beef. He believed that using rotational grazing (imitating the foraging of bison in the wild) would be healthier for everyone—land, animals, and humans. After tests confirmed higher CLAs (conjugated linoleic acid, a healthy fat shown to fight obesity, cancer and diabetes in lab animals), he was convinced. In 2000, U.S. Wellness Meats was born from a collaboration of four families—the Woods, the Suters, the Leesers, and the Crums. Since its inception the business has expanded beyond 100 percent grass-fed beef and now includes chicken, pork, rabbit, and a host of other products like cheeses and even raw organic ice cream. Farmers who sell through U.S. Wellness must adhere to their strict farming guidelines. They have partnered with farmers in neighboring states, so not all of their farmers are from Missouri. Their mission is simple: Do what is good for our animals, good for our planet, and good for you. Their website is full of recipes, tips, and health information.

Products: Cuts from lamb, beef, bison, and pork, sausages like chicken apple sausage links, gourmet rabbit, dairy, and unusual items like pemmican.
Where to buy: On-line, Local Harvest Grocery, Hy-Vee in Kirksville, several retail locations in Illinois, and the brisket is served at Local Harvest Café. Check the retail link on their website.
Address: P.O. Box 9
Phone: 877-383-0051
Email: eathealthy@grasslandbeef.com
Website: grasslandbeef.com
Agritourism: Call for information.

Central Region

Altai Meadows, Higbee

Jeff Cook is new to farming, and he will tell you with a laugh, "The tuition is expensive, but you learn a lot." He was always attracted to farming and did a lot of research prior to starting his farm in 2009. Based on his research he decided to focus primarily on beef and to use a technique called "mob grazing" or "ultra high density grazing." A biologist in Africa noticed that in areas where the animals are pushed around by predators, the grassland flourished. The animals naturally bunch together and tend to feed voraciously. When applied to farming, this means moving the animals at least once a day and utilizing electric fencing to break the land into smaller swaths. He has 80 to 100 cattle on 210 acres and is learning what his land can hold. Already he has observed that when most folks were moving their cattle to hay, he had at least a month of grass supply left for his cattle. Through and through, this farm is dedicated to 100 percent grass-fed/grass-finished beef raised without the use of hormones, vaccines, or antibiotics.

Products: Beef for sale mainly by cuts and some eggs.
Where to buy: On the farm, at Danjo Country Store, and he hopes to be in a Columbia Farmers' Market in 2012.
Address: N/A
Phone: 660-651-9189
Email: altaimeadowsllc@yahoo.com
Website: altaimeadows.com
Agritourism: Farm tours available by appointment.

Mob Grazing

Mob grazing imitates grazing patterns of herd animals where grasslands flourish. Farmers move the animals at least once a day (often more) to small swaths of land, on which the animals then graze intensely over a short period of time.

Angel Acres, Bland

Karen grew up on a farm in South Dakota and as an adult wanted to move to the country and become self-sufficient. Seven years ago she and her husband started Angel Acres in Bland. Their 300 acres is now home to about 150 head of registered Belted Galloways, an old Scottish breed. They work hard to nourish the land by utilizing rotational grazing, feeding the hay to the animals in the pasture, and using the tractor only when necessary. And they are dedicated to producing great-tasting and healthy beef. In 2011 they seeded winter wheat to provide more forage for the animals in winter—better grass means better beef.

> **Products:** 100 percent grass-fed/grass-finished beef.
> **Where to buy:** Freddie's Market, Local Harvest Grocery, and Sappington Farmers' Market carry their beef, and Angel Acres is served in Annie Gunn's, Big Sky, Five Bistro, Local Harvest Café, and Lucas Park Grille, all in the St. Louis area.
> **Address:** 1356 Hwy. D
> **Phone:** 573-943-6947
> **Website:** gallowaybeef.com
> **Agritourism:** This farm is open to visitors and possibly apprentices.

Buttonwood Farms, California

Matt Tiefenbrun always wanted to be a farmer despite his urban St. Louis upbringing. At just twenty-three years old, he has quite a setup: a beautiful farm in Central Missouri where he raises chickens on the land, a few cows he currently sells on the commodity market, turkeys, and about an acre of produce. Many farmers will tell you that you have to be quite handy and mechanically inclined to farm—you never know when you'll need to fix a tractor or plow. Matt has put his tinkering to good use. He converted his diesel truck to run on fryer oil and can travel three hundred miles round trip for about ten dollars. Just follow the smell of French fries to find his farm.

Products: Pasture-raised chickens and turkeys and some produce.

Where to buy: You can buy his chickens and some produce at Local Harvest Grocery, and in shares at Maude's Market and Fair Shares. His product is served at Cardwell's, Farmhaus, Fresh Gatherings at SLU, Harvest, Local Harvest Café, Sqwires Restaurant, and Winslow's Home, all in St. Louis.

Address: 65092 Pilot Grove

Phone: 314-402-6756

Website: N/A

Agritourism: Call for a tour.

Crooked Lane Farm, Wellsville

Gene and Linda Langford have farmed for around twenty years. In 2005 they decided to add animals. They make the most of their ten-acre diversified farm. All animals are pastured and raised with no hormones or steroids, and the animals provide great manure for their acre of produce.

Products: Beef, pork, and some produce (sweet corn, green beans, tomatoes, squash, peppers, and eggplant). Gene sells most of his meat in pieces and parts (think roasts, hamburger, and pork chops). His biggest seller is his pork.

Where to buy: O'Fallon Farmers' Market, on the farm, or call Gene to reserve a side or whole beef or pork.

Address: 703 East Hudson

Phone: 573-220-9404

Website: www.crookedlanefarm.vpweb.com

Agritourism: N/A

Houston's Home Grown, Hermann

Paul grew up truck farming so he was somewhat familiar with farming practices when he and his wife bought their farm in Missouri two years ago and decided to give it a go. Paul did a lot of research and decided to raise heritage animals as naturally as possible. Their laying and meat birds are a mix of breeds like Barred Rock, Buff Orpingtons, New Hampshires, and Cornish Crosses. And if it is turkey you're after, Paul raises Midget White, Bourbon Reds, Chocolate Turkeys, and Broad Breasted Whites. The hog herd is made up of Red Wattle, Large Black, and Gloucestershire Old Spot as well as some crosses. All the animals are free-range and receive no hormones or antibiotics. This diversified farm also has three acres in vegetables, fruits, and even some flowers that are grown using organic practices.

Products: Cuts of hogs, whole chickens, eggs, and a variety of vegetables.
Where to buy: Buy from Paul on the farm or at Hermann Farmers' Market and Wright City Farmers' Market.
Address: 1604 Stolpe Rd.
Phone: 573-294-6040
Email: paulhouston70@gmail.com
Website: N/A
Agritourism: People can come and visit the farm.

JJR Family Farm, Tebbetts

John and Julie Rice raise USDA-Certified Organic beef, pork, chickens, and eggs. This family farmed conventionally for seventeen years before switching to Certified Organic farming in 2007. John said he became concerned about the antibiotics and didn't like the confinement processes that are prevalent in conventional animal farming. Since he has switched to Certified Organic he says he hasn't had any sick animals. They believe in responsible farming and invite customers to visit.

Products: Beef, pork, and eggs; JJR Farm sells cuts, ground, sausages, brats, nitrate-free bacon (which is in high demand), and 100 percent beef hot dogs.
Where to buy: Columbia Farmers' Market, Clovers in Columbia, and a health food store in Jefferson City.
Address: 4029 State Road AA
Phone: 573-295-6292; 573-680-2390
Website: N/A
Agritourism: Customers are invited to visit the farm.

Legacy Beef, Salisbury

Mark Mahnken used to raise over five thousand head of cattle on his land. A third-generation rancher, he decided to downsize and return to the roots of his ranch and the methods of his grandfather. Now he raises about two hundred head of cattle on his land. They are never confined and receive no antibiotics because, as he says, they are never sick when raised correctly. Although his cattle mostly eat grass, Mark believes the meat tastes better when the cows have had some grains, and feeds his cows a high-fiber supplement.

Products: Beef, cuts, and ground beef.
Where to buy: Columbia Farmers' Market, Hy-Vee in Jefferson City and Columbia, Clovers in Columbia, and on-line.
Address: 31369 Hwy. 129
Phone: 660-788-3555
Website: www.missourilegacybeef.com
Agritourism: Check with Mark for availability.

ar Company, Inc., Osage Beach

...au perhaps to think about caviar in Missouri, but that is exactly what L'Osage Caviar Company produces from their "paddlefish ranching program" in the Missouri Ozarks. L'Osage Caviar considers themselves the only "green" caviar because the Paddlefish at their operation "feed on only a natural diet of phytoplankton and zooplanktons."

Products: Caviar, 1.5 oz. and 4 oz. jars.
Where to buy: On-line.
Address: N/A
Phone: 573-348-1190
Email: losagecaviar@usmo.com
Website: www.osagecaviar.com/paddlefish-caviar.asp
Agritourism: N/A

Neuner Farms (Westphalia Vineyards), Westphalia

Wagyu cattle, a breed of cattle from Japan, are typically used for Kobe beef, an often-touted luxury item at steakhouses and in Japanese restaurants. Terry Neuner was hooked on Kobe beef after living in Japan for more than eight years. He decided to breed his own Wagyu cattle and now boasts a herd that is 75 to 88 percent Wagyu as a result of years of cross-breeding imported Wagyu sperm with Angus cattle. While his cattle do not get massaged daily, they do have a wonderful life strolling among the grapevines of Westphalia Vineyards and are given a supplement of brewer's grains for tenderness of flesh.

Products: Kobe beef.
Where to buy: Local Harvest Grocery, Local Harvest Café, Broadway Brewery.
Address: P. O. Box 5
Phone: 573-455-2950
Website: westphaliavineyards.com
Agritourism: Call for information.

Patchwork Family Farms, Columbia

This co-op of family farms is a program of Missouri Rural Crisis Center, which is a non-profit family farm membership organization. This group has worked tirelessly to support the family hog farms and to keep CAFOs (confined animal feeding operations) out of Missouri. Farms that sell under the Patchwork name raise their hogs on the land and only use antibiotics if their animals are sick. To get involved in supporting family farm agriculture, please call Tim Gibbons at the Missouri Rural Crisis Center.

Products: Hams, bacon, brats, ground pork, and cuts.
Where to buy: Local Harvest Grocery and Café in St. Louis and the Root Cellar and all Hy-Vees in Columbia. They also sell to over thirty restaurants.
Address: 1108 Rangeline St.
Phone: 573-449-1336
Email: timgibbons@morural.org
Website: patchworkfamilyfarms.org
Agritourism: N/A

Reisner Ranch, Rolla

Craig and Susan Reisner actually started their farm with horses. After working horses for a few years, they felt that cattle would be a better fit for their farm and for them. They utilize intensive grazing and do not use hormones or antibiotics. Their cows are offered grain along with grass during the last ninety days. This active duo has rented some additional acreage, and the calf/cow operation is their new work in progress.

Products: Whole beeves as well as half and quarter sides to individuals. Some cuts available on the farm.
Where to buy: Nature's Girl in Rolla, Sappington Farmers' Market, directly to consumer.
Address: 5231 Hwy. O
Phone: 573-729-7277
Email: reisner4@embarkmail.com
Website: reisnerbeef.com
Agritourism: Always open to visitors, but call ahead.

Sassafras Valley Farm, Morrison

A desire for the traditional "Christmas goose" led Connie and her family to convert their farm to goose production. In recent years the farm had mainly produced hay—essentially enough to pay the taxes. So in 2006, Connie Cunningham introduced geese to the farm. She raises goslings to maturity on the natural pasture on the farm. The fields reflect the careful planting of foods of local origin and the local microclimate to ensure a healthy diet for the geese. The natural forage is supplemented with seasonal vegetables, fruits, and grains that they grow. The goose population on Sassafras is thirty-six geese per acre. Great Pyrenees act as guardians and protect the geese from predators like coyotes, hawks, and feral dogs. Bob Cunningham, Connie's brother, helps market and sell these fantastic birds. Bob also distributes pasture-raised grass-fed veal from Lucas Farms in Meta, Missouri.

Future plans include renovating the original farmhouse to a bed and breakfast where you can eat a traditional goose dinner during your stay. Connie hopes to have this open in spring 2012. In 2011, they also added French Rouen ducks, which can be purchased on-line or on the farm.

Products: Most of the geese are frozen immediately after harvest, but some are smoked first. You may purchase them either way. Ducks are also available for purchase on-line and on the farm.

Where to buy: On-line, seasonally through Local Harvest Grocery and Swiss Meats in St. Louis, and on the farm.

Address: P.O. Box 11

Phone: 866-684-2188

Email: acermay@aol.com

Website: sassafrasvalleyfarm.com

Agritourism: By appointment only.

Stanton Brothers Eggs, Centralia

What started as a home project in first grade is now a huge egg business for nineteen-year-old Dustin and his younger brother Austin. Dustin's father, Andrew, bought him twenty-five pullets (baby chickens) when Dustin was just seven years old because Dustin wanted to care for his own farm animals. Andrew Stanton raises cattle, and they have over 540 acres of land. Twelve years later, Dustin and Austin, with help from their dad, raise about 8,500 chickens on the land. You read that correctly—8,500 free-ranging chickens.

These birds are free to roam anywhere they please during the day and return on their own each night to the barn where they roost and lay their eggs. A commercial egg washer enables them to clean and prepare the thousands of eggs they sell each week. Dustin attends college full-time and his younger brother is still in high school. In 2011, Dustin was the National FFA Competence winner in Agriculture Sales. Apparently it was worth getting into trouble in the sixth grade for taking a cell phone call from Café Berlin, which was placing an egg order.

Products: Free-range eggs.
Where to buy: Columbia Farmers' Market, Hy-Vee's in Jefferson City and Columbia, Natural Grocer's and Clovers in Columbia, C & R in Centralia, among others. The following eating establishments use Stanton Brothers eggs (there are at least thirty-four, and Andrew couldn't remember them all): Wine Cellar and Bistro, Café Berlin, Broadway Diner (all in Columbia), Bubba's in Moberly, all MU dining halls, some nursing homes, and Columbia College.
Address: 21101 North Tri City Lake Rd.
Phone: 573-682-4285 (Andrew's phone)
Website: Facebook
Agritourism: Does tours all the time.

Land and Livestock Farm, Gerald

Dennis Sahm have farmed their 380 acres since 2001. Gail and Dennis raise animals for breeding stock, which is not that unusual until you learn that most of the animals they raise are on the critically endangered list. At the farm you can find Arapawa Island goats, Brabant Belgian draft horses, Black Minorica chickens, and Blue Slate turkeys to name a few. Gail says these breeds are longer lived, more parasite resistant, utilize their feed better, and in general are heartier. Every October they host a "Mid-Missouri Horse, Mule, & Ox Farming and Historical Crafts Days," attended by 1,500-plus people. Be sure to visit their prairie with more than 400 identified plant species.

Product: Endangered breeding animals.
Where to buy: On the farm.
Address: N/A
Phone: 573-764-2629
Email: tenacity@fidnet.com
Website: witnessstreefarm.org
Agritourism: They would welcome people to come help, or please attend the festival held the first weekend in October.

St. Louis Region

Big Bison Meat Company, Ste. Genevieve

Many people know Crown Valley Winery but don't know that bison roam over one thousand acres alongside the vineyards. These pasture-raised animals are hormone- and antibiotic-free and enjoy the natural creeks found on the land. The three-hundred-plus herd is always on pasture but receives grains (85 percent of the grain comes from their farm) throughout their life. The grain is actually spread across the fields and the animals "forage" this along with grasses.

Products: All things bison—jerky, sausages (Summer, Breakfast, and Polish), bison bacon, ground, roasts, and steaks. The products are in high demand and sell out quickly. Black Branded Beef (brand name) can also be purchased at Crown Valley. Three thousand head of the Black Angus Cattle share the 10,000 acres that make up Crown Valley Wine Properties. You can also purchase produce from the farm at Crown Valley at their seasonal farmers' market.

Where to buy: On-line, at Crown Valley Winery, Local Harvest Grocery and T-Bones Natural Meats in O'Fallon (Terry Yake, former Blues Hockey player is the owner of T-Bones) for retail. Train Wreck Saloon for bison burgers and Mike Shannon's serve the bison in their restaurants.

Address: 23589 State Route WW

Phone: 866-207-9463, ask for Bryan Siddle

Email: bsiddle@crownvalleywinery.com

Website: crownbluebison.com

Agritourism: Crown Valley is a wonderful place to visit. You will, of course, find the winery, but you will also find a restaurant with lots of local flavor since they use their own produce, beef, and bison. April-November they host a farmers' market. You can see the bison grazing in the area below the winery. Worth a trek to Ste. Genevieve.

A bison herd at Big Bison Meat Company

Eckenfels Farm, Ste. Genevieve

Bob Eckenfels is a fifth-generation farmer who got the farming bug the day his dad first let him drive a tractor. He processes about twelve head a year direct to consumers but wants to increase this as the market for his product grows. This family farm has had cattle since its inception in 1851. Bob offers 100 percent grass-fed/grass-finished cows.

Products: Twenty-one-day dry-aged 100 percent grass-fed beef.
Where to buy: Soulard Farmers' Market (first Saturday of the month except when frigid outside), Farmington Farmers' Market, Crystal City Farmers' Market, and at the farm.
Address: 549 Glenda St.
Phone: 573-883-0337; 813-839-8861
Email: bseckenfels@yahoo.com
Website: eckenfelsfarms.com
Agritourism: N/A

The Farmer's Larder, Washington

The Farmer's Larder is truly a family business. Tom Matoushek dreamed up the concept, and Anne, his wife, and their son, Lucian, make the products. Tom works another full-time job but still makes time to raise the farm animals and source any other meat needed to make their products. The Farmer's Larder is both a farm and a producer of value-added products. On this small farm they practice management-intensive grazing and biodiversity to protect the water and soil. Using animals from their own small farm and from small farms in their area, the Farmer's Larder produces small batches of kielbasa, andouille, frankfurters, ham hocks, and bacon, to name a few. They use only organic herbs and spices, dry curing, hardwood smoking, and no additives, fillers, or synthetic nitrates.

Products: A variety of beef and ham products like kielbasa, frankfurters, ham hocks, bacon, andouille, and herb-encrusted pork loin.
Where to buy: Ferguson Farmers' Market, Maplewood Farmers' Market, Tower Grove Farmers' Market, Clayton Farmers' Market, and Webster Groves Farmers' Market.
Address: N/A
Phone: 636-667-1901
Email: info@farmerslarder.com
Website: thefarmerslarder.com
Agritourism: N/A

Todd Geisert Farms, Washington

Todd's family has been "doin' it the natural way" since the 1880s. Visit Todd's farm and see the pigs roaming the land, cooling in the stream, and burrowing in the mud. Todd is dedicated to sustainable farming, and he rotates his hogs and produce.

Products: Pasture-raised pork and vegetables. Don't miss the pork burgers. You will find a wide variety of brats, sausages, braunschweiger, and pork cuts. One very popular product is Todd's apple cinnamon breakfast link and apple cinnamon sausage. He also sells tomatoes, pumpkins, and squash at his farm stand and to a few stores.
Where to buy: For retail, buy at his farm stand, in St. Louis at Local Harvest Grocery, Old North Co-Op, Sappington Farmers' Market, at Connie's in Cottlesville, K&R Market in Marthasville, L&F Foods in Washington. Check his webpage for updates, but the following restaurants serve some of his products: In St. Louis at Almonds, Big Sky Café, Foundation Grounds, Latitude 26, Mike Shannon's, Mosaic, Vertali's, Yia-Yia's, and at Washington University; in Washingon you can find his product at Cowan's.
Address: 4851 Old Hwy. 100
Phone: 314-791-6942
Email: toadspigs@yahoo.com
Website: toadspigs.com
Agritourism: Todd has an honor system farm stand. Shocking in today's world, but a must-see if you feel a nostalgia for a quieter and simpler time. Buy juicy tomatoes and tender squash along with pork products like bacon, green bean sausages, brats, brat burgers, and Todd's favorite, the pork burger. Farm stand is always open. To schedule a tour, please call the farm.

Ladd's Family Farm, Farmington

Karin and her husband, Norman, are transplants from Oklahoma. When they moved to the farm they had very little farm experience. In fact, if you had asked Karin ten years ago if she ever thought she would kill a chicken, she probably would have laughed at you. This small diversified farm has it all—produce, rabbits, chickens, turkeys, and eggs. The chickens are in moveable pens (chicken tractors) and the turkeys are on the land. They butcher the chickens and turkeys on-site, and for that reason you must buy them directly from the farmers.

Products: Produce, eggs, chickens, and turkeys.
Where to buy: You can only buy the meat on the farm. Produce and eggs are available at the Farmington Farmers' Market. Chickens and turkeys must be pre-ordered. Call Karin to arrange.
Address: 6583 Hwy. F
Phone: 573-747-1889
Website: N/A
Agritourism: N/A

Meyer Hog Farm, Ste. Genevieve

Kenny Meyer is a third-generation farmer, but until recently he never had Berkshire or Duroc heritage hogs on the farm. Kenny was hooked on farming at an early age and has always wanted it to be his profession. His animals are not given antibiotics and most of his hogs are in outside pens. Kenny has noticed that more people want to know their food and know their farmer, and he is working on expanding his direct marketing. He likes knowing his customers, having direct feedback, and having control over the pricing as opposed to selling on the commodity market.

Products: Cuts of Berkshire and Berkshire-cross hogs.
Where to buy: Call Kenny to buy a hog or try his meat at the Grapevine Grill at Chaumette Winery.
Address: N/A
Phone: 573-883-3286 (farm); 573-880-2252 (cell)
Website: N/A
Agritourism: N/A

The Old Homestead, Washington

Fran Fister loves chickens and fresh eggs. Even before she moved to her thirty-acre farm in 2009, she kept a few chickens for eggs. Now she's swimming in eggs—about twenty-five to thirty dozen a day from her four hundred chickens. Her chickens are free-ranging. To keep out land predators she uses electrified poultry netting which she loves. Of course, as she points out, it can't keep out the hawks and owls that get a few of her chickens a week. She is gradually reseeding her land in clover so her chickens will have even better foraging options. Fran also makes a luxurious goat's milk soap from her Nubian goats.

Products: Eggs and soap.
Where to buy: Find her eggs in the St. Louis area at Freddie's Market, Kirkwood Farmers' Market, Local Harvest Grocery (eggs and soap), Sappington Farmers' Market, and Planet Health. L&F in Washington also sells her eggs and her soap.
Address: 766 Turning Leaf Dr.
Phone: 314-920-0004
Email: fister@toast.net
Website: N/A
Agritourism: Not at this time.

Free ranging at the Old Homestead

Price Family Farms, Troy

David and Lana Price are in some ways accidental farmers. In 2000, they started raising a cow or two for themselves and friends and the next thing they knew, they were adding more cattle to keep up with the requests. A former teacher, David says taking care of cows is a lot easier than a roomful of students. David finishes out about ninety beef a year using rotational grazing. Ninety days before slaughter they are also offered the option to eat from a self-feeder. The cattle are never taken off pasture and have their choice for that ninety-day period. One benefit of this system, according to David and a few other farmers featured in this book, is that it allows you to harvest the animals year round. To have the most flavor, the animals need to have access to a reliable food source for the last three months. During winter, for instance, the forage is not as lush or as available. Cattle on this farm never receive hormones or antibiotics. And the animals that David sells directly to customers are slaughtered on the farm. The animal is then taken to a processing plant for aging and packaging.

Products: Beef products are available by the quarter, half, or whole. You can also buy beef bundles with clever names like Crockpot Pack and Grill Pack. This convenient bundling is perfect for folks who don't have a lot of storage but want to buy a variety of meats at one time.
Where to buy: You can pre-order sides from David or buy/order beef bundles from Green's Country Store in Lake St. Louis.
Address: 149 Strack Farm Ln.
Phone: 636-338-1418
Website: www.pricefamilyfarm.com
Agritourism: Call if you want to visit the farm.

Rutherford Farms, Silex

Desiree has been farming since 2005, but her husband has farmed his whole life. Lindell and Desiree Rutherford run this small Certified Naturally Grown farm in Silex, much like the farms of yore. Red Wattle hogs, a heritage breed, roam the acreage along with Sexlinks chickens and ducks and lots of produce. Her newest foray into Black Mottle miniature turkeys has been quite successful, but you have to pre-order to get one. Desiree is an active member of the Missouri Organic Association and is featured in a movie by Slow Food, USA.

Products: Chicken and duck eggs, cuts of pork, vegetables, and wild crops.
Where to buy: Café Osage, Clarksville Station Restaurant, Ellisville Farmers' Market, and at the farm. The Rutherfords also have a winter CSA.
Address: 741 Hwy. TT
Phone: 636-322-9042
Website: N/A
Agritourism: Can visit, but call to set up.

Tri-Pointe Farm, Jefferson County

Joe and Jennifer Althoff have been farming since the late 1990s. They have over fifty acres for their animals and rent additional land for crop farming. The crop farming allows them to grow their own grain for their animals along with selling on the commodity market. You will find beef, pork, and chicken on the farm. The hogs are loose in a big hoop building, and the chickens and cattle are on the land. In addition to the farm, Jennifer and Joe have a feed store they operate, and it is their dream to be able to sell their products at their store. Permits are in the works.

Products: Eggs, hogs, and beef.
Where to buy: Call to order beef or pork. They mainly sell halves and whole but can do quarters.
Address: 9091 Tripointe Farm Rd.
Phone: 636-262-0725
Email: jenny@tripointefarm.com
Website: tripointefarm.com
Agritourism: N/A

Kansas City Region

A & B Homecoming Beef, Leeton

Glenn Varner has farmed cattle for twenty years, but in 2006 he took his cattle off grain. Originally he did this because he says, "I was tired of the middle man getting all the money." Since then, he has researched the 100 percent "forage" diet and believes it is the right thing to do. Glenn points out that to survive as a cattle farmer you either need a whole lot of cattle or a niche market. His closed herd is rotationally grazed on his eighty-acre farm.

> **Products:** Currently you can buy a split half, half, or whole beef, but Glenn plans to go to farmers' markets in 2012 so he can sell to folks who prefer to buy smaller quantities.
> **Where to buy:** Directly from Glenn and in 2012 he hopes to be at the City Market in Kansas City (Sunday) and Brookside Farmers' Market (Saturday).
> **Address:** 303 NE Hwy. 2
> **Phone:** 660-221-1918
> **Email:** sales@abhomecomingbeef.com
> **Website:** abhomecomingbeef.com
> **Agritourism:** Yes, but please call.

Paradise Meats (How a Cow Becomes Beef)

It used to be that almost every farming community had its own meat locker/processing facility. This made it easy for farmers to process their animals and get their products to consumers. Farmers around the Kansas City area can take their animals to Paradise Meats. The original locker was built in 1946. In 1995 Mario and Teresa Fantasma bought the business. After a fire in Paradise, they rebuilt and relocated to Trimble. The Fantasma family (Mario, Teresa, Nick, and Louis) keep busy. They work with 50 to 75 farmers and process 100 to 150 animals a week.

Barham Cattle Company, Kearney

Barham Cattle is more than just cattle. Kenny Barham and his family offer pasture-raised chickens and eggs as well as turkeys for Thanksgiving. The chickens are in moveable pens that are relocated twice a day. The cattle are born and raised on the farm. They offer their cattle a locally grown grain until they reach their harvest weight. In 2012, he has a farmer who is going to grow a non-GMO corn that he can use for his chickens, turkeys, and cows. Check out this one-hundred-year-old family farm.

Products: Beef, chicken, eggs, and turkeys for Thanksgiving. Kenny also offers beef sticks, beef and bacon brats, summer sausage, and hot dogs. In addition to cuts, you can buy whole and half beef.
Where to buy: Liberty's Farmers' Market, Big V Country Mart has their eggs, Green Acres Market carries their eggs and beef. Offer by the cut, filets, strips, ground beef. They also offer a CSA—information is available on the website.
Address: 16600 NE 128th St.
Phone: 816-628-4567; 816-365-2445
Email: barhamcattleco@embarqmail.com
Website: barhamcattleco.com
Agritourism: Call if you would like a tour.

In addition to their processing business, they have a retail operation and sell their own line of cured and smoked products, sausages, bacon, hams, braunschweiger, etc. All the animals used in their products are from farmers who raise their animals on the land and use no hormones or antibiotics. The Fantasma family is passionate about supporting small farms and the natural food movement. As Nick says, "Food is not supposed to make us sick, it's supposed to make us healthy."

Address: 405 W. Birch St.
Phone: 816-357-1229
Email: nick@paradisemeats.com
Website: paradisemeats.com

Benedict Builders Farm, Knob Noster

Calvin and Laura Benedict have farmed for more than twenty years but have been "clean food farming" for ten. Both Calvin and Laura grew up in families and communities where conventional farming was prevalent. After some health issues in their immediate family they decided to pursue what Laura calls "clean food farming." For the Benedicts, this means 100 percent grass-fed beef, all animals raised on the land, and no hormones or antibiotics.

> **Products:** They sell individual cuts of beef and pork as well as sausages and summer sausage. You can also buy quarter and half sides of beef. The turkeys and chickens are processed on the farm and are available at the farm or by delivery. Eggs are sold at farmers' markets.
> **Where to buy:** From the farm, Brookside Farmers' Market, and Briarcliff Village Farmers' Market.
> **Address:** N/A
> **Phone:** 660-563-3309
> **Website:** N/A
> **Agritourism:** Open to visitors except on Sunday, but please call.

Breezy Hill Farm, Centerview

This farm has been in the family for more than 130 years, making this Certified Naturally Grown farm a Missouri Century Farm. Debra and Art Ozias moved back to the family farm twenty-five years ago and immediately started raising cattle. Art, a voracious reader, read lots of books about diversified natural farming and attended Joel Salatin workshops. They now sell directly to the consumer. They have three hundred acres and raise some of their own grain. When possible, they do not use GMO grain with their chickens. They have several loose partnerships with farmers near them and they help each other with marketing and selling each other's products.

Products: 100 percent grass-fed beef, raw milk, and fresh eggs. Some honey because they keep bees on their property for another farmer.

Where to buy: Contact directly. They sell directly to customers, and they deliver beef within a one-hundred-mile radius of their farm.

Address: 62 SW State Route 58

Phone: 660-656-3409

Website: breezy-hill-farm.com

Agritourism: Call if you would like to see the farm.

D & R Farms, Cameron

Don and Ruth Lowenstein have been raising cattle for nearly twenty-five years, organically for twenty. Both grew up in big cities, but Ruth always wanted to live on a farm. When they found this lovely farm in Cameron, they knew they were home. Don admits that when he bought his first two cows, he had no idea what he was doing. Over the years, though, they have figured out a perfect balance for their land, their time, and their cows. For Don this meant figuring out how to make their farming operation profitable and at the same time understanding what the land will healthily sustain without external inputs. Don has read a lot of older farming books, and one that changed his life was *Grass Productivity*, by Andre Voison. He sees himself as a Grass Farmer, and the farm's by-product is the calf crop.

Products: Don and Ruth have a small herd, and they butcher their 100 percent grass-fed/grass-finished beef once a year in November.

Where to buy: Sells directly to the customer. Don and Ruth have a lot of regulars and currently do not actively market their products. But call if you are interested because sometimes they have extra.

Address: N/A

Phone: 816-632-7996

Email: don.lowenstein@laapc.com

Website: N/A

Agritourism: N/A

Golden Rule Meats, Walker

Mark Curtis plans to one day be a full-time farmer. Help make his dream come true. He has been farming part-time since 1989 and in 2007 made the switch to 100 percent grass-fed/grass-finished beef. The genetic makeup of his cows is great for grass-finished beef because it marbles easily and the cows fatten easily on forage. Mark plants annual forages for his herd for a richer flavor and more marbling. With four hundred acres, his closed-herd cows are fat and happy.

Products: Black Angus 100 percent grass-fed beef cuts, and he also sells by the whole.
Where to buy: The City Market in downtown Kansas City.
Address: 13376 S. Hwy. AA
Phone: 417-876-3371
Email: markcurtis@centurylink.net
Website: www.goldenrulemeats.us
Agritourism: N/A

K.C. Buffalo, Belton

With thirty years of experience, K.C. Buffalo has a lot to offer. Peter Kohl fell in love with buffalo meat and worked long hours and many different jobs to make his dream of buffalo farming a reality. He and his wife, Susan, now have a 250-head herd and sell their hormone/antibiotic-free meat all around the Kansas City area.

Products: Ground, roasts, steaks, brats, bison hot dogs, summer sausage, jerky, and filets.
Where to buy: They have a store on the property and also sell at the Kansas City Farmers' Market in Kansas City. Western Crown Center, the Majestic Steak House, the Le Froo Frog, and the Roadhouse serve their bison. You can purchase their meat at Green Acres, Nature's Market, Nature's Pantry, Consentino's Market, and Hy-Vee's (check with yours).
Address: 2201 E. 203rd St.
Phone: 816-322-8174
Email: kcbuffaloco@sbcglobal.net
Website: kcbuffalo.com
Agritourism: Yes, they are located just outside of Kansas City.

Parker Farms Natural Meats, Richmond

In 2006 Tom Parker added a meat CSA and began direct marketing to his customers, which made it possible for him to farm full time. Tom and Paula raise all the animals organically, but they do not have certification. The cattle and Katahdin Hair sheep are 100 percent grass-fed, and the chickens and hogs are raised on the land. When the couple started the year-round meat CSA, they worried about how they would transport the products, but it was a useless worry. The CSA members were asked to help, and they pitched in more than the Parkers could have imagined. The members compiled a distribution list, determined the drop-off points, and ran the deliveries. This keeps costs down and is truly a cooperative effort. Tom believes that if you find the customers, the farmers will come.

> **Products:** Grass-fed beef and lamb, hogs, chickens, and eggs.
> **Where to buy:** CSA (two times a month for twelve months) and BADSEED Farmers' Market.
> **Address:** 43602 Hwy. F
> **Phone:** 816-470-3276
> **Email:** parkerfarms@peoplepc.com
> **Website:** parkerfarmsmeat.com
> **Agritourism:** Possibly.

Pisciotta Farms, Kidder

Russell Pisciotta and Julia Kisser have farmed for ten years. All of their animals are on a pasture rotation that mimics nature. The cattle are given some grain for flavor, but animals are not given any hormones or antibiotics. Russell and Julia just added hogs to their farm, and turkeys are available seasonally.

> **Products:** Beef, pasture-raised chickens, eggs, turkey, and pork.
> **Where to buy:** City Market in Kansas City and folks can also pick up products at the farm. Russell and Julia will make deliveries for orders over two hundred dollars.
> **Address:** 4755 NW State Route W
> **Phone:** 816-803-9001
> **Email:** pisciottafarms@hughes.net
> **Website:** N/A
> **Agritourism:** N/A

RSK Farms, Chilhowee

Sue Stropes is an example of a farmer with plenty of product for direct-to-consumer sales. Now she is ready for some more customers who want to enjoy her high-quality beef. She has worked hard to develop the genetics of her cows and they are not given hormones, antibiotics, or grains. She currently runs seventy to eighty cow/calf pairs and harvests three to five animals a year for direct sale. The remainder goes to the sale barn. You will also find free-range Freedom Ranger chickens (pre-order) and eggs.

> **Products:** Grass-fed beef (quarter, half, whole beeves), eggs, and free-range chickens (pre-order only on chickens).
> **Where to buy:** Blue Springs Farmers' Market (near Kansas City) and on the farm.
> **Address:** 189 SW State Route 2
> **Phone:** 816-405-9545 (cell)
> **Email:** sue.stropes@gmail.com (If you email Sue, please list a product in the subject line or it gets thrown out.)
> **Website:** N/A
> **Agritourism:** Can see the farm when you pick up products.

Troque Farms, Buckner

Frank Kuhnert and his sister Frannie Graves farm 125 acres right outside of Kansas City. In 1994 they fully implemented sustainable agriculture. The cows and sheep are 100 percent grass-fed, and the broilers and layers are all free-range. A six-acre vegetable garden is planned for spring 2012. Frank also distributes and uses Fertrell's organic feed supplements and fertilizers. Fertrell's is the oldest organic fertilizer in the U.S.

> **Products:** Troque Farms sells direct to the consumer—chickens, lamb, veal, beef, and turkeys.
> **Where to buy:** Troque Farms store.
> **Address:** 31710 E. Oakland School Rd.
> **Phone:** 816-215-9925
> **Email:** troquefarms@aol.com
> **Website:** troquefarms.net
> **Agritourism:** Yes, you must buy from the farm.

Southwest Region

Alger Family Farm, Miller

Tammy and Steve Alger moved to a small farm from Chicago in the early 1990s and then ten years later bought fifty-five acres and a fixer-upper so they could grow for more than just their family. They did a lot of reading about how they wanted to farm and found a lot of wisdom from farmers like Joel Salatin. Their farm is very much a family business—their twenty-year-old and twelve-year-old both own cows on the farm. The Algers harvest their 100 percent grass-fed cattle after spring when they have had access to lots of good forage. In 2011, they harvested about six hundred pasture-raised chickens supplemented with non-GMO corn rations.

> **Products:** Lamb, chicken, beef, turkeys, and eggs. They also sell bread and some soap.
> **Where to buy:** Place an order on-line. (All pick-up is at the farm, which keeps the prices lower.)
> **Address:** 10304 Lawrence 2030
> **Phone:** 417-452-2049
> **Email:** info@algerfamilyfarm.com
> **Website:** algerfamilyfarm.com
> **Agritourism:** Her kids occasionally will do farm tours for interested customers.

Autumn Olive Farms LLC, Bois D'Arc

Started in 1999 by Kim and Jackie Glass, Autumn Olive Farms has a lot to offer folks interested in healthy eating. They grind their own feed from non-GMO grains, which are fed to their hogs, chickens, and turkeys. The beef and lamb are 100 percent grass-fed and grass-finished. Their chicken business has grown substantially over twelve years—the first year they harvested three hundred, and now it is up to about six thousand a year. The chickens are moved every day, and electric fencing protects them from land predators.

> **Products:** Pastured pork, beef, lamb, and chickens, as well as free-range turkeys available for Thanksgiving, but they also have ground turkey around July.
> **Where to buy:** MaMa Jean's South Store, the Greater Springfield Farmers' Market (year-round), and at the farm.
> **Address:** 2169 N. Farm Rd. 71
> **Phone:** 417-732-4122
> **Email:** glassmagic@sbcglobal.net
> **Website:** eatfromthefarm.com
> **Agritourism:** Possibly.

Bechard Family Farms, Conway

This family farm, located on 115 acres, can meet most of your needs for pasture-raised meats and then some. Started in 2000 by this family of nine, they ensure that their animals live on chemical-free pastures and do not give them hormones or antibiotics. In 2011, the Bechards located a source for non-GMO corn for their chickens and turkeys. Teddi and Armand love their adopted home (they moved from the Denver suburbs in 2000) and welcome you to visit their small farm store where you will find products from their farm along with handmade crafts and local honey.

Products: Beef, turkey, lamb, chickens, pork, eggs, whole wheat bread, raw milk (must call to reserve it), twelve flavors of handmade jams, a soap-making kit, and handmade lye soaps.

Where to buy: Marshfield Farmers' Market (May-Oct.), on the farm Mon-Sat. 10-6, and some delivery drop-off points in Springfield. Please check the website for more information about drop-off sites. Frozen birds are available most of the year, but fresh chicken and turkey should be reserved. Their handmade lye soaps are available at MaMa Jean's in Springfield, J & T Country Store in Roach, and Heartland Antique Mall in Lebanon.

Address: 13700 Athens Rd.

Phone: 417-589-4152

Email: grassfedmeats@bechardfarm.com

Website: bechardfarm.com

Agritourism: Visit their farm store, Mon-Sat. 10-6.

Circle B Ranch, Seymour

Marina and John Backes left New Jersey for a quieter farming life in Missouri. Marina comes to the farming business from a food background and knows the importance of quality products. Their ninety-acre farm is now home to Berkshire, Duroc, and Red Wattle Hogs who breed, farrow, and live outside for their whole lives in rotating paddocks. There are lots of acorns and foraging material for these heritage hogs. Circle B Ranch is humanely certified. Their first harvest will be in 2012.

Products: Half, whole, or cuts. Marina also has her own line of products—Marina's Cranberry Chutney, Big John's BBQ Sauce, and Marina's Italian Sauce.

Where to buy: Farmers' Gastropub, Chateau on the Lake (Branson), Farmers' Market of the Ozarks, MaMa Jean's, and Local Harvest Grocery in St. Louis carries the chutney.

Address: RR2 Box 2824

Phone: 417-683-0271

Email: marina@circlebranchpork.com

Website: circlebranchpork.com

Agritourism: Call for information.

Ozark Natural Beef/Ozark Natural Pork, Springfield

Alan and Meera Scarrow raise Angus cattle and Berkshire hogs on Certified Organic pastures. Their cattle are never given grain, hormones, or antibiotics. The hogs also do not receive hormones or antibiotics. In business since 2007, the Scarrows want to provide consumers with healthy, safe, and delicious beef and pork.

    Products: Beef and pork products.
    Where to buy: Springfield Farmers' Market.
    Address: 2128 S. Cross Timbers Ct.
    Phone: 417-838-1682
    Email: alan@ozarksnaturalbeef.com
    Website: ozarksnaturalbeef.tripod.com
    Agritourism: N/A

Rainbow Trout and Game Ranch, Inc., Rockbridge

Rainbow Trout and Game Ranch is a unique combination of fish hatchery, hunting and fishing, hiking, lodging, and dining. The fish hatchery produces 200,000 fish yearly. The cool spring-fed stream is a perfect place to learn to fish.

    Products: Smoked trout.
    Where to buy: MaMa Jean's, on location, and on-line.
    Address: P.O. Box 100
    Phone: 417-679-3619
    Email: info@rockbridgemo.com
    Website: rockbridgemo.com
    Agritourism: Yes.

Rockin H Ranch, Norwood

Look no further than Rockin H Ranch to find a farm family that lives, breathes, eats, and proselytizes holistic farming. Cody has been farming his whole life—his high-school 4-H project of seven cows blossomed into their now-diversified thousand-acre ranch, on-farm market, and agritourism business. During those thirty-nine years, Cody has tried a lot of things and, as he and Dawnell will both tell you, have made lots of mistakes. About twelve years ago they began changing the way they farmed and now run a very holistic farm and are working toward certification from the Animal Welfare Association. Animals at Rockin H Ranch are raised on the land without the use of antibiotics, hormones, or vaccinations. The cattle are 100 percent grass-fed and grass-finished, and all of their animals are rotated through their clover-rich pastures. The chickens and turkeys also receive a non-GMO grain supplement. In addition to raising cows, hogs, chickens, lambs, goats, bison, and turkeys, both Cody and Dawnell find time to write blogs and articles in *Acres USA*, and Cody just published a book called *Ranching Full-Time on 3 Hours a Day*. Dawnell runs the marketing side of their business along with home-schooling their daughter, Taylor, who plays an important role in this family business. She takes care of the hogs, oversees the pastured fryers and turkeys, and tends the Great Pyrenees guard dogs.

Products: Beef, pork, chicken, lamb, goat, turkey (seasonal), raw milk, and eggs, as well as seasonal produce. They also run a produce CSA and plan to get certification to sell their goat milk and goat milk products.

Where to buy: On the farm, Homegrown Foods, Well-Fed Neighbor Market, Wild Root Grocery (Eastland Farmers' Market), Spring Valley Herbs and Natural Foods (all-in Springfield). They sell most of their products directly to consumers through a home delivery system in the Greater Springfield Area. Interested customers place their order via email. Minimum $25 order for delivery. Contact Dawnell for information.

Address: 6156 Curtner Rd.

Phone: 417-259-BEEF (Cody); 417-259-CHKN (Dawnell)

Website: rockinh.net

Agritourism: People can visit the farm, and they have customer appreciation days the first Saturday of June and first Saturday of November. They also host an annual "Cowboy Gathering" where participants get to live like a cowboy for five days. Experience real chuckwagons, camping, and horseback riding while enjoying the beautiful countryside. Cody also runs a Stockman's School for Profit to help folks learn how to have a financially successful calf/cow operation. Check the website for more information.

Troutdale Farms, Gravois Mills

Most people don't know that it takes about as long to grow a trout to harvest weight as it does some cows—fourteen months. Dennis and Merrit Van Landuyt have lots of interesting fish tidbits to share, and they should. Since 2005, this high-energy couple has invested a lot of time and money in trout. Their trout farm was founded in the 1930s and is fed by an underground Ozark Spring that is at a constant temperature of 56 degrees—perfect for trout. When they bought this farm as their "retirement" activity, they had no idea the amount of work and effort it would take to refurbish the runways and get the farm back into shape. Troutdale Farms is unusual in Missouri because they raise trout to sell wholesale and directly to customers, not to stock ponds or streams. Stop by Columbia Farmers' Market and meet these two intriguing people, and learn something while you're there.

Products: Trout—whole or filleted.
Where to buy: Columbia Farmers' Market, Local Harvest Grocery, and served at some of the finest restaurants in St. Louis, including Big Sky Café, Niche, Taste, Annie Gunn's, Bottleworks, I Frattelini, Local Harvest Café, Brasserie, and in Columbia at Sycamore's, Wine Cellar and Bistro, Les Bourgeois Bistro in Rocheport, and Glenn's Café and Abigails in Boonville. (This list evolves, so be sure to ask at your favorite local restaurant if the trout is from Troutdale Farms.)
Address: 12726 Troutdale Ln.
Phone: 573-372-1900
Website: N/A
Agritourism: Call to set up a tour.

Southeast Region

Black Bell Acres, Alton

Albert and Kirsten Kosinski have been farming and ranching in Missouri for seven years and are very involved with their community of farmers. They are in a very rural location, and low population density sometimes works against them in terms of sales. They raise 100 percent grass-fed/grass-finished lamb and beef. They also have a team of draft horses for moving firewood and logs, alpine dairy goats, and some chickens.

Kirsten and Albert raise Scottish Highland cattle, an extremely old breed known for their heartiness and adaptability. The cattle are excellent foragers and produce a meat that is lean, well marbled, and flavorful. These beautiful cattle have long shaggy fur that protects their eyes from insects and despite the large horns are considered very even tempered.

Brownie, a two-plus year-old heifer, Black Bell Acres

Products: They sell the animal "on the hoof." They would like to expand their direct-to-consumer business.
Where to buy: On the farm.
Address: Route 3 Box 3544
Phone: 417-778-6009
Email: blackbellacres@yahoo.com
Website: blackbellacres.com
Agritourism: Yes, you can visit. You need to call or email for directions or products.

Farrar Out Farms, Frohna

Colby grew up going to his uncle's dairy farm and spent summers working on the farm with his cousins. At age fifteen, he started working on the newly established Farrar Out Farms. Now the whole family is involved. His parents have a farm nearby, and Colby bought the Farrar Out Farms business. His brother also raises some animals, which Colby sells for him at markets. Colby is known for his pasture-raised Thanksgiving turkeys, heritage pork products, and eggs. He also has chickens available seasonally April-November, as well as lamb. All his animals are raised on pasture with no hormones or antibiotics.

> **Products:** Eggs, lamb, pork products, chickens, produce, and holiday turkeys.
> **Where to buy:** Buy products at Maplewood Farmers' Market, Kirkwood Farmers' Market, and Local Harvest Grocery. The following restaurants use his products: Five Bistro, Winslow's Home, Foundation Coffee Grounds, Local Harvest Café, and Schlafly Bottleworks.
> **Address:** N/A
> **Phone:** 573-579-9550
> **Email:** farraroutfarms@hotmail.com
> **Website:** N/A
> **Agritourism:** Call if you want to set up a visit.

Hinkebein Hills, Cape Girardeau

Carlios Hinkebein is dedicated to raising his animals on the land. He has been farming for twenty to twenty-one years and has always raised beef and pork. He finishes his cattle two different ways—some are grass finished and others are grain finished. Customers have their choice. Carlios also has a processing plant on his farm. He can process meats for individual customers as well as other farmers. However, because it is not a USDA-inspected facility, he cannot sell those products in retail operations. The animals for sale at retail locations are slaughtered and packaged at a USDA-inspected facility.

Products: Pasture-raised pork, grass-fed/grain-finished beef. Try his brats, and don't miss his salt and pepper sausages featured in *Sauce Magazine*.

Where to buy: Local Harvest Grocery, Mud House, Blood and Sand, Restaurant 360, La Dolce Via, Onesto Pizza, Stellina Pasta, Mad Tomato, Farmhaus. In Cape Girardeau you can find his products at Molly's, Celebrations, and a small grocery called Natural Health. You can also order half, quarter, and whole animals directly from Carlios.

Address: 434 Whispering Wind Ln.

Phone: 573-332-8530

Website: hinkebeinhillsfarm.com

Agritourism: N/A

Janzow Farms, Cape Girardeau

Julie and Micah Janzow are very busy part-time farmers. They started to raise their own food because they wanted better food than you typically find in a grocery store and soon realized it was fairly easy to raise food for their family of four. It wasn't long before they found other people willing to buy their products—people who wanted better-quality food. They now raise beef, lamb, pork, chickens, and rabbits. Their animals are given no additional hormones or antibiotics and are pasture raised. Their cows are Mexican Steers that they finish off on grass. These former rodeo steers are raised on a plant-based feed prior to living at Janzow Farms.

Products: Eggs, pork, lamb, and beef.

Where to buy: Cape Farmers' Market (April-November on Thursdays) and only beef at Family Friendly Farm store and by appointment at the farm to buy directly from them.

Address: 530 Buffalo Ln.

Phone: 573-450-1922

Email: janzowfarms@hotmail.com

Website: janzowfarms.com; Facebook

Agritourism: Have done tours in the past. Please call to arrange.

Jones Heritage Farm & Market, Jackson

After one of his children got sick from E. coli, Gerry Jones started to look into food issues. What he learned led him to farming and growing his own food. And in 2009, Gerry started Jones Heritage Farm. Gerry and his farm-to-chef manager, Stephen Sauer, focus on raising healthy and happy heritage breeds on this farm and market. You won't find antibiotics or added hormones, but you will find free-ranging chickens, pigs, goats, beef, and lamb. The farm is just under one hundred acres and houses a small farm store where you can buy fresh cuts of meat as well as other farm products.

> **Products:** Berkshire pork, chicken, lamb, beef, free-range eggs, and produce.
> **Where to buy:** On the farm, Annie Gunn's, Cardwell's, Cielo at the Four Seasons, Harvest, Range, Scottish Arms, Yia-Yia's.
> **Address:** 5739 State Hwy. W
> **Phone:** 573-332-7447
> **Email:** stephensauer@jonesheritagefarms.com
> **Website:** jonesheritagefarms.com
> **Agritourism:** Can buy at the store market Mon.-Fri. 10-6, Sat. 8-4, closed Sunday. Once a month they host a farm-to-fork dinner with well-known chefs. Check the website for information.

Meramec Bison Farm, Salem

Jim and Joan Sample have been raising bison since 1993. Their herd of about 100 rotationally grazes on the 760-acre farm outside of Salem. Jim is careful to make sure the land is not over grazed and rotates the bison through three major sections of his farm. He has built up a nice customer and retail base across Missouri which values the hormone- and antibiotic-free meat as well as the health value from eating lean bison meat.

Products: Bison products including cuts, ground, bison snack sticks, and summer sausage.
Where to buy: On the farm, at health food stores across the state, and in St. Louis at Sappington Farmers' Market.
Address: 605 South Main P.O. Box 707
Phone: 573-729-3148; 800-827-3403
Email: bison@fidnet.com
Website: meramecbison.com
Agritourism: N/A

Missouri Best Beef Co-Op, Koshkonong

Ron McNear had a very winding path to farming, but once he arrived more than twenty-five years ago, he stayed. In about 2004, Ron had an idea to start up a co-op of cattle farmers. He researched the laws to decide how to set up the operation and stumbled upon something called Chapter 274 that was written over one hundred years ago. He started Missouri Best Beef Co-op as a charter non-profit agricultural cooperative under this law and says there is really nothing else like it in the whole United States. The co-op does all its own processing and distribution, which keeps the money in the co-op and expands the economic opportunities for the ranchers. There are thirty-five ranchers in the co-op throughout the southern part of Missouri, which Ron says is perfect land for cattle. Members of the co-op agree to raise their cattle on the land, breed within their herds, and not feed hormones or antibiotics to their animals. The cattle are always on grass, but the last ninety days they are given a grain supplement. You can find their products labeled under "Ranchers All Natural Beef," and it is available fresh or frozen.

Ron says that they want to increase their direct-to-consumer relationships by selling more wholesale to local restaurants, to individuals, and at stores in Missouri.

Products: Beef products, fresh and frozen. They also sell smoked beef sausage and snack stix that are all natural (no nitrates or MSG).
Where to buy: Sappington Farmers' Market, buyers' clubs (see website), and sold directly to individuals.
Address: Route #1, Box 149
Phone: 417-867-8501
Email: mobest@centurylink.net
Website: mobestbeef.com
Agritourism: Call and talk with Ron about tours.

Missouri Grass-Fed Beef, Salem

Jeremy Parker is a fourth-generation farmer, and his family has raised cows for decades. Over the last few years, the Parkers have been direct marketing their 100 percent grass-fed beef to customers. Jeremy will tell you that he is primarily a grass farmer because the quality of the grass is the quality of the cow. This is a closed herd, which means the cows are all born and raised on the nine-hundred-acre farm. Jeremy is passionate about what he does and why he does it, so be sure to meet him at a farmers' market or check out his website.

> **Products:** 100 percent grass-fed beef. Buy whole cows, half, or individual cuts.
> **Where to buy:** Tower Grove Farmers' Market, Maplewood Farmers' Market, Local Harvest Grocery, Baumann's Fine Meats, Winslow's Home, Old North Grocery Co-op, and he sells halves and whole directly to customers. His beef is also featured at Local Harvest Café and Winslow's Home. Check website for updates.
> **Phone:** 314-570-5858
> **Website:** eatmograssfedbeef.com
> **Agritourism:** Jeremy welcomes visitors, but you have to call to set up a time.

R & C Beefalo, Arcadia

Beef + Buffalo = BEEFALO. To be considered beefalo, the animal must be 37.5 percent bison and the rest is bovine beef cattle. Richard Childers relays that it takes seven generations to create a beefalo. Anything over 37.5 percent bison is considered an exotic breed. Richard used to raise regular Angus, but he likes that beefalo aren't heat exhausted in the summer and that they are very efficient foragers. He is a one-man operation and harvests eight to nine beefalo per year. Richard does not use hormones or antibiotics, and his fields are not treated with any chemicals or fertilizers.

> **Products:** Quarter, half, or whole beefalo. The beefalo are processed to your specifications.
> **Where to buy:** On localharvest.org, and to individual customers. There is a waiting list so call to reserve early.
> **Address:** 2920 CR 110 (mailing)
> **Phone:** 573-546-6501
> **Email:** apexgs12@hotmail.com
> **Website:** N/A
> **Agritourism:** N/A

Rain Crow Ranch American Grass Fed Beef, Doniphan

Dr. Patricia Whisnant and her husband started raising grass-fed beef when a friend (a vegan at the time) requested a grass-fed cow. This friend had decided to start eating meat and thought that if she was going to eat meat, then she wanted her cow to be solely raised on grass. That cow officially led to American Grass Fed Beef. In the late 1990s, they began marketing their beef on the Internet. The Whisnants will tell you that they have made every mistake in the book as they built up their now 1,200 head of cattle. They are now the largest 100 percent grass-fed beef producer in the country. No antibiotics, no hormones, closed herds, and the pastures are Certified Organic. This farming operation is unique because they now control every aspect of the beef—from birth to harvest to table. In 2005 they purchased Fruitland American Meats, where they had processed their meat for years, and by 2006 the plant was Certified Organic. Their son Pete manages the plant, which employs fifty people. This is certainly one of the larger farms in the book, but an example of a Missouri farm with local, regional, and national appeal.

Products: 100 percent grass-fed/finished beef products—cuts, ground.
Where to buy: On-line, Whole Foods, Schnucks Markets, Fair Shares, Niche, Straub's, The Crossing, Mike Shannon's, Washington University (check website for extensive listing). If you travel to New England you can find their beef in many Whole Foods stores.
Address: HC4 Box 253
Phone: 573-996-3716; 866-255-5002
Email: customerservice@americangrassfedbeef.com
Website: americangrassfedbeef.com; raincrowranch.com
Agritourism: Call to schedule a tour.

Sayersbrook Bison Ranch, Potosi

In 1976 (the Bison-tennial), Skip and Connie Sayers started raising bison on the family farm, which was started in 1920 by Skip's parents. Sayersbrook Bison Ranch, bordered by the Mark Twain National Forest on three sides, is now a destination for families and other groups. Not only can consumers purchase meat from the farm, but Sayersbrook also hosts executive and group retreats at their lodge. The farm houses a herd of six to eight hundred bison. The bison graze in the field, and during their last ninety days are offered a blend of natural grains that the Sayers believe enhance the flavor and tenderness of the meat. Sayersbrook Bison Ranch offers tours April-November.

Products: All things buffalo, including lunchmeat, brats, steaks, roasts, jerky, ribs, and dog treats.
Where to buy: Schnucks (all butcher counters and freezer), Straub's, John's Butcher Shop, Good 4 You Nutrition, Earth Mother Foods, Freddie's, Baumann Fine Meats, and Maude's Market. Sayersbrook Bison is also available in many fine dining establishments.
Address: 11820 Sayersbrook Rd.
Phone: 573-438-4449
Email: connies@sayersbrook.com
Website: Americangourmet.net (for bison meat) and sayersbrook.com for ranch and information
Agritourism: Open tours most Saturdays at 10 a.m. April-November, $6-$12. Includes a video, tour of the herd, and a visit to the county store. Call to make sure the ranch is not booked for a private event. Check website for information on the deluxe tour and lunch tour.

Missouri ranks tenth in the nation in the number of dairy cow operations and twentieth in the number of dairy cows, at 99,000 milk cows (as of 2010). That number, as large as it looks, actually represents a decline in the total number of dairy cows in the state. Although the number of traditional feed-based dairy operations in Missouri is declining, the number of pasture-based operations is growing. The farms we feature are all pasture-based.

But if we are tenth in the nation in number of dairy cow operations, why are there so few dairies in this chapter? First, running a dairy is hard work and can have a marginal return on investment. Most dairy farmers in Missouri belong to a cooperative. In fact, there are relatively few large dairy operations that sell milk and other dairy products locally, or at least in ways that are easy to track. (One way of tracking that we like is through the website "Where Is My Milk From?"—www.whereismymilkfrom.com.) There are a handful of dairy cooperatives doing business in Missouri, including Dairy Farmers of America, Prairie Farms, and Lone

Star Milk Producers. Ozark Mountain Creamery also sells their milk to a milk cooperative, and they hope to increase sales enough that they can discontinue this. Most of the cooperatives sell Grade-A milk products, although at least two also sell Certified Organic milk.

Missouri used to have small dairies all over the state. But as with other farming operations, smaller dairies were bought out or shut down when it became too costly for families to operate them. The increase in the cost of grain and lower milk prices are two main reasons many dairies have gone out of business. Most of the individual farms listed in the chapter either sell from their farms or bottle on-site.

A lot of dairy farmers are on the lookout for new and innovative ways to operate their farms. Several farmers in Missouri who want to continue to sell to cooperatives and stay in business have found ways to decrease their inputs and increase their profitability. Primarily, this has been through the practice of intensive grazing operations like rotating cows to fresh pasture every twelve to twenty-four hours, which significantly decreases the amount of grain they eat. Meier's Dairy in Monett, run by Mike and Janan Meier, is one farm that saved its farming operation through these practices. When you take away or drastically decrease the amount of feed, you reduce or eliminate the corn price volatility. It is much better to be left with only one volatility—milk prices. Another business model borrowed from New Zealand, from where a number of our state's dairy farmers originated, is sharemilking, whereby a future farm partner starts on the dairy farm as an employee, moves up into management, then part ownership, then full ownership.

Because most cow's milk is bought and sold through cooperatives that deal in Grade-A pasteurized milk, and because cow's milk is, for the most part, the only kind of milk that consumers want, the dairies featured in this chapter tend to raise goats and sheep (although a few also raise cows), and they tend to be cheese producers rather than milk producers. Missouri is developing a strong artisanal cheese industry (*St. Louis Post-Dispatch*, April 2010), with a growing local following. In fact, the state even boasts its own artisanal cheese cooperative: the Big Rivers Dairy Artisan Guild. Artisanal cheese has become so popular and mainstream that even large supermarket chains now carry many of the local brands, including Goatsbeard and Heartland Creamery cheeses. To be considered artisanal, the cheese is generally made from the milk of cows, sheep, or goats that are owned by the cheesemaker, so the dairy farm not only raises and milks the animals, but it also sustains a cheesemaking operation on-site (called a farmstead producer by the state milk board). One of the perceived benefits of such an arrangement is the presence of a terroir, or flavor-sense of the land/territory where the milk animal was raised. Artisanal cheese is also typically made from raw milk, which farmers cannot sell commercially in the state (although they can sell it directly from their farms to individuals). Needing raw milk for cheese production effectively means that cheesemakers must also provide the raw milk, hence the number of farmstead operations.

Whether you love handcrafted, cave-aged cheddar, herb-encrusted chèvre, or lots of choices in between, Missouri is fast becoming a player in the world of artisanal cheese, giving Wisconsin, Vermont, and California a run for their money.

Raw Milk

Many small Missouri farmers produce and distribute raw cow's milk, goat's milk, or sheep's milk from their farms or have pick-up points in nearby communities. There are far too many to list here, but most likely there is a farm or distribution point near you. In Missouri, it is illegal for stores and retail outlets to sell raw milk. Consumers must purchase directly from the farmer. Raw milk is a necessity if you want to make cheese or even churn your own butter. To find a location near you, check out this website: www.realmilk.com/where05.html#mo. This link will take you directly to sites in Missouri, but a listing for all states is available on the site.

Northwest Region

Green Hills Harvest, Purdin

Barb and Ken Buchmayer have over five hundred acres and around sixty cows. They own and operate their Certified Organic dairy and process their milk right on the farm. One thing that is unique about their farm is that they milk most of their cows only once a day. After talking with some farmers in Illinois and reading several articles, they made this switch in 2002 and it has worked fairly well for them. The savings in time and labor made it worthwhile. Ken has planted a mix of forages on the fields so that regardless of the weather something besides fescue will be available for forage. The cows' diet is supplemented with organic grains.

Products: Milk and eggs.
Where to buy: Hy-Vee in Columbia (eggs), Clovers, Schnucks in Columbia.
Address: 14649 Hwy. M
Phone: 660-244-5858
Email: GHHarvest@juno.com
Website: N/A
Agritourism: No.

Northeast Region

Heartland Creamery, Newark

Heartland Creamery is a large farm, boasting more than 17,000 acres. Formerly this creamery made and distributed large quantities of fresh milk in glass bottles. In 2010, they closed the milk operation and began focusing solely on their cheeses. Using only the milk from their own cows and goats, Heartland produces a wide variety of cheeses, including chèvre and "Gouda-like" cheeses.

> **Products:** Cheddar, goat-milk cheddar, chèvre varieties including fine herbs, lavender, honey & almonds, cranberry pecan, garlic & chive, olive & pimento, natural and lemon pepper, and several cheeses they describe as "Gouda-like."
> **Where to buy:** Local Harvest Grocery, Schnucks, and Sappington Farmers' Market.
> **Address:** N/A
> **Phone:** N/A
> **Website:** www.heartlandcreamery.com
> **Agritourism:** N/A

Weiler Dairy, Rutledge

Nevina and Debra Weiler started bottling milk on their farm in 2004. Prior to that they sold their milk to Prairie Farms. This small family-owned and operated dairy makes the most of their twenty-five to thirty cows with products in stores around Columbia and Kirksville.

> **Products:** Half-gallon glass, plastic pints, and quarts—skim, 2%, and whole, cream, chocolate milk, and lemonade in the summer.
> **Where to buy:** Clovers, Hy-Vee in Columbia and Kirksville, C & R Store in Macon, Bratchers in Moberly, and the Root Cellar in Columbia.
> **Address:** RR 1 Box 90
> **Phone:** 660-883-5839
> **Website:** N/A
> **Agritourism:** The Weilers have a small store on their farm where you can purchase milk. Open 8-5, Mon.-Fri. Call for directions.

Central Region

Goatsbeard Farm, Harrisburg

Ken and Jennifer Muno, with help from their two young sons, run their small family farm with great care. Utilizing intensive grazing methods and with a dedication to environmental stewardship, this family proves you can practice sustainable farming, have fantastic products, and make a living. The Munos have eighty acres of pastures and woods and a herd of about fifty goats. The cheeses are made right on the farm using the milk from their herd. Goatsbeard Cheeses can be found throughout the state both in restaurants and retail.

> **Products:** Fresh rounds, fresh tubs, soft-ripened cheese, feta, and raw milk cheese.
> **Where to buy:** Clovers Natural Market, Hy-Vee Supermarket, Root Cellar, Local Harvest Grocery, The Smokehouse Market, The Wine and Cheese Place, and The Wine Merchant; Restaurants: The Main Squeeze, Les Bourgeois Winery, Sycamore, Uprise Bakery, The Wine Cellar and Bistro, American Place, Duff's, Harvest, Stellina Pasta, 40 Sardines, Starker's Reserve, Café Via Roma, and White Stone Inn.
> **Address:** 11351 Callahan Creek Rd.
> **Phone:** 573-875-0706
> **Website:** www.goatsbeardfarm.com
> **Agritourism:** N/A

Sinking Creek Dairy, Rocheport

Brent and Heidi Netemeyer own and operate this small goat farm in Central Missouri. Brent grew up farming, but goats are a new endeavor for both of them. Heidi says they have a great clientele who treasure the fresh goat milk, goat milk soap, and eggs from their free-range chickens. For Brent and Heidi, their animals are more like pets than livestock, and they enjoy sharing their lives with them. Feel free to stop by, but not during milking time.

Products: Raw goat's milk, goat milk soaps, and eggs.
Where to buy: On the farm at their farm stand. Soap is available at the Peace Nook and Clovers in Columbia.
Address: 501 N. Route O (between Rocheport and Columbia)
Phone: 573-424-1314
Email: sinkingcreekdairy@yahoo.com
Website: www.sinkingcreekdairy.com
Agritourism: Open to visitors.

St. Louis Region

Baetje Farms, Bloomsdale

Steve and Veronica Baetje (pronounced BAY-jee) began retailing their award-winning cheeses in 2007. The couple ensures that their herd of seventy-five goats receives the best care, even giving pregnant females herbal teas to settle restless nerves. The care shows. The Baetje cheeses have received numerous awards in their short time on the market, garnering bronze and silver awards at the World Cheese Awards in 2010 in Birmingham, UK. The American Cheese Society in 2010 awarded top placement to five of their cheeses. See their website for an extensive list of the awards.

Products: Coeur de la Crème (heart-shaped goat cheese in a variety of flavors), Sainte Genevieve, Fleur de la Vallee, Cherbourg, Coeur de Clos, and Bloomsdale.
Where to buy: Stores and Markets: Winslow's Home, Local Harvest Grocery, Sappington Farmers' Market, Jones Heritage Farms, Grapevine Wine and Cheese, Southbound Fuel-Phillips 66, Tower Grove Farmer's Market, Maplewood Farmer's Market, Clayton Farmer's Market; Restaurants: In St. Louis at Farmhaus, Five Bistro, Café Osage, Local Harvest Café, Bixby's, Niche, and Chaumette Vinyards and Winery (Ste. Genevieve).
Address: 8932 Jackson School Rd.
Phone: 573-483-9021
Website: www.baetjefarms.com
Agritourism: The Baetjes do not give tours of their farm. Samples are always available at farmers' markets, and Steve or Veronica often attend the markets to meet with customers and answer questions about their cheeses.

Kansas City Region

Green Dirt Farm, Weston

Sheep farmers will tell you that sheep's milk makes the best cheese, and the two women who founded Green Dirt Farm are no exception. These two are proving that you don't have to go to France for gourmet cheese. You will find that these cheeses, made in the tradition of French farmhouse cheeses, become creamy as they age, with a rind that imparts a unique flavor. The 100 percent grass-fed lambs graze in the steep terrain that overlooks the surrounding countryside. Sarah and Jacqueline use intensive grazing management to protect the plants from overgrazing. Eat this cheese year-round and notice the change in flavor that reflects the varied plants, legumes, and flowers consumed by the sheep. Green Dirt Farm is an Animal Welfare Approved Farm.

Green Dirt Farms offers tours, farm dinners available by reservation, and cheese classes and tastings. Join their email list or check their website for events. The farm dinners fill quickly. Chefs from around the Kansas City area create dinner for the thirty guests using lamb and cheese from the farm and seasonal vegetables. Each dinner is unique, and the menu is a surprise for the guests and the farm owners. The community dinner, situated inside the farmhouse, is a food-lover's paradise.

> **Products:** Woolly Rind (2010 American Cheese Society Competition Winner), Dirt Lover (2010 American Cheese Society Competition Winner), Bossa (2009 American Cheese Society Competition Winner), Prairie Tomme, and Fresh (2009 American Cheese Society Competition Winner).
>
> **Where to buy:** Green Acres Market, The Better Cheddar, Cosentino's, Community Mercantile, Cellar Rat Wine, and Brookside Wine (in Kansas City); Local Harvest Grocery and Whole Foods in St. Louis; Restaurants: Blue Grotto, Bluestem, Café Sebastienne, Room 39 in Midtown, The American Restaurant, and The Farmhouse.
>
> **Address:** 20363 Mount Bethel Rd.
>
> **Phone:** 816-386-2156
>
> **Website:** www.greendirtfarm.com
>
> **Agritourism/Activities:** Tours are available May-October by appointment. To schedule a tour contact tours@greendirtfarm.com.

Shatto Milk Company, Osborn

Shatto has been in operation as a dairy for more than sixty years. In 2003, Shatto Milk Company began processing and bottling their milk right on the farm. They wanted to make sure that the customer had the freshest and best milk possible from cows not treated with rbST or rbGH (growth hormones). To that end, they bottle all their milk products in returnable glass bottles to keep the milk at the coldest temperature, which they believe is more desirable. Shatto Milk Company has a wide variety of products that are available throughout the Kansas City area.

Products: Whole milk, 2%, 1%, and skim in half gallons, quarts, and pints. They also produce cream, half and half, chocolate milk, banana milk, strawberry milk, root beer milk, butter, cheese curds, eggnog, and ice cream.

Where to buy: They mostly sell in the areas around Kansas City. Please see their webpage for a complete list of locations: www.shattomilk.com/where.html. Larger stores include Hy-Vee and Country Mart.

Address: 9406 N. Hwy. 33

Phone: 816-930-3862

Website: www.shattomilk.com

Agritourism: Barb and Leroy Shatto want everyone to experience the joy of the family farm. Their country store is open seven days a week. You can stop in for merchandise and to schedule a tour of the farm and bottling facilities. Check the website for special events.

Southwest Region

Lorenae Dairy, Galena

Robert and Debbie Salisbury planned a nice quiet retirement near Table Rock Lake, but after three years of living the supposed good life, they found they were bored to tears. So they did what most folks would do—start a dairy! In 2004 Robert and Debbie started selling their cheddar cheese curds. They now also make a dry ricotta and two years ago became a licensed distributor for raw milk. As of 2012, they are now the only licensed raw milk bottler remaining in Missouri. They hope to add aged cheeses as soon as they can find a little extra time. This farm boasts fifty-one beautiful acres with forty Jersey cows.

> **Products:** Cheddar cheese curds, raw milk, and a dry ricotta.
> **Where to buy:** On the farm, Springfield Farmers' Market, Country Marts in their area, Taste of Missouri in Branson, Buckner's Orchard in Reed's Spring, MaMa Jean's, Homegrown, and Well-Fed Neighbor in Springfield, Woody's Market in Highlandville, and Porter's in Crane.
> **Address:** 27141 State Hwy. 413
> **Phone:** 417-357-2873
> **Email:** lorenae@lorenaedairy.com
> **Website:** lorenaedairy.com
> **Agritourism:** They are always open because they have an honor box. Stop in and get fresh cheese curds on your way to Branson.

Ozark Mountain Creamery, Mountain Grove

David and Dwight Fry continue what their parents started in 1957 with help from their wives, Teresa and Lori, and the kids. The brothers take care of the animals and farm and Teresa and Lori run the creamery. Until 2009, Fry Family Dairies sold their milk exclusively to co-ops. For many reasons this arrangement was no longer profitable for the farm, and the families wanted to find another way. As Teresa tells it, "We started talking about it (opening the creamery) just so we would have something happy to talk about." The more they all talked about it, the more it made sense. In 2010 they opened Ozark Mountain Creamery LLC, and their number of customers and converts keeps growing.

They continue to farm the way they always have, which means they raise their cows on the land, grow alfalfa and corn for supplemental feed, never give growth hormones, and only give antibiotics if an animal is sick (the milk from these animals is not used while the cow is treated). Additionally, to keep the milk as natural as possible, they use vat pasteurization. Vat pasteurization uses lower temperatures, which safely pasteurizes the milk but allows the milk to retain its natural flavor, nutrients, and enzymes. As of December 2011, Ozark Mountain Creamery was the only licensed vat pasteurization plant in Missouri. Teresa says that many people who are lactose intolerant can drink their milk. The creamery also offers a non-homogenized whole milk called "cream line milk." The name says it all. You can see the separation of the cream because it has been left intact, leaving a "line." You can scoop off the cream or shake to mix prior to drinking.

Products: Half gallons in returnable glass bottles: skim, 2%, whole milk, and whole chocolate milk.

Where to buy: See website for all locations: Town & Country Stores (Ava, Bourbon, Cabool, Gainesville, Houston, Licking, Mansfield, Mountain View, Willow Springs, and Harville), Summer-Fresh (Mt. Vernon and Marshfield), Shetler's in Cabool, Richards Supermarket (Mountain View), Jean's Healthway in Ava, Mace's Supermarket in Cuba, Frick's Market in Sullivan and Union, Foods for Health and Nature Girls in Rolla. In Springfield at Homegrown Foods, MaMa Jean's, Hormann Meats, and Smillie's IGA. At Paul's Supermarkets in Eldon, Lake Ozark and Osage Beach, Hy-Vee in Osage Beach, Jefferson City, and Springfield, and at Country Mart Stores in Dixon, Mountain Grove, Rolla, St. James, Salem, Steelville, West Plains, and St. Clair.

Address: N/A
Phone: 417-926-FARM (3276)
Email: ozarkmtncreamery@yahoo.com
Website: ozarkmtncreamery.com
Agritourism: N/A

Spring Hill Dairy, Mountain Grove

Duncan Smith grew up on a dairy farm, and in 1992 he and his wife, Tara, bought the farm from Duncan's parents. This innovative farm family has sold milk through the commercial market and has tried a variety of ways to increase profitability while still maintaining a family life. As that got harder and harder, Duncan and Tara decided to diversify with a line of farmstead cheeses. David Kline, formerly of Nannie Cheese, is consulting with Duncan and has helped to develop some delicious aged cheeses. Using vat pasteurization (145 degrees for 30 minutes), they keep the cheeses as fresh as possible. In fact, most days the milk goes directly from the cow into the pasteurizer. This means it is not chilled or stored before beginning the cheese-making process. Spring Hill Dairy keeps their cattle on grass and believes it is important to minimize the grain intake for the best product. They have big dreams at Spring Hill Dairy, including future plans to add yogurt, kefir, and possibly even cottage cheese. Keep an eye on this expanding dairy and look for their products in specialty stores in your area.

Products: Baby Swiss, provolone, Tomme, and possibly cheddar in the future.
Where to buy: Check the website for a listing of retailers.
Address: 5673 County Line Rd.
Phone: 417-259-2080; 417-926-5945
Email: springhilldairy555@gmail.com; salina@springhillpumpkinpatch.com
Website: springhillpumpkinpatch.com; dairy website coming soon: www.springhilldairy555.com
Agritourism: They plan to provide tours. The farm also hosts a pumpkin patch in the fall with lots of activities for families and children. Information is available on their website.

Stoney Acres, Competition

Established in the late 1990s, Stoney Acres was the first sheep dairy in Missouri. Rick and Debra Christman moved from Wisconsin with the dream of opening a sheep dairy. With the knowledge that sheep's milk has the highest concentration of vitamins and minerals, they were excited to offer the milk to Missouri residents. Since opening, they have had several setbacks, most recently the loss of most of their herd to a "big cat"—most likely a mountain lion. The Christmans have plans to increase their herd once it is again safe. In the meantime, they still provide frozen sheep's milk and make fudge and soap using the milk.

Products: Frozen sheep milk ($7 a gallon), fudge, and soap.
Where to buy: At the farm or on-line at www.localharvest.org.
Address: 11399 Claxton Rd.
Phone: 417-668-5560
Website: www.stoneyacres.biz
Agritourism: If you want to work on your vacation, Rick and Debra welcome the help. Pitch a tent and learn to bale hay and milk sheep. Stay for one night or a few. Just be sure to call ahead and make arrangements.

Terrell Creek Farm, Fordland

Lesley Million and her family have been raising goats since 2006. By early 2012 they plan to have their artisan cheese creamery up and running. This small Certified Naturally Grown farm is family owned and operated by Lesley, her husband, and their two adult children. They use organic grains, utilize rotational grazing, and are seeking certification from the Animal Welfare Association. All the cheeses are made using the milk from their own herd of goats.

> **Products:** Plain and flavored chèvre, feta, blue goat cheese, and smoked Gouda.
> **Where to buy:** At Marshfield Farmers' Market and they deliver to Springfield area.
> **Address:** 508 Fordland Hills Dr.
> **Phone:** 417-209-0021
> **Email:** terrellcreekfarm@yahoo.com
> **Website:** terrellcreekfarm.com (in progress)
> **Agritourism:** The farm plans to have some customer appreciation days. Because of the nature and standards of cheese-making, they will not give regular tours.

Walnut Haven Farm, Osceola

Jayne Ramsey and her husband didn't start farming until they moved to Southwest Missouri. They have been raising goats since 1998, and Jayne will tell you that you have to love it to do it. Her day starts every morning at 4 a.m. They make farmstead cheeses, including feta, mozzarella, chèvre, and, by request, cottage cheese. She also sells goat milk by the gallon and makes lots of soaps and lotions using goat milk.

> **Products:** Goat milk farmstead cheeses, goat milk, and goat milk soaps.
> **Where to buy:** Cheeses and milk are sold on the farm. She sells her soaps and lotions at craft shows and on-line.
> **Address:** 450 SE 1131 Rd.
> **Phone:** 417-309-9597
> **Email:** willie_64776_1999@yahoo.com
> **Website:** walnuthavengoats.freewebspace.com; jellybeangoatsoapsandlotion.yolasite.com
> **Agritourism:** See the farm when you buy products from them. Call ahead for product availability.

Southeast Region

Family Friendly Farm, Cape Girardeau

It was hard to decide in which section to place this diverse farm run by Matthew and Rachel Fasnacht. They raise chickens for meat and eggs, dairy cows for milk, and also vegetables. All their animals are raised on pasture with no hormones or antibiotics. The beef and Jersey cows are 100 percent grass-fed except for hay and a bit of kelp. This hard-working family also teaches classes on how to make cheese, butter, and yogurt. Customers are welcome to visit the farm and see how the animals are raised, help collect eggs, or watch on a chicken processing day. The Fasnachts believe this allows the customer to feel like it is their farm too.

Matthew and Rachel want small farmers to succeed. They have a farm store on their property where they sell products for other farmers as well as their own products.

Products: Eggs, cow's milk, pastured meats, honey, sprouted grain breads, organic rice and popcorn, and locally made soaps. Check their website for complete listings. There are also several farms not listed in this book whose products are available at Family Friendly Farm.
Where to buy: At the store; hours are Tues. 3-6 p.m. and Sat. 9-3.
Address: 834 State Hwy. V
Phone: 573-335-1622
Email: info@familyfriendlyfarm.com
Website: familyfriendlyfarm.com
Agritourism: They welcome visitors.

Oak Ridge Goat Dairy, Advance

Enos Kauffman is passionate about farming and believes in the necessity and importance of small farms. He has farmed his whole life and has raised cattle, lambs, and now goats. Enos and his wife and kids relocated to Missouri in 2006 and decided to raise goats. His wife grew up on a dairy farm, and this seemed a good fit for the area. Initially, they sold milk to Morningland Dairy for raw goat milk cheese, but when Morningland Dairy closed, Enos had to revamp. After much research and talking with people across Missouri, they decided to start making and selling their own goat milk cheeses. Their goal is a Grade-A dairy with bottled goat milk. In the meantime, they are focusing on making delicious goat milk cheeses. The goats receive no hormones or antibiotics, and Enos uses rotational grazing as much as possible. Enos says it's harder with goats because they tend to be more "browsers" when it comes to grazing and therefore they supplement with alfalfa hay and some grains.

Enos says you have to wear three hats when you are making cheeses on your own farm: first you must run the dairy barn, which is a full-time job; then you are the cheese maker in the processing room; and always you are the marketer. It's a lot of jobs for one person, and he's hopeful that, as his children get older, they will play a larger role in the family business. In addition to the cheese operation, this industrious and creative family also sells homemade donuts at the markets. Diversification is key when you run a small farm, and the donuts are a great draw.

Products: Aged cheddar, fresh chèvre, plain feta, herbal feta, hot pepper feta, and tomato basil feta. They also sell fresh cheese curds—plain and one with onion and basil seasonings. The fresh cheeses have a short shelf-life, so they are sold mostly at farmers' markets.

Where to buy: Cape Girardeau Farmers' Market, Poplar Bluff Sale Market, Sikeston Farmers' Market, and the Jackson Farmers' Market on Tuesday. You can also find their cheese at the Celebrations Restaurant in Cape Girardeau. Several Schnucks grocery stores also carry Oak Ridge Goat Dairy products, including the store in Webster Groves, the Schnucks on Arsenal in St. Louis City, and a Schnucks in Cape Girardeau and Columbia.

Address: N/A

Phone: 573-803-7207

Website: N/A

Agritourism: They hope to add farm tours in the future.

Riverbluff Farm, Bem

April Adkison has dairy goats, sheep, chickens for eggs and eating, and cows on her farm. It's hard to separate the farm from the General Store (three miles from her farm) that she opened in the spring of 2011. The store is open only on the weekends and is a great place to visit for local products, repurposed items, and vintage goods.

Products: Raw goat and cow's milk, eggs for part of the year, and handmade soaps using milk from her goats. At the store you will also find items from a local blacksmith and woodworker, locally produced honey, some antiques, and April's farm products.
Where to buy: General Store.
Address: 2133 Hog Trough Rd. (farm); 4059 S. Hwy. 19 (farmstand)
Phone: 314-659-9844
Website: farmhousekitchenlab.blogspot.com
Agritourism: Talk with April.

Shepherds Crook Dairy, Belleview

Roger Weible had acres of land with very rough terrain and he wanted to farm. Produce wouldn't work, but the land is perfect for sheep or other grazing animals like goats. After a lot of research, Roger decided that more sheep's cheese would be a wonderful addition to the growing cheese market in Missouri. Roger's first batch of cheese sold in June 2011. He plans to grow his herd to sixty sheep from his current forty.

Products: Blue cheese, Manchego, Ozark farmhouse, which is a modified cheddar, and garlic peppercorn.
Where to buy: Local Harvest Grocery (availability will expand in 2012).
Address: N/A
Phone: 573-269-1440
Website: N/A
Agritourism: N/A

Cheese-makers and Recipes

Alpine Dairy, Webster Groves

Sometimes known as the "cheese lady" or the "goat lady," Merryl Winstein is passionate about cheese and goats. Her urban farm, located in St. Louis County, features raw goat milk, raw cow cream, and a host of cheese-making supplies, including liquid rennet and citric acid powder. Her farm is her home, so please do not just drop by—be sure to call first.

> **Products:** Cheese-making classes and supplies, and raw goat's milk.
> **Where to buy:** Call for appointment.
> **Address:** N/A
> **Phone:** 314-968-2596
> **Website:** www.cheesemakingclass.com
> **Agritourism:** Merryl offers cheese-making classes at her home, in Columbia, and other areas around the state and in Springfield, Illinois. Contact her or check her website.

Cheese-making with Janet, Hermann

Janet Hurst is a true lover of artisan and homestead cheese, and through her work she is preserving the artisan cheese-making heritage. Janet shares her love of cheese and her talents in classes around the state and has published a book called *Homemade Cheese*, which is perfect for folks who want to learn to make cheese out of their home. Janet's writings have been featured in numerous magazines, and she was recently a guest on NPR's "The Splendid Table." Take one of Janet's classes and learn to make four types of cheese from Missouri's own expert. She sources her milk from local farmers for the freshest possible cheese. Help Janet with her goal to bring cheese-making back to Missouri. (P.S. Janet is writing a second book called *The Goatkeeper's Companion*.)

Products: Cheese-making classes.
Where to buy: She has classes around the state. Check her website for updates.
Address: P.O. Box 89
Phone: 660-216-1749
Website: cheesewriter.com
Agritourism: N/A

Feta-Style Cheese

Merryl Winstein (www.cheesemakingclass.com)

Heat one gallon of milk to 86°F. Raw milk works best. (Supermarket pasteurized milk seldom works for cheesemaking.) Add ⅛ tsp. mesophilic starter culture powder, or ¼ cup cultured buttermilk with live cultures. Let ripen one hour at 86°F. Then add ⅛ tsp. liquid rennet enzyme, and stir in thoroughly.

Let sit perfectly still. Within 10-20 minutes, the milk should thicken like gravy. In about 45 minutes, it should be as firm and sleek as yogurt or tofu. If this doesn't happen, the milk is not acting right. Perhaps you used pasteurized supermarket milk.

When the sleek, firm coagulated milk comes away from the side of the pot about ⅛-inch or more, cut into 1-inch cubes. Cut across into 1-inch strips, turn pot a quarter turn, cut across to make squares, then cut underneath with the knife to make cubes. For feta, irregular pieces will be fine. Let the cubes sit 10 minutes. Then stir them gently for a minute. Let sit another 10 minutes, and stir again. Then drain them through a cloth-lined colander.

The wet curds will quickly pack down as they drain. Tie two opposite corners of the cloth over the long handle of a wooden spoon. Tie the other two corners over too. Then hang the spoon across the two rims of a deeper pot so the bag of cheese will drain overnight. In the morning, take out the firm cheese, and salt it all over. Return it to the cloth and hang again, at room temperature. Salt morning and night for three days, out in the kitchen at room temperature. If it becomes slippery during the hot humid summer days, let it drain and salt it in the refrigerator, uncovered so it will dry.

You may eat the delicious soft fresh cheese as soon as it is made. At first it is very mild. By the first morning, it's delicious. The flavor improves each day as the bacteria do their work. It won't be very salty unless you soak it in brine. You may preserve the feta for two months in a covered container of salty brine in the refrigerator. If it is too salty, cut off the serving you want and soak it in many changes of plain water for a few hours till the salt dissolves out. Add a few drops of vinegar to the water so the cheese won't get mushy.

BRINE
One quart of water or whey saved from draining cheese
½ teaspoon vinegar (acid is needed to keep the cheese from dissolving into the tap water)
Enough salt (about a cup) to make the cheese float. If it won't float, add more salt until it pops up.

Nuts & Honey

Two other types of Missouri foods that may be of interest are honey and nuts. We may tend to think of these when baking season starts in the fall, partly because that's when nuts are harvested, but both nuts and honey are available year-round.

Although the state nut tree in Missouri is the black walnut, the state is a sizeable pecan producer as well. In fact, the world's largest pecan can be found in Brunswick, Missouri. Despite that claim to fame, Missouri's Northern pecans tend to be smaller and sweeter than those grown farther south, but they are in just as much demand. Pecans are easier to shell than black walnuts, and can be bought shelled and unshelled. Thankfully, black walnuts, on the other hand, are usually sold shelled. Both walnuts and pecans are welcome additions to baked goods and sweets like candies and ice creams, but are also quite delicious on their own or slightly toasted. Be sure to store nutmeats in the freezer in an airtight container if you do not plan to use them right away.

Another nut that is gaining popularity in Missouri is the chestnut. A blight in the early twentieth century wiped out the American chestnut, so most chestnuts grown in Missouri are Chinese chestnuts, which are reliably hardy in the region. Chestnuts evoke wintertime scenes of open fires with a pan full of roasting nuts. That's because the nut is much better cooked, and the outer skin and hull are easier to remove when the nut has been heated. This process can happen in the microwave just as easily, but much less festively! Chestnut meats are commonly incorporated into soups, stews, and stuffings, and the dried nuts are too tough to eat as whole nuts, but can be ground into flour. They have a lower fat content than pecans and walnuts, but their high water and carbohydrate levels require that they be refrigerated, frozen, or dried soon after purchase.

Another common ingredient in baked goods and other foods is honey. Honey is a natural sweetener, produced by the very bees that help the farmers featured in this book by pollinating their crops. Because of that, many farmers either raise bees or invite beekeepers to establish hives among their crops. In addition to the trend in establishing and maintaining a symbiotic relationship between bees and crops, there is also a trend in beekeeping, as in farming, to raise bees as naturally as possible. Mite infestations began in the 1980s and have caused serious damage to beehives. In fact, prior to mite infestations, many longtime beekeepers will tell you that beekeeping was much easier than it is now. Although beekeepers are using more natural methods like essential oils, altering breeding techniques, and reclaiming local swarms to deal with mites, many rely on chemical treatments to treat the mites and keep healthy hives. Most beekeepers interviewed for the book minimize treatment and monitor their hives carefully.

Many of the beekeepers in this chapter swear by the benefits of raw honey, or honey that has not been pasteurized and is strained only once to remove the large particles of wax. This process retains much of the pollen that gives local honey its unique flavor, and some maintain it also helps alleviate allergy symptoms. Raw honey thickens and becomes crystallized after a month or so. Color can be used as a guide to honey's flavor; generally, lighter honeys have a milder flavor and darker honeys are stronger. The color and flavor of honey depends on the floral source of the nectar, although heat and storage time may also affect the color. In Missouri, depending on the season, honey bees are attracted to clover, sorghum, wildflowers, and certain trees like black locust, basswood, and tulip trees. Of course, vegetable crops and fruit trees are an important source of pollen and nectar.

Some honey is sold along with the honeycomb. The comb is edible and can be spread on bread or simply chewed until the honey flavor is gone. The remaining wax can be discarded. You can also make beeswax candles from the wax, or use it in various ways around the house (see "10 Uses for Beeswax" by Harry Sawyers, *This Old House Magazine*, www.thisoldhouse.com/toh/article/0,,1206547,00.html).

Honey and nuts are always welcome additions to your locavore pantry. In the fall and winter you can use them in cookies, cakes, and candies; in the summer mix them into ice cream or add honey to iced tea and lemonade; or in the spring sprinkle them on that first harvest of strawberries, layer them in a breakfast parfait, or add nuts to a spring mix salad, and use honey in the salad dressing. However you like them, the beekeepers and nut growers featured in this chapter will tell you that Missouri produces some of the best when it comes to honey and nuts like pecans, black walnuts, and chestnuts.

Northwest Region

Gerald Auffert, Conception Junction

Gerald Auffert started raising bees as a hobby when he retired. He now has seventeen hives and can't keep up with the demand for his honey. Gerald does not use any chemicals on his hives. As president of the "Missouri Bee Busters" he also gives classes on beekeeping and is connected with many other beekeepers in his area. Gerald is passionate about bees and in awe of the complexity of the colonies.

> **Products:** Raw honey.
> **Where to buy:** A small store called Something Country and at his house.
> **Address:** N/A
> **Phone:** 660-944-2535
> **Email:** auffert@grm.net
> **Website:** N/A
> **Agritourism:** N/A

Cedar Ridge Honey Bees LLC, Maitland

Kent Brown, his father, and even his four-year-old are all raising bees together. They have fourteen hives now, and Kent says they will "let nature dictate how big they get." Instead of buying bees to get started, they found a hive on a farm they visited, and they now get hives from beehive rescue and relocation operations. In other words, if the bees swarm or people want a hive removed from their property, the Browns remove the hive and keep those bees. They build their own equipment and help other folks get started. Kent said they have a waiting list for people who want hives of their own.

Products: Pure raw honey, and he recovers wax for folks wanting blocks of beeswax.
Where to buy: Sells primarily at his workplace, but in 2011 also sold to the Klub in Mound City. He sells in one-, two-, and three-pound jars.
Address: N/A
Phone: 660-442-5485
Email: cedarridgebees@gmail.com
Website: N/A
Agritourism: N/A

Bee Thankful Honey Co., Barnard

When Kevin Helzer acquired some land he was thrilled to have the opportunity to start raising bees. Kevin had wanted bees from an early age. So when he saw an ad from a beekeeper who wanted to teach others, he jumped at the chance. He now has thirty hives, and most of them are on his property. Kevin wants to grow his business and has requests from people who want him to put hives on their property.

Products: Raw honey.
Where to buy: Sells from his house and the Barnard Farmers' Market in the summer.
Address: P.O. Box 23
Phone: 660-541-1411
Email: Kevin@simply-bee.com
Website: N/A
Agritourism: Will give tours and talks about honeybees.

King Hill Farms, Inc., Brunswick

Paul and Kathy Mason along with Paul's brother and wife run King Hill Farms. Paul and his brother were born and raised in Brunswick. While many of the pecan trees in the Brunswick area have been around for hundreds of years, some as old as four hundred years, they continually add new trees through grafting. Paul has been grafting trees for thirty-five years and has taught his children how to do it. They have three thousand producing trees and a cracking and shelling facility on their farm. In addition to their own pecans, they also buy pecans from the area and, in bad pecan years, from nearby states and process them on their farm. Pecan trees are wind pollinated, and the cool damp springs the past couple of years did not allow for optimal pollination. That, coupled with flooding, hurt the crop yield. Another factor for pecan growers across the state was buyout from China. Brokers came to the area (and to neighboring states) and secured contracts with independent pickers who usually sell to businesses like King Hill. In a lean pecan year like this, it was nearly impossible to buy extra pecans from within the state or outside of it. As Paul says, "There is always hope for next year."

Products: Whole, cracked, or shelled Brunswick-area pecans and custom harvesting. They also sell jellies, walnuts, jams, honey, and sorghum at the retail shop on their farm.

Where to buy: On the farm at their retail store. They wholesale to stores across the country, but in-state you can also find them at Prenger Foods and for fundraising projects for groups like FFA.

Address: 22842 Hwy. 24

Phone: 660-548-3972

Email: kinghillfarmpecans@gmail.com

Website: kinghillfarms.com

Agritourism: Store is open seven days a week Sept.-Dec. They also sell produce and the Masons will tell you they are open if they have something to sell. During winter you can mail-order pecans or call to pick up.

Miller Pecan Farms, Inc., DeWitt

Dean Miller is a fourth-generation farmer who at one point said, "Boy, when I grow up, I am *never* going to look at another pecan in my life." He obviously changed his mind because he and his wife, Ruth, started Miller Pecans in 1972 and turned it into a wonderful business. They have about fifteen hundred native pecan trees in their orchard along with a cracking and shelling facility. They have a store on-site and often host motorcoach tours.

> **Products:** Diverse line of nuts and specialty items along with their own pecans.
> **Where to buy:** The best place to get them is at their store, although they sell wholesale as well.
> **Address:** 25097 CR 381
> **Phone:** 660-549-3389
> **Website:** N/A
> **Agritourism:** 8 a.m. to 5 p.m. Mon.-Sat.; 1-5 p.m. Sunday. Closed Jan. 10-Apr. 15.

Neidholdt Pecan Farm, Brunswick

Melvin and Hildreth Neidholt began Neidholdt Pecan Farm in the 1950s. The business stayed in the family, and Pam Benson (their daughter) and her husband, John, now own the business and run it with help from her cousin. Her cousin maintains the orchards, and Pam and her husband do all the processing. With more than fifteen hundred trees on one hundred acres, it is a lot of work. In a good year, they average about five thousand pounds from each grove of trees. In 2011 the average was about five hundred pounds. The only good thing about a bad year, according to Pam, is that her back doesn't hurt. Harvesting and processing pecans is labor intensive, and each pecan is touched about twenty times before sale.

> **Products:** Three-pound bag shook (same amount of kernels, cracked, but shaken and blown-out shells), or five-pound bag cracked. Specialty items like honey and sorghum along with candied nuts are also for sale at their on-site store.
> **Where to buy:** At the store.
> **Address:** 28095 Hwy. 11
> **Phone:** 660-548-1025 (shop); 660-233-0825 (cell)
> **Website:** N/A
> **Agritourism:** Open seasonally from the end of Oct. through the end of Dec.

Byron Miller, Ravenwood

Byron Miller was born and raised in Ravenwood. After a long teaching career, Byron decided to raise bees, and now twenty years later he sells over four thousand pounds of honey a year, teaches beginner and advanced beekeeping classes, and works to get others interested in beekeeping. He has about forty hives of his own and also sells honey he buys from Falls City, Iowa. He raises Italian bees and believes those are the most productive.

> **Products:** Two-pound and five-pound jars as well as buckets of honey. Also sells beeswax and bee pollen.
> **Where to buy:** At the Maryville Coop or call Byron to buy directly.
> **Address:** N/A
> **Phone:** 660-254-5200
> **Website:** N/A
> **Agritourism:** N/A

Northeast Region

Hollenbeck Honey Farms LLC, Kirksville

Cliff Hollenbeck started keeping bees when he was thirteen years old—thirty-eight years so far. He has commercially raised bees for twenty years and has no plans to do anything else. His hive number averages about three hundred, and he can produce fifty thousand pounds of honey each year with very intensively managed hives. Lots of variables play into hive management—prolific queens, maintaining strong hives, and manipulating the boxes for better production. All beekeepers have their own ways of working bees, and Cliff says with a small laugh that most beekeepers wouldn't understand how he maintains his hives. Most of it comes from experience and knowing his bees. He does not move his hives around and therefore understands the nuances of his hive locations. For good honey production, Cliff says you want boisterous hives, and they are not easy to move. He raises his bees as naturally as possible but will use mite treatments when necessary to save a hive. Cliff eats the honey too so he wants to limit this as much as he can. Cliff sells some of his honey retail, but most of it is sold to small honey packers and to small beekeepers who need extra honey to fill their orders.

Products: Honey, bulk beeswax, propolis, and his wife makes some beeswax candles.
Where to buy: Hy-Vee in Kirksville, Kirksville Farmers' Market (periodically), and he does sell directly to customers. Best way to reach him is to call him.
Address: 3001 Spencer Ln.
Phone: 660-665-2542
Email: hollhoneyfarm@cableone.net
Website: N/A
Agritourism: N/A

Sandhill Farm, Rutledge

This intentional community has been around since 1974 and farms on 135 acres in rural northeast Missouri. They grow and raise most of their own food for the community members who live at Sandhill, and also produce and sell sorghum syrup and mustard. The sorghum harvest is every fall in September and October. Sorghum syrup is their biggest agricultural income source. Sorghum syrup comes from sweet sorghum (also called "sorgo"), which is grown for its stalk, which has a higher sugar content. Stalks can grow up to ten feet tall.

Products: Sorghum and mustard.
Where to buy: Please check the website for new listings, but here are some of the places you can find Sandhill sorghum: In Kansas City at Whole Foods Market; Nature's Pantry in Independence; in St. Louis at Whole Foods, New Dawn, Local Harvest Grocery, Sappington Farmers' Market, and Black Bear Bakery; in Southern Missouri at Foods for Health in Rolla; and in Columbia at Clovers, Hy-Vee, the Root Cellar; Northern Missouri at C & R Market in Centralia; Zimmerman's in Rutledge; IGA in Salisbury; Hy-Vee in Trenton; Prenger's in Centralia; and in Kirksville at Hy-Vee, Farm & Home, and Countryside Market.
Address: RR 1 Box 155
Phone: 660-883-5543
Website: sandhillfarm.org
Agritourism: This is an intentional farming community, and they welcome people to visit or come to help with sorghum harvest. Please email to set up a visit.

Shepherd Farms, Clifton Hill

In 1971 Jerrell Shepherd planted lots and lots of pecan trees (or as his son Dan laughingly tells it, Dan planted lots and lots of pecan trees) hoping one day they would produce. On the first experimental twenty-acre orchard they grafted the best native pecan trees they could find. Ten years later they planted the more than 180 acres now in production. All together there are roughly 8,000 trees with seven or eight main varieties. These days when they want to plant more trees, they simply plant the nut because they found that transplants didn't really do any better. They have their own processing building where nuts are cleaned and dried. At their store building they wash, dry, and crack nuts for resale. They also have pecan shelling equipment but like to do that in cold winter months when you can't work outside. Most of their pecans are sold at their store, and a smaller amount is sold to other roadside stands and a few grocery stores. Dan says, "I don't really like selling to a

sheller because I like to have one thousand customers for my pecans instead of just a very few."

Products: Pecans.
Where to buy: At the store or shipped.
Address: 1580 CR 2010
Phone: 660-261-4567; 800-327-0211
Email: dan@cvalley.net
Website: shepherdfarms.com
Agritourism: They have occasionally given tours to large groups, but it is not common.

Pecan tree shaker, Shepherd Farms

Central Region

Capps Chestnut Orchard, Versailles

Teresa and Tommy Capps were both born and raised in the Versailles area and now have a farm of their own. Teresa remembers all the "horrible sprays" on the apple orchard where she grew up, and she and her husband wanted to raise something naturally and easily without using sprays and chemicals. They learned about chestnut trees from a conservation agent and decided to give them a try. In 1998 they started planting and now have close to 250 trees on the property. They specialize in colossal chestnuts and are growing them as organically as possible—no sprays and they fertilize with cow manure. Chestnuts are fairly time consuming, but they love that you can keep them for a year in the freezer. Every year they save fifty of the biggest nuts and grow their own replacement trees. You can meet Teresa and Tommy at the Chestnut Festival in New Franklin that is held each October. Teresa's specialty is Chestnut Chili (see recipe on page 196). Teresa recently learned a new way to cook chestnuts at the festival. Boil the chestnuts for two to three minutes (no need to score them this way) and then just peel the skin away using a sharp knife and eat them.

Products: Chestnuts.
Where to buy: At their house. In 2011, they sold some to Maude's Market in St. Louis.
Address: 406 N. Van Buren
Phone: 573-378-8531
Website: N/A
Agritourism: Call if you would like a tour.

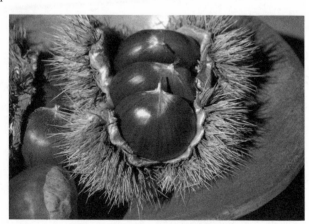

Chestnuts from Capps Orchard

Fadler Farm, Centralia

When Brent and Valorie Fadler's son was attending the University of Missouri they learned about chestnut trees from his coursework. They wanted to start a farm for extra income in retirement but knew they were not interested in livestock or raising vegetable crops. So after some research and purchase of land, they planted Qing and Eaton chestnut trees in 2005. It took three to four years to get chestnuts, but now their 140 trees are starting to produce in larger quantities. The trees grow twenty to thirty feet tall and need lots of sun. Brent says you need to prune them for maximum sun exposure. With help from their two sons and their wives they harvest, sort, and process each nut. They do not use pesticides or insecticides on the trees.

Products: Chestnuts along with some blackberries, apples, peaches, and grapes.
Where to buy: Buy on-line, at C & R Market in Centralia and the Southside Farmers' Market in Macon. They plan to increase their retail outlets and also want to add a retail store on the property.
Address: N/A
Phone: 573-682-4356
Email: bfadler@centurytel.net
Website: missourichestnuts.com and on Facebook
Agritourism: Call if you are interested in a tour.

Walk-About Acres, Columbia

Art and Vera have a very diverse farm in Columbia. You will find Auracana chickens, Pilgrim geese, heritage turkeys, goats, Mulefoot pigs, emus, and lots of honeybees. They moved to Walk-About Acres in 1992 and started leading tours in the late 1990s. Now nearly three thousand students a year visit the farm to learn about the animals, bees, and gardens. This couple keeps busy with beekeeping classes, selling bee kits, selling at farmers' markets, and maintaining their farm.

> **Products:** They call themselves a diversified farm with a big emphasis on honeybees. Most of their products revolve around honey. At the farmers' market you will find honey lemonade, honey ice cream, and of course honey.
> **Where to buy:** On-site at Papa's Store and the Columbia Farmers' Market.
> **Address:** 6800 N. Kirchner Rd.
> **Phone:** 573-474-8837
> **Website:** www.walk-aboutacres.com
> **Agritourism:** Tours available from Apr. 1-Nov. 1. All tours, visits, field trips, and rentals need to be scheduled in advance. Check website for prices.

Missouri Chestnuts

Chestnuts are not a huge crop in Missouri, but researchers at the University of Missouri Center for Agroforestry are encouraging farmers to add the chestnut tree to their orchards. Most chestnuts are imported, and they believe this would add another reliable source of income for farmers.

The chestnut is not actually a nut, but a fruit. Chestnuts grow in a thick husk or burr—it almost looks like green needles are growing out of the skin. You do not want to grab these with your hands unless you are wearing thick leather gloves, and even then the burr can penetrate the glove. Inside each burr you will find one to three chesnuts. Although not commonly used in the Midwest, chestnuts are a great source of protein and are more like a grain than a nut. While you could eat it raw (most do not), cooking the chestnut brings out its natural sweetness. The chestnut is much more suited to savory dishes like stuffings, soups, and even chili. Dried chestnuts can be ground into a "chestnut flour" and used for baking. Check your local farmers' market in the fall to find chestnuts.

St. Louis Region

Bosancu Honey, Union

Juliana Bosancu's father-in-law was determined that her family raise bees. He has always had bees and thought they needed their own honey. So, he bought them equipment, they ordered a starter set of bees, and began with one colony. That was in 2007, and Juliana says they now have ten hives and her husband adds two to three more each year. The Bosancus are fans of black locust honey (as are many beekeepers) and, weather permitting, take their hives to an area where there are black locust trees. She says that her first batch of honey is usually 95 percent black locust honey and the second batch is 70 percent black locust and 30 percent wildflower honey. Using only glass jars with distinctive shapes, she packages her honey on its own and also submerges nuts in her honey for an elegant and delicious snack or gift.

Products: Raw honey, raw black locust and wildflower honey, and gifts. Please view her website to see her beautifully packaged honey as well as decadent treats like almonds and pecans suspended in honey.
Where to buy: On-line.
Address: 664 Scenic View Dr.
Phone: 636-259-0145
Website: bosancuhoney.com
Agritourism: N/A

A worker bee visits about fifty to one hundred flowers during each trip.

(National Honey Board)

Femme Osage Apiaries, Foristell

Ian and Pamela Brown were introduced to the benefits of raw, local honey because they had a son who was "allergic to everything." An allergist suggested raw honey, and it really helped their son. They figured you couldn't get more local than doing it yourself, and Ian said the business grew from a hobby that "got out of control." Thirty years later they have two hundred hives and are busy with all things bees—colony rental to farmers, manufacturing bee equipment, swarm removal, and honey production. Ian and Pamela are both Certified Master Beekeepers who believe in raising bees as naturally as possible with no chemicals. And when renting colonies to farmers, they work with the farmer to ensure the bees aren't exposed to spraying by moving the colony before the plants or trees are sprayed with fungicides or pesticides. They gut their boxes every three years or so to help keep the bees healthy and have incorporated techniques they learned from beekeepers on a trip to Uzbekistan.

Ian and Pamela want more young folks to start beekeeping, and they encourage people to keep a hive or two in their backyards. When asked about a good book for beginning beekeeping, Ian recommended *First Lessons in Bee Keeping* by Keith Delaplane. And if you decide to start a hive, these folks are a great source for equipment and advice.

> **Products:** Raw honey, beekeeping equipment, pollen. One note about pollen: Ian says he sells a lot of pollen to truck drivers. Ian will tell you that it increases your energy, stamina, and can jumpstart your immune system. He hasn't had a cold in fifteen years and has no joint or arthritis pain. Bee pollen is also high in Vitamin E. If you decide to try bee pollen, Ian says to be sure to introduce it slowly and build to one tsp. a day.
> **Where to buy:** You can find Femme Osage products at Mr. Fuel, Short Stops, and Center Field in Foristell, two convenience stores in the New Melle area, and Grayson's Produce in O'Fallon. They do two shows a year for Missouri State Beekeepers and sell their assembled equipment at the shows. You can also call to place an order for equipment.
> **Address:** N/A
> **Phone:** 636-398-5014
> **Email:** femmeosage1@aol.com
> **Website:** N/A
> **Agritourism:** N/A

Bob Finck, Fenton

Bob blames his wife for his beekeeping obsession. He took a class on beekeeping in the late 1970s, and his wife gave him his first hive in 1979. And it grew from there to eighty hives while he still had a full-time job. Now that he is retired he keeps about 120 hives in St. Charles County and South County. He doesn't use any chemicals and keeps the bee colonies in areas where farmers are not using pesticide or chemical sprays.

> **Products:** Raw honey and beeswax.
> **Where to buy:** Directly from Bob (at his house), St. Peter's Nutrition Stop, OK Hatchery in Kirkwood, Fenton Feed Mill, Diehl Feed Store in Fenton, Imperial Farmers' Market, and seasonally at Stuckmeyer's.
> **Address:** 1361 Montevale Court
> **Phone:** 636-305-8818
> **Email:** bjfinck@aol.com
> **Website:** N/A
> **Agritourism:** Bob is involved with the Eastern Missouri Beekeeper Association and Three Rivers Beekeepers. He often mentors new beekeepers and helps with workshops each year.

Finer Things from the Land of Milk and Honey, St. Louis

Sandy Brooks has been making candies for decades. And now, with the addition of her own honey and fresh local milk and cream, she says her candies are even better. About four years ago Sandy started keeping bees and says the hives are really "coming into their own." Sandy is a Master Gardener and knows the importance of bees. She says there are not a lot of competing bees in her area, and that increases her production. She has eight hives spread around St. Louis County, which produce plenty of honey for her candy-making and her special creamed honey. The landscape around her property is edible, and her blueberries and strawberries feature prominently in her creamed honeys.

Products: Creamed honey and truffles.
Where to buy: On-line through Localharvest.org or call Sandy.
Address: N/A
Phone: 314-965-4975
Email: pedsptedd@prodigy.net
Website: Go to Localharvest.org and type in Finer Things to order
Agritourism: N/A

Robins Apiaries, St. Charles

Jim's dad, Leonard, started Robins Apiaries in 1922. Jim grew up raising bees. In fact, he will tell you with a smile that it was forced servitude and he didn't really like helping with the bees. It wasn't until his early teens that he realized that maybe it wasn't so bad. Well, that was nearly sixty years ago. Leonard Robins studied honeybees with the men who originated commercial beekeeping. At their busiest they had over eight thousand hives. Jim now maintains between four and five hundred hives and has co-authored eight research papers. Until recently they only sold their honey wholesale. When he turned seventy-five Jim decided he wanted to do something new so he began retailing his honey himself and loves it.

Products: Raw honey and honeycomb.
Where to buy: Tower Grove Farmers' Market (and Winter Market), Local Harvest Grocery, or from Jim.
Address: 37 Sharon Dr.
Phone: 636-946-3664
Website: N/A
Agritourism: N/A

Seven Gables Farm, Villa Ridge

Timothy and Mechelle Ortmann have big plans for their ten acres near Shaw Nature Reserve. In 2005 they planted cherry, peach, pear, and apple trees, which are producing along with blueberries, strawberries, and some grapes. They recently added almond trees (yep you read that correctly), chestnut trees, black walnut, and eighty pecan trees. And they run a small CSA, which includes fruit, vegetables, and some eggs. Timothy says they will soon be a Certified Naturally Grown farm. Their first goal is to grow the best fruits and nuts possible. Then they plan to market themselves beyond their CSA. In 2011, they grew lots of pumpkins and sold to Ladue Market in St. Louis, which was very successful. Other plans include adding an on-site farm store, lodging for weekend getaways, and to be a place people can go year-round for health and wellness.

> **Products:** Seasonal produce, fruits, and nuts.
> **Where to buy:** Through the CSA so far. Look for their pumpkins at Ladue Market in St. Louis.
> **Address:** N/A
> **Phone:** 636-451-5745; 314-581-2644
> **Email:** timothyortmann@yahoo.com
> **Website:** www.sevengablesfarmorganic.com
> **Agritourism:** N/A

Stinger Honey, Clayton

Joy Stinger is well-known in St. Louis for her honey and her candles. This energetic woman keeps busy with a variety of projects, including beeswax ornaments made using antique molds. She hand paints them and sells them at various craft shows and out of her house. She also packages and sells honey in a variety of sizes, including in the honeycomb.

> **Products:** Honey, honeycomb, rolled beeswax candles, beeswax candles crafted with antique molds.
> **Where to buy:** Local Harvest Grocery, at her home, and Clayton Farmers' Market.
> **Address:** N/A
> **Phone:** 314-862-0509
> **Website:** N/A
> **Agritourism:** You can buy directly from Joy, who has a small "urban farm" with chickens, hives, and a garden.

Kansas City Region

Camp Branch Bee Ranch, Harrisonville

Rod Rictor is a man who wears many hats—preacher, paramedic, farmer, and beekeeper. He was somewhat familiar with bees because his dad kept them during his youth, but it was not in his plans to become a beekeeper. In fact, he started his colonies out of necessity. In 2006 they planted a vegetable garden and found themselves hand pollinating the squash because there were not enough bees. He started with two colonies, the next year he had seven, and now he has fourteen. Rod is unusual because he gets his bees from bee removal and from swarming. He loves the idea of truly local bees and like a few other beekeepers featured in the book believes the hives are stronger when you use feral bees or "mutts." He uses very minimal treatments (organic acids for mites) and uses no pesticides, unnecessary treatments, or antibiotics. Rod harvests the honey two times a year and his honey is available starting in late July or early August.

Products: Raw honey. You can also call Rod for swarm or bee removal.
Where to buy: He sells most of his honey at work or at church. He plans to have a lot more honey in 2012 and may expand his outlets. Call Rod to buy directly from him.
Address: N/A
Phone: 816-405-1671
Email: cbeebr@gmail.com
Website: N/A
Agritourism: N/A

Cooper's Honey, Peculiar

Cooper's Honey packages over 250,000 pounds of honey each year and sells to many stores in the Kansas City metropolitan area. They do have their own hives, but also much of their honey is from other local beekeepers in the area. The beekeepers they partner with are all local and family farmers located across Missouri, Southern Iowa, and Southeast Nebraska. Their honey is not pasteurized, but is heated to 120 degrees for easier bottling.

> **Products:** Raw honey, beeswax, and pollen.
> **Where to buy:** They sell to many stores—too many to list here. Please go to their website and enter your zip code to find the store nearest to you.
> **Address:** P.O. Box 748
> **Phone:** 816-779-1144
> **Website:** cooperhoney.com
> **Agritourism:** N/A

Five Oaks Honey and Christmas Tree Farm, Higginsville

Bob and Carolyn Rauch raise Christmas trees and honey. Rauch began raising bees in the 1980s when he needed additional pollination for his fruit trees. He started out very small but quickly established fans who wanted him to sell his honey in their stores. As he says, it was "a hobby that ran amok." He now produces about fifteen thousand pounds of honey a year from the two hundred hives he keeps in Lafayette and Johnson counties. In addition to the honey business, Carolyn and Bob have run a Christmas tree farm for eleven years. This farm is "u-cut" or "we-cut" and draws folks from all over the area.

Products: Christmas trees are "u-cut" or "we-cut"—scotch pine, spruce, and white pine. Clover/wildflower honey and some years locust honey. Bob only sells his honey wholesale, so be sure to look for it in stores and at seasonal orchard stands/stores.
Where to buy: You can buy Five Oaks honey on 24 Hwy. at Sibley Orchard, Rasa's, Schreiman's, and Templeton's Orchard and in Osceola at Gordon's Orchard or Osceola Cheese Store. Also sold at most grocery stores in Johnson, Lafayette, Ray, and Saline counties, including Patricia's Foods.
Address: Two miles north of I-70 on Hwy. 13 towards Higginsville
Phone: 660-584-7375
Email: fiveoakshoneytreefarm@yahoo.com
Website: fiveoaksfarm.net
Agritourism: U-cut or we-cut Christmas tree farm is open Thanksgiving to Christmas on weekends only, 9 a.m.-dark.

Miller's Honey Farm, Independence

Les Miller had an interesting path to bees. He always wanted to raise bees but was allergic to them. A bee sting in the late 1990s relieved his arthritis pain and intensified his wish to raise bees. Now twelve seasons later he has eighty to one hundred hives and keeps all of his hives in town to minimize exposure to pesticides and herbicides.

Products: Honey, pollen, honeycomb, and beeswax.
Where to buy: The BADSEED Farmers' Market, Independence Farmers' Market, and Rosedale (organic) Farmers' Market.
Address: 1414 S. Northern; farm at 500 S. Sterling, Sugar Creek
Phone: 816-254-3702 (Les); 816-461-7363 (Eleanor)
Email: les.miller36@aol.com
Website: N/A
Agritourism: N/A

Donald and Kay Tilman, Harrisonville

Donald Tilman knows his bees, and he should. He has kept bees off and on (mostly on) for almost fifty years. He said when he has quit in the past he just "missed the little guys" and went back to it. He keeps thirty-five to fifty hives for honey production—just enough to keep honey production, but not so much that he can't travel when he wants to. Mites and the introduction of the African honeybee have presented new challenges for beekeepers like Donald. He is active in the local beekeeper's association and works with other keepers to find solutions to these issues. We have not verified this, but Donald says that most germs can't survive in honey for longer than twenty-four hours and the rest are killed within forty-eight hours. He has used it himself to help an infected incision and says that it was used on soldiers in Iraq. Donald also does bee removal.

Products: Raw honey and some honeycomb.
Where to buy: Byrd's Pecans (in Virginia), Kansas, Bannister Federal Complex Farmers' Market, Harrisonville Farmers' Market, and Belton Farmers' Market. You can also call him for direct sales.
Address: N/A
Phone: 816-884-5221
Email: dtilman1940@gmail.com
Website: N/A
Agritourism: N/A

Southwest Region

Byrd's Pecans, Butler

Mary Ann and her husband, L.V. Byrd, started Byrd's Pecans in 1964. L.V. was passionate about pecans and trees in general, calling them the "lungs of the planet." His granddaughter Jennifer said that he would talk for hours about pecans. It was his passion that inspired his kids (Cindy Bays, Denise Byrd, and Mark Byrd), grandkids, and wife, Mary Ann, to carry on Byrd's Pecans after his death in 2003. Jennifer said they are all "weekend warriors" who hold other jobs outside the farm. With four thousand pecan trees and over five hundred acres they are some busy folks. They have a small shop three miles down the road where they process the pecans.

Products: Pecans, one pound ready to cook, cracked native pecans, cracked thin-shelled pecans (from grafted trees), and shelled and blown three-pound bags of nut meats. They also sell Hammons walnuts at their store, fresh-baked pecan pie, local honey, and other pecan goodies.

Where to buy: Buy from their general store or on-line.

Address: 3 RR Box 196 (located on Hwy. 52, exactly eight miles west off of Hwy. 71 or twelve miles east on Hwy. 52 from Hwy. 69 in Kansas)

Phone: 866-679-5583 (store number)

Email: jason@kidrocketinc.com; mabyrd@ckt.net

Website: byrdspecans.com

Agritourism: Store is open 9 a.m.-5 p.m., seven days a week from Nov. 1 to Jan. 1 and after that on weekends only.

Green Thumb Farm, Stockton

According to Linda, she and her husband, Neil Brunner, were "back to the landers" in the early 1970s. They moved to Missouri from Wisconsin because they liked the longer growing season and land was much cheaper. They have had farms and kept bees off and on throughout their marriage moving around Missouri and then to California. They moved back to Missouri in 1996 and for awhile they had a CSA and were a Certified Naturally Grown farm. Now Neil keeps bees. They have some chickens and big gardens, but mainly for themselves. Linda says they do not use any chemicals on their bees and that their bees have little exposure to pesticides. Neil has about fifteen hives and also makes and sells bee equipment.

> **Products:** Raw honey and beekeeping equipment.
> **Where to buy:** Hammons Store in Stockton, New Life Natural Foods in Bolivar, and MaMa Jean's in Springfield.
> **Address:** N/A
> **Phone:** 417-276-4252
> **Email:** grnthumb@windstream.net
> **Website:** ourgreenthumbfarm.com
> **Agritourism:** N/A

Hammons, Stockton

In 1946 Ralph Hammons realized that Missouri had a treasure in black walnuts. He owned a small grocery store in Stockton and couldn't keep black walnuts on the shelf. He was shipping black walnuts to Virginia and figured he should see who else might want this Missouri native. So, he got a cracking machine from Tennessee and set up an operation. The first year they shelled 100,000 pounds. Brian Hammons, his grandson and head of Hammons, says they now shell that in one day. Brian says they are "blessed to do something no one else in the world does." Black walnut harvesting is a true community effort. Hammons has two hundred total buying stations spread across twelve states, with 115 to 130 stations in Missouri alone. Anyone who has access to black walnuts can bring them in to sell at the buying stations. These are wild hand-harvested crops and Brian says the only shaking that happens is from people who climb the trees themselves. (Pecan orchards utilize tree shakers to retrieve pecans.) Very few black walnut trees are grown in an orchard although they are working with some growers to initiate more. Hammons is the world's premier processor and supplier of American black walnuts. Cracking and processing black walnuts on your own is a serious proposition and advice on Hammons' website even includes running over the nuts with your car to remove the first outer covering. There is a wonderful video on the website under the Media tab called "corporate video." You will see how they are harvested and processed along with the history of Hammons.

Products: American black walnuts in bulk and packages. They have a store in Stockton on the square with a lot of walnut products (think black walnut ice cream and fudge). Their Black Walnut Oil was a 2011 Sofi Silver finalist award recipient and their Black and Gold Mix featuring walnuts covered in dark chocolate with caramelized black walnuts is a decadent delight.

Where to buy: Because they are the main producer of American black walnuts, you will find their nut meats in stores all over Missouri and the country. Cheese Store, Costco (Independence, Kansas City), Country Mart, CVS (Springfield), Dierbergs, Dillons, Dover Supermarket, Food 4 Less, Food Pyramid, G&W Foods, Hammons Nut Emporium (Stockton), Harp's Supermarket, Harter House, Hen House, Kithcart Orchard, Local Harvet Grocery (St. Louis), MaMa Jean's Market, Missouri Dept. of Agriculture, Osceola Cheese, Price Chopper, Price Cutter, Rameys Supermarket, Redmon's Travel Center (Springfield), Sam's Club, Save-A-Lot stores, Schnucks, Summerfresh, Tom's Mad Pricer, Tom's Priced Right Foods, Tom's Supermarket, Town & Country, Wal-Mart, Walgreens (Branson, Joplin, Ozark, Springfield), Woods Supermarket. Brian says they are mainly available in the fall when folks are baking. Look for them in the baking aisle.

Address: Hammons Nut Emporium in Stockton is at 2 Public Square.

Phone: 417-276-5181; 417-276-5800

Website: www.hammonsproducts.com

Agritourism: N/A

The Black Walnut is the official tree nut of the state of Missouri.

Honey Heaven Bee-stro Café, Springfield

Find all things honey at the Honey Heaven Bee-stro Café. Opened in 1998, this store and café features honey and many honey-inspired dishes and sells an assortment of honey edibles and health and beauty products. They use honey from their own hives and honey from other local producers.

> **Products:** Raw honey, honey mustard, BBQ sauce, flavored honeys, honey butter, creamed honey, and bee pollen. And obviously they sell lunch at their Bee-Stro Café.
> **Where to buy:** At their store open Mon.-Fri.: 10 a.m.-6 p.m., Sat.: 10 a.m.-3 p.m. Bee-Stro Café is open Mon.-Sat. 10:30 a.m.-2:30 p.m. They also operate a store in Silver Dollar City and sell their honey and honey products at the Greater Springfield Farmers' Market.
> **Address:** 2516 S. Campbell Rd.
> **Phone:** 417-869-0233
> **Email:** contactus@honeyheaven.com
> **Website:** honeyheaven.com
> **Agritourism:** N/A

Missouri Northern Pecan Growers, Nevada

Drew Kimmell, managing partner, grew up in the pecan business, helping his dad with his orchard. Missouri Northern Pecan Growers joined the organic market when they received their first organic certification in 2003. While they had always guaranteed that their pecans were free of pesticides, herbicides, and fungicides, this extra step lets consumers know they are serious about protecting the environment. A listing of the growers who are part of Missouri Northern Pecan Growers is on their website. They all have Missouri Certified Organic groves. In Drew's orchards there are trees over 250 years old. These trees were around when George Washington was president. "Trees don't care if it's a recession or depression. And that just gives a feeling of serenity."

Products: 100 percent organic pecans.
Where to buy: Check the website for listings of locations. Found at most large grocery stores and many smaller stores and health food stores across the state.
Address: N/A
Phone: 417-667-3501
Website: mopecans.com/index.php
Agritourism: N/A

Pecans & More, LLC, Rich Hill

Jay and Charlotte Payne were looking for a nice place to retire and ended up with about fourteen hundred pecan trees ranging in age from two to twelve years old. One thing led to another, and eight years later they have a cracking facility they use for their pecans as well as to harvest, clean, and crack for other pecan growers nearby. This family doesn't rest much. Charlotte runs their store and deli. At the store you will find a variety of locally produced jams, jellies, and honey.

> **Products:** Pecans, flavored pecans, fudge, honey, sorghum, jams, and jellies. At the store you will also find a deli where you can buy sandwiches.
> **Where to buy:** On-line and on-site at their store.
> **Address:** Rt. 3 Box 191 (1½ miles south of Rich Hill). Hwy. 71 has a "cut across" to their store. Soon Hwy. 71 will be expanded and you will need to take the Rich Hill exit.
> **Phone:** 417-395-4242
> **Email:** charlotte@pecansandmore.com
> **Website:** pecansandmore.com
> **Agritourism:** The store is open seven days a week, 9 a.m.-6 p.m., year-round (closed on serious snow days, Christmas, Easter, and Thanksgiving).

Southeast Region

Goods from the Woods, Licking and Salem

Pinyon Penny (Penny Frazier), as she is known, champions the pinenut on her website and is a proponent of wild harvesting. She and her husband, George, along with help from their son Zeb, are in the business of tending wild crops and foraging. She is known as "Pinyon Penny" because she and George go out West each year and harvest lots and lots of pinenuts. They are crazy about pinenuts and sell them through their website. In Missouri they also wild-harvest black walnuts and hickory nuts and make their own 100 percent organic and alcohol-free hydrosols using sustainably harvested witch hazel, yarrow, elderflower, and wild bergamot. The Fraziers own twenty acres of Ozark forest land and lease one hundred additional acres for harvesting wild-growing plants. The Fraziers demonstrate that you can make a profit and create a livelihood from the forest while simultaneously restoring and preserving it.

> **Products:** Missouri-grown products for sale include black walnuts, hickory nuts, and hydrosols that they distill themselves. They also have lots of wild-growing forest plants they harvest such as fiddlehead ferns, pawpaws, and persimmons.
> **Where to buy:** On-line.
> **Address:** 667 County Rd. 4060
> **Phone:** 573-729-6725
> **Website:** pinenut.com
> **Agritourism:** N/A

Mo' Honey, Jackson

Grant Gillard has long been interested in honey bees. In fact, his mother scolded him and his brother for stomping the bees in the dandelions and educated them about bees and honey at an early age. But it was a class in college called "Entomology 222: Beekeeping" that he took for a supposed easy A that sealed his fate as a beekeeper. He now has hives on his property and on nearby farms. Grant believes in capturing wild honeybee swarms and raises new queens from those swarms. He thinks the most effective defense in fighting mites is raising bees that are resistant to mites—and it seems that the bees he has captured in wild honeybee swarms have for the most part been mite-resistant. If he does get mites or the bees are ill, he treats using organic treatments or essential oils. Grant is the president and founder of the Jackson Area Beekeepers and president of the Missouri State Beekeepers.

Products: Honey.
Where to buy: At the house (they have a self-serve honor box), Natural Health Organic Foods, Cape Girardeau; Pioneer Market, and Jones Heritage Farm in Jackson; Family Friendly Farm in Cape Girardeau; in Perryville at Rozier's Food Center, ALPS Always Low Price Store and Hair Essentials and Tea Store; and at Begg's BerryWorld in Benton. You can also find his honey seasonally at Cape Girardeau Farmers' Market and Jackson Farmers' Market.
Address: 3721 N. High St.
Phone: 573-243-6568
Email: gillard5@charter.net
Website: mohoney.homestead.com
Agritourism: N/A

TNT Chestnut Chili, Capps Chestnut Orchard

2 pounds of chopped Missouri-grown chestnuts
3 pounds of ground chuck
1 pound of Italian sausage
1 pound of regular sausage (hot if you prefer)
1 large yellow onion, chopped
1 large purple onion, chopped
3 squares of bittersweet baking chocolate (Yes, chocolate!)
4 pkgs. McCormicks mild or hot chili seasoning
Plus extra chili powder to your liking!
1 Tablespoon of minced garlic
1 chopped green pepper (optional)
2 chopped fresh jalapeño peppers (optional)
½ gallon tomato puree
½ gallon diced tomatoes (we grow our own and freeze)
1 teaspoon Tabasco sauce
3 cans of light red kidney beans
3 cans of dark red kidney beans
Salt and pepper to taste

Prepare chestnuts: cut the chestnuts in half with garden pruners. Steam 3 minutes in a colander that will fit in a large pot over 2 quarts of water. Peel while warm. If the skins start to stick, pop back into steamer.

Brown the ground chuck and sausage (drain the meat) then add the chopped onions and chopped peppers.

Stir in the chocolate and cook over medium heat with meat, onion and pepper mixture until the chocolate is melted. Add chili seasonings and minced garlic, along with the tomato puree and diced tomatoes. Continue cooking over medium heat adding water or tomato paste to your preferred consistency. Add beans and chestnuts and simmer uncovered, stirring frequently for 1 hour. Make a day ahead, and the flavors will meld.

Freeze chestnuts; they are a fruit and will mold if not used in a day or two.

Recipes & Tips

What do you do with all the great produce, meat, and dairy products once you get it home from the market? How about that CSA or other box of local "shares"? In this chapter, we offer some recipes, meal-planning ideas, and, a personal favorite, advice about preserving foods before they become compost. There are hundreds of excellent cookbooks that extol the virtues of eating locally sourced foods, and it is not our intention to compete with them. Instead, we provide a handful of recipes from some of our farmers along with helpful hints and advice for cooking and serving your bounty, and saving some for later.

A typical box from a CSA or other food share program will have lots of produce, so many of our recipes emphasize the veggies, but we include meat and dairy recipes as well. And because there is enough food in those boxes for several meals, we offer suggestions for using your local foods in a variety of ways. We start with a handful of meal suggestions, including brunch or breakfast, a picnic lunch, a romantic dinner, kid-friendly foods, a cocktail party, and a winter supper.

Meals

During the week, your go-to breakfasts should include hot grains with maple syrup or preserves, fruit, and milk. Wheatberries, oats, or even leftover rice make a great and hearty breakfast. Most of these can be cooked ahead of time and stored in your refrigerator during the week (see below). In the summer, a fruit smoothie is quick and refreshing. Use an immersion blender to blend an assortment of fruit, juice, and, if you like, yogurt. Try blending these combinations: fresh mint and a handful of blueberries, strawberries, and melon with a splash of juice, water, milk, or yogurt drink.

Weekend **breakfasts** or **brunches** often includes eggs, meat, fruit, and bread or muffins. For an easy but impressive brunch dish, try a **frittata**, which is basically vegetables, grated cheese, meat (if you want), and beaten eggs to bind it all together. It's a great way to use leftover vegetables or a big bunch of greens that are a mainstay of CSA boxes.

Pre-heat your oven to 350°F. In an oven-proof skillet, use a little butter or oil to sauté the vegetables and meat until soft and/or cooked. Remember, a bag of greens can be cooked down to a cup or so when sautéed. Don't be shy about using it up! Whisk enough eggs together in a bowl to surround the ingredients in the pan, and season with salt and pepper and/or fresh herbs to taste. Depending on the number of people you plan to serve, you can use as few as 2 or 3 eggs and as many as 8. Combine the eggs, cheese, and vegetables together and pour the egg mixture into the skillet. (Be sure to melt a little more butter or oil so the eggs don't stick to the pan). Let it set undisturbed over a medium flame for 10 minutes or until the bottom is firm, then transfer to the oven to continue cooking on top (about 10-20 minutes). Cut into wedges and serve hot, or cool and serve at room temperature. This dish can be eaten hot or cold, so it also makes great leftovers or an elegant dish for a brunch potluck.

A variation on this theme is a crustless quiche from Dry Dock Farms, one of our featured farmers.

Crustless Swiss Chard Quiche, Dry Dock Farms

This is a great *easy* recipe using chard or spinach.

Serves 8

1 teaspoon olive oil
½ sweet onion, chopped
½ bunch Swiss chard, washed, dried—trim ends; roughly chop (leaving the stems intact)
2½ cups shredded cheese of choice-cheddar, Swiss, or whatever you have!
4 eggs
1 cup milk
salt
pepper

Preheat oven to 375°F.

In a medium fry pan heat olive oil. Add chard and onion to pan. Sauté until chard stems are tender. Do not overcook. Salt and pepper to taste.

Whisk eggs. Add milk and cheese. Fold in the onion-chard mixture. Add salt and pepper to taste.

Pour into a pie dish that has been lightly oiled. Bake for 35-45 minutes or until golden brown and no liquid seeps out when you test the center with a knife.

Strawberry Rhubarb Coffeecake, Wilsdorf Berry Patch Cookbook (WilsdorfBerryPatch.com)

This coffeecake is not overly sweet, with a satisfying combination of strawberries and rhubarb.
Serves 12-15

Fruit mixture:	1 cup sugar
	⅓ cup cornstarch
	½ cup water
	3 cups rhubarb (½-inch pieces)
	3 cups sliced strawberries
	2 Tablespoons lemon juice

Preheat oven to 350°F; baking time: 40-45 minutes; pan: greased 13 × 9.

Combine sugar and cornstarch in a saucepan. Stir in water. Add rhubarb, strawberries, and lemon juice. Cook over medium heat until thickened, stirring frequently. Cool.

Batter:	3 cups all-purpose flour
	1 cup sugar
	1 teaspoon baking soda
	1 teaspoon baking powder
	½ teaspoon salt
	¾ cup butter or oleo, softened
	1 cup buttermilk
	2 eggs
	1 teaspoon vanilla

Combine dry ingredients. Cut in butter to make fine crumbs. Beat buttermilk, eggs, and vanilla together. Stir into dry ingredients until just moistened. Spread half of batter in pan and top with strawberry/rhubarb mixture. Spoon remaining batter over fruit.

Topping:	¾ cup sugar
	½ cup all-purpose flour
	¼ cup butter or oleo, softened

Combine sugar and flour. Cut in butter to make fine crumbs. Sprinkle topping over batter. Bake until lightly browned and a toothpick inserted in center comes out clean.

For your *picnic lunch/basket* how about sandwiches, slaws, vegetable salads, spreads, and cheese? Round it out with some fruit and drinks, pack it in a pretty basket, and you're good to go.

Sandwiches can be made from just about anything you can fit between slices of bread. Try sliced apples, cheddar or Brie, and fresh spinach with a grainy mustard spread on multigrain bread. How about herbed goat cheese with pickled onion, radish, and cucumber slices with a small mound of micro-greens on a baguette; ham and Swiss (and/or Swiss chard); roast pork with grilled peaches or peach chutney; roast chicken, roasted red peppers, fresh spinach, and aioli on flatbread? Buy good local bread or make your own, and then let your imagination go.

Slaw usually starts with cabbage as its base, and you can find lots of cabbage in Missouri. The variety you have on hand may lead you in one direction or another when it comes to preparing your slaw, but the basic ingredients are cabbage, other vegetables like carrots, peppers, onions, radishes, etc., and a dressing to bind it all together. Substitute potatoes for the cabbage and you have yet another picnic favorite. Here are some variations on the dressing. All of these are based on a bit of trial and error, so feel free to experiment with the proportions and ingredients until you get the flavor you prefer. To take the tang out of some of these, add a touch of sweetener like sugar, agave nectar, or honey (even orange juice can be used).

Here are a few slaw variations:

• **Creamy**: Mix 1 cup plain yogurt with 2 Tablespoons mayonnaise (homemade or purchased). Add a teaspoon of Dijon mustard and the juice of one lemon or a splash of vinegar (tarragon or cider is best) to taste. Season with salt and pepper and/or your favorite herbs (celery seed, tarragon, fines herbes, dill).

• **Asian**: Mix equal parts rice wine vinegar, sesame or canola oil, peanut butter (¼ cup each, for example). Add a half-part soy sauce (⅛ cup) and a little sweetener to taste (honey, agave nectar, or brown sugar). Add some minced ginger root and garlic to taste (about 2 Tablespoons each). This one is good made with napa cabbage and carrots with sliced scallions and sesame seeds.

• **Sweet and Sour**: Mix equal parts white sugar (½ cup) and cider vinegar (½ cup) with half part water (¼ cup). Add 1 teaspoon salt, ½ teaspoon mustard seed, and ½ teaspoon celery seed and shake in a covered jar until the sugar dissolves. Refrigerate until ready to use.

• **French or mustard vinaigrette**: Mix 1 Tablespoon finely chopped shallot or onion, 1 teaspoon Dijon mustard, ¼ cup red wine vinegar, salt, and freshly ground pepper to taste. Slowly add ¾ cup extra virgin olive oil while whisking the mustard-vinegar mixture until emulsified.

• **Tarragon vinaigrette**: Same as above but use tarragon vinegar instead of red wine vinegar, and add fresh or dried tarragon to taste. This one is also delicious with red potato salad (sliced boiled red potatoes, celery, radishes, onions, or scallions, and hard boiled egg, if you like).

Other vegetable salads are a nice addition to your picnic lunch. One that we like conceptually is the **"50-mile" salad**, formerly served at the now-closed Terrace View Café in St. Louis. Dressed in a vinaigrette and served in mason jars, this salad was composed of whatever fresh produce was available from within a fifty-mile radius of the café and included corn, radishes, potatoes, carrots, peppers, tomatoes, and chunks of farmer's cheese, to name a few of its many (changing) ingredients.

Panzanella uses fresh tomatoes and cubes of stale or toasted Italian or French bread tossed with a vinaigrette, salt, and maybe some fresh herbs like basil. For an interesting variation on that theme, try tossing cooked spaghetti or linguini with fresh tomatoes (halved cherry tomatoes or chunks of large ones), salt, and basil, adding some softened Brie (or grated Parmesan for a different approach) to the hot pasta before the other ingredients. This one can then be served at room temperature or hot—either way it's delicious.

*****

For a *romantic dinner*, you want to go simple but elegant. Easy and impressive choices are steaks or pork chops, a simple vegetable or greens (creamed spinach is a classic side with steak), soufflé or custard (easier than you think!), and a nice Missouri wine. If you plan to cook a grass-fed steak, follow these directions from Rain Crow Ranch:

• Since grass-fed beef is extremely low in fat, coat with virgin olive oil, truffle oil, or a favorite light oil for flavor enhancement and easy browning. The oil will also prevent drying and sticking.

• Do not overcook. Grass-fed beef is best rare or medium. If you prefer well-done, make sure to cook it at a low temperature so it doesn't dry out.

• Consider using a meat tenderizer (Rain Crow Ranch recommends Jaccard meat tenderizer). If you don't own a meat tenderizer, consider marinating your beef before cooking, especially lean cuts like N.Y. strip and sirloin, but use slightly less than you would use for grain-fed beef. Grass-fed beef cooks more quickly, so the marinade won't have as much time to cook off. For safe handling, always marinate in the refrigerator.

• If you do not have time to marinate and don't own a meat tenderizer, coat your thawed steak with your favorite rub, place on a solid surface, cover with plastic and pound your steak a few times to break down the connective tissue. As an added benefit, the rub will be pushed into your beef. Don't go overboard and flatten your beef unless your recipe calls for it. If you don't have a meat mallet, use a rolling pin or whatever you feel is safe and convenient—the bottom of a small, heavy saucepan does the job well.

• Stovetop cooking is great for any type of steak . . . including grass-fed steak. You have more control over the temperature than on the grill. Use butter in the final minutes when the heat is low to carry the taste of fresh garlic through the meat just like steak chefs.

• Grass-fed beef will usually require 30 percent less cooking time and will continue to cook when removed from heat. For this reason, remove the beef from the heat source ten degrees before it reaches the desired temperature. Use a thermometer to test for doneness and watch the thermometer carefully.

• Let the beef sit covered and in a warm place for 8 to 10 minutes after removing from heat to let the juices redistribute.

• Bring your meat to room temperature before cooking . . . do not cook it cold straight from a refrigerator.

A good alternative to a beef steak is a pork chop (think Chop House!). Here is a great recipe from Jones Heritage Farm & Market that will definitely impress that special person in your life. This recipe serves six, so, for a romantic dinner, cut the recipe or plan to have leftovers. Kids may also enjoy these pork chops, despite the bourbon marinade, which cooks off in the process. If you are concerned about using alcohol in this recipe, use two or three healthy dashes of vanilla extract and extra water or peach juice (preferably from peaches you have canned yourself!).

Berkshire Pork Chops from Jones Heritage Farm & Market

Serves 6

5-6 large Berkshire pork chops
1 cup fine bourbon
⅔ cup cold water
¼ cup table salt
½ cup Dijon mustard
1 Tablespoon teriyaki sauce
3 teaspoons ground paprika
4 Tablespoons pure maple sugar
2 garlic cloves, minced
1 heaping Tablespoon brown sugar
5-6 strips peppercorn bacon

In a large mixing bowl, add bourbon, brown sugar, minced garlic, ground paprika, maple syrup, Dijon mustard, salt, and water; mix vigorously. Marinate Berkshire chops for at least 30 minutes. In a separate dish rub brown sugar into bacon and wrap each Berkshire chop with bacon. Pin with soaked wood chip. Grill on hickory plank or straight on grill until internal temperature is 150°F, about 5-7 minutes per side. Serve hot and enjoy.

This dish would be great with a simple side of grilled peach halves. Cut peaches in half and remove the pit. Brush a little oil on the cut side, place the halves cut-side down on the grill, and cook until desired doneness. The peach halves develop a delicious caramelized surface on the grill.

Cheese Soufflé (yes, you can!)

Serves 6

3 Tablespoons butter
2 Tablespoons grated Parmesan
2 teaspoons flour
½ cup milk
½ cup grated Gruyere or cheddar or any other cheese you like (Gorgonzola is great, but maybe not so romantic. . . .)
pinch of cayenne pepper
pinch of nutmeg
2 egg yolks
2 egg whites
pinch of salt

(You can also add chopped spinach, arugula, kale, or other vegetables. Just be sure to cook them first and squeeze the liquid out. Chop them finely enough to distribute throughout the egg batter or else they will sink and the soufflé will not rise properly.)

Pre-heat oven to 375°F. Grease one 16-ounce or two 8-ounce ramekins with 1 Tablespoon of butter. Coat with the Parmesan, then tap out the excess. Set aside.

In a small saucepan, over medium heat, melt the remaining butter. Stir in the flour and cook 1 minute. Whisk in the milk and cook, stirring constantly, until the sauce boils (about one minute). Remove from heat and stir in the cheese until melted. Blend in the cayenne and nutmeg. Whisk in the yolks one at a time. Set aside. (The recipe can be made to this point up to one day ahead. Cover with plastic wrap and refrigerate.)

In a clean bowl, beat the egg whites with the salt until stiff (but not dry) peaks form. Make sure NO fat, including egg yolks, are in the whites or they will not stiffen. Stir ¼ of the egg whites into the cheese sauce to loosen it. Gently fold in the remaining egg whites. Spoon into the ramekins. Bake until puffed and browned, 40 minutes for a 16-ounce soufflé, 20 minutes for two smaller ones. Serve immediately.

Kids love "junk food" (and so do we!). Some **kid-friendly** but healthful choices include pizza, cauliflower mac and cheese, baked fries and sweet potato fries, baked potato and vegetable chips, fried rice, and chicken tortilla soup.

Pizza dough is fairly easy to make, and you can add all sorts of great toppings: chopped greens, onions, tomatoes, basil, mushrooms, ham, or whatever. If possible, use fresh mozzarella slices for the cheese. You can even make smaller individual pizzas for a special kids' night supper—let the kids choose their toppings.

This recipe is enough for one 12-inch pizza. Increase quantities for more pizzas. There are other great pizza dough recipes out there that require more rising time, which can also be frozen and used later. This one is especially good for those times when you (or your kids) want pizza NOW! Preheat oven to 450°F. If you have a pizza stone (highly recommended if you like pizza), preheat it with the oven.

Quick and Simple Pizza Dough

1 (¼-ounce) package active dry yeast
1 teaspoon white sugar
1 cup warm water (110°F)
2½ cups bread flour (which has more gluten than all-purpose flour)
2 Tablespoons olive oil
1 teaspoon salt

In a medium bowl, dissolve yeast and sugar in warm water. Let stand about 10 minutes until dissolved and proofed. Stir in flour, salt, and oil. Beat until smooth. Let rest while you prepare your toppings (or at least 5 minutes).

Turn dough out onto a lightly floured surface and pat, stretch, or roll into a round, being careful not to tear the crust. Transfer crust to a lightly greased pizza pan or baker's peel dusted with cornmeal (if you plan to transfer the pizza to a stone). Spread with your toppings and bake in preheated oven for 15 to 20 minutes, or until golden brown. Let baked pizza cool for 5 minutes before serving.

You can also grill pizza on the barbecue. It takes a bit of practice, but the kids will love it! Start with hot coals (or gas) on one side of the grill. Brush one side of the shaped pizza dough with oil and turn it onto the hot side. Let it grill for a few minutes until you can turn it. Brush the uncooked top with a little oil. When you can easily turn it, flip it over to the cooler side and add your toppings and cheese. Cover and grill until the cheese melts.

Baked fries and chips are also easy. Cut up potatoes, sweet potatoes, and/ or other root vegetables into sticks or thin slices. (Use a mandoline or V-slicer for chips, and note that most root vegetables like beets or turnips are best as chips rather than fries.) Heat the oven to 400°F and place one or two baking sheets in the oven to heat. Put the sliced vegetables into a large bowl and pat dry. Add enough oil to coat them lightly (1 or 2 Tablespoons) and toss them with the oil and some salt and pepper. Carefully remove the hot baking sheets and spread the vegetables evenly in a single layer. (This part is important so that the fries/chips get crispy and don't just steam cook.) Bake them until they begin to brown (around 30 minutes). Flip the fries/chips and continue baking until desired crispness. Sprinkle again with salt and pepper if you like. For a great variation, try salt and vinegar chips: dredge the raw chips in malt vinegar before tossing in the oil and baking. Another trick to try with the chips is to use wire cooling racks on the baking sheets and bake the chips on the racks.

Mac and cheese is a classic kids' favorite. When you add cauliflower to the cheese sauce, the result is creamy and delicious and you can use a bunch of that cauliflower you bought (or grew). Your kids may not even notice!

In *The Food Matters Cookbook*, Mark Bittman has a great version that cuts a lot of fat out of the more traditional recipes:

Creamy Cauliflower Mac

Serves 4

2½ cups vegetable or chicken stock
2 bay leaves
1 cauliflower, cored and cut into large pieces
8 ounces whole-wheat elbow macaroni, shells, ziti, or other cut pasta
½ cup grated cheese (such as sharp cheddar, Gruyere, Emmental, or a combination)
2 Tablespoons olive oil
1 Tablespoon Dijon mustard
⅛ teaspoon nutmeg
Salt and black pepper
¼ cup grated Parmesan cheese
½ cup whole-grain breadcrumbs

Heat oven to 400°F. Boil a pot of salted water. In a saucepan, warm stock and bay leaves on medium-low heat for five minutes; turn off heat.

Cook cauliflower in boiling water for 25 minutes. Drain and put cauliflower in a food processor or blender. Cook pasta in boiling water for 5 minutes. Drain and rinse to cool; put pasta in a greased, nine-inch square baking dish.

Process cauliflower with stock (discard bay leaves), cheese, oil, mustard, nutmeg, salt, and pepper, working in batches. Pour sauce over pasta, toss, and spread evenly in dish. Top with Parmesan and bread crumbs. Bake 20 minutes.

Fried rice can be as easy as tossing some leftover rice with cooked eggs and leftover vegetables and maybe a little beef, pork, or chicken. Stir-fry vegetables and meat (if using) in oil and soy sauce. When done, set aside. Beat a few eggs (3 or 4) together, add more oil to the stir-fry pan, and briskly scramble them. Remove the cooked eggs and break them up. Add a bit more oil and add the rice. Heat the rice through, then add the other ingredients together, mixing and stir frying them. You can season the fried rice with garlic and fresh ginger while you stir fry the vegetables. Garnish with chopped scallions.

A lot of kids love to prepare their own food. We gave you one suggestion with pizza, but have you thought about **soup**? Here are two suggestions for kid-friendly soups that they can have a hand in. Cold tomato soup starts with a base of tomato or vegetable juice and lemon to taste (the desired taste is in line with V-8). Some people like to mix the juice with equal parts buttermilk, but that's not necessary (it's really good, though). Provide bowls of chopped vegetables like peppers, tomatoes, onions or scallions, celery, radishes, and avocado, and a bowl of homemade (or not . . .) croutons. Let kids fill their serving bowls with their choice of vegetables, then pour on the soup and enjoy. Use this same approach with chicken soup in the form of tortilla soup—just substitute the tomato soup with chicken soup (just seasoned broth and chicken) and instead of croutons use baked or fried tortilla strips. Mom and Dad may want to add hot sauce to these soups, and for the chicken-tortilla soup, a bit of crumbled farmer's or Mexican Cotija cheese.

*****

Missouri's wine production is well-known to locals (and well-covered elsewhere), and, of course, we revel in our state's role as savior to France's wine grape crop in the mid-nineteenth century. But locally distilled spirits are becoming a phenomenon in Missouri, so we have to include ideas for a *cocktail party*.

Everyone has a favorite cocktail recipe, so we won't discuss them except to say that infusions are easy and delicious and will surely impress all your guests! The following ideas are different from infused drinks like limoncello, which take longer and use sugar as part of the infusion, although those are worth the effort and make great holiday gifts (cranberry liqueur is great in Cosmos). Mix a bottle of good-quality vodka with some crushed (but not pulverized) berries, peaches, pears, apples, citrus zest, ginger, hot peppers, coffee beans, or herbs and let it sit for a week, shaking the bottle every day. Strain the vodka through a cheesecloth or coffee filter and discard the solids. Use the infused vodka in your cocktails (hot pepper vodka is perfect for Bloody Marys).

Another refreshing summer drink is a gin and tonic or vodka tonic with a sprig of rosemary lightly muddled in the glass before making the drink. Rosemary is strong, so be careful not to crush it too much—in fact, you may want to just stir the drink with a sprig of the herb and leave it in the glass. Another classic herb for cocktails is mint, but basil can also be a good substitute in Mojitos or other light drinks. For the adventuresome among you, bourbon infused with bacon is excellent by itself or in a Manhattan or Old Fashioned. Cook a pound of smoked bacon and save the fat. Eat the bacon (or save it for a party appetizer later). Pour the hot fat, plus one or two slices of the cooked bacon, into a large, clean jar and fill with good-quality bourbon. Let it cool to room temperature, then freeze it. Once the fat is frozen, pour off the bourbon through a cheesecloth or coffee filter and discard the bacon fat (or use it for cooking).

For nibbles, consider the burgeoning charcuterie market. Locally cured meats and sausages have become wildly popular and can be found all across the state. A large platter of meats and cheeses served with sliced baguette or crackers (home-made crackers are easy and tasty), crudités (all those vegetables!), some spiced nuts, and maybe a dip or two makes a nice spread. Add some homemade pickles (see page 217) and kale chips. No one will want to go to a party at anyone else's house. Ever.

Kale chips are a great snack and a great way to use up the ubiquitous mound of kale familiar to anyone who ever subscribed to a CSA. Heat the oven to 325°F. Rinse and dry a batch of kale. Cut or tear into medium-sized pieces. Toss with oil mixed with salt and/or other seasoning like chili flakes or garlic (tahini with garlic and sesame oil is great) and place on a baking sheet (preferably lined with parchment paper). Bake until crisp (check after 10 minutes so they don't burn). You may want to turn them once in the oven. You can also bake them at a lower temperature (250°F) for more time (30 minutes or so). The effect is that the oven dries them more than bakes them. Make a bunch and store any leftovers in an air-tight container, if you can stop eating them! If you leave them whole with the stems intact, you can serve them in a tall glass or jar like a bouquet.

*****

No matter what time of year it is, you know winter will always come and with it the desire for something hot and hearty. Some great *winter warm-ups* include soups, stews, casseroles, and roasts. A slow cooker is a great appliance to have on hand in the winter so you can put together your one-pot meal in the morning on your way to work and come home to supper almost on the table.

Butternut squash soup is nearly synonymous with fall and winter. You can use just about any winter squash or a combination of them for a creamy and satisfying soup. Roasting the squash in advance deepens the flavor. A lot of people peel and cube squash before roasting, which is fine but not necessary (and can be difficult if the skin is tough and hard). Using a heavy chef's knife, you can get away with removing the stem and cutting the squash in half, scraping out the seeds, brushing the cut side with oil, sprinkling it with salt and pepper, and roasting it in a shallow baking dish at 400°F until it's soft (time depends on the size of the squash, but start checking it after 30 minutes). You can, of course, also do this with pumpkin. Scrape out the flesh to use in your soup. If you peel and cube the squash in advance, try roasting it with other vegetables to make your soup more complex: apples, onions, potatoes, carrots, parsnips, or other root vegetables. Some good herbs to use include sage or thyme.

For the soup, slowly sauté a chopped onion, a chopped carrot or two, and a rib or two of chopped celery. Add some minced garlic to the sauté. When these are nicely soft and aromatic, add them to the cooked squash in a large Dutch oven or stock pot. Add a cup or two of vegetable or chicken stock and use your immersion blender to blend all the vegetables together. When they are blended, add another three or four cups of stock and season with chopped sage, salt, and pepper. Serve with a dollop of plain Greek yogurt and either chopped scallions or fried sage leaves (quickly pan-fry fresh leaves in a little hot olive oil).

This soup can also be made with leftover roasted root vegetables—just heat them up in the soup pan and add enough stock to blend, then add the remaining stock. If you want a chunky soup, skip the blender. A garnish of roasted wild mushrooms would take this soup to a whole new level.

Vegetable soup with or without meat is great in the winter, especially because you will have frozen vegetables left from your summer bounty. The key to really great soups is to sauté the aromatics slowly beforehand to let them develop a richness and depth for your soups. Vegetable soup can start with chopped onions, carrot, and celery as the aromatics. Once those are ready, add them to a pot of stock (beef, chicken, or vegetable) and then add whatever vegetables you have on hand. You might add cooked beans (kidney or white), grains (barley, wild rice, or wheatberry), or meat. If you use fresh meat, be sure to sauté it first. If it's left over, just chop it up and add it to the pot. Chopped canned tomatoes or tomato sauce takes the soup in a different direction; adding chopped or sliced zucchini, cooked pasta, and kidney beans to the tomato-based soup makes it more of a minestrone, and adding cooked pasta, chopped greens, and cannellini beans makes it a pasta e fagioli.

Here's a recipe from Rain Crow Ranch for another great winter warm-up—pot roast:

Pot Roast, Rain Crow Ranch

3 pounds grass-fed beef roast
3 Tablespoons olive oil
2 cups sour cream
2 teaspoons dill seed
1 package onion soup mix
1 teaspoon sea salt
¼ teaspoon freshly ground black pepper
1 cup water (red wine or tomato juice can be substituted for water)

Brown roast on all sides in olive oil. Season with dill seed, salt, pepper, onion soup. Add water. Cook covered in Dutch oven approx. 3 hours at 275°F, turning occasionally to keep moist. When the meat is fork-tender remove from the pot; do not overcook. Reduce pan drippings or add water to make 1½ cup liquid. Add flour and stir until thickened (if needed, put in blender to make smooth). Add sour cream. Slice roast and serve with sour cream gravy.

Variations:
Add mushrooms, carrots, and potatoes the last 60 minutes of cooking. When done remove roast and vegetables. Add flour to pan drippings and stir until thickened, season as needed. Slice roast and pour gravy over meat. Serve with the vegetables. This roast can easily be cooked in a crockpot to have dinner ready when you come home.

Ken and Jennifer Muno of Goatsbeard Farm suggest this recipe for a unique spin on bread pudding (adapted from *Food and Wine*, March 2005). It would make a great side dish for pot roast.

Spring Onion, Spinach, and Goat Cheese Bread Pudding, Goatsbeard Farm

1 pound country-style bread, crust removed, cut into ¾ inch cubes
5 Tablespoons unsalted butter
2 bunches scallions, cut into ½-inch lengths
8 ounces spinach, tough stems removed, washed well and coarsely chopped
2 large cloves garlic, finely chopped
salt and pepper
4 large eggs
1½ cups half and half
¾ cup sour cream
¼ teaspoon freshly grated nutmeg
10 ounces Goatsbeard Farm fresh goat cheese, crumbled

Preheat oven to 400°F. Toast breadcrumbs on a cookie sheet until golden—about 10 minutes. Melt butter in a large skillet and sauté green onions until soft, about 3 minutes. Add garlic and spinach and stir, cooking just until spinach wilts. Season with salt and pepper.

In a large bowl, whisk eggs, half and half, sour cream, and nutmeg. Fold in bread cubes, vegetable mixture, and half the goat cheese. Season with salt and pepper. Let stand at least 30 minutes, or overnight. (Bring to room temperature before baking.) Transfer mixture to a 9 × 12 baking dish. Sprinkle with remaining goat cheese. Place baking dish in a larger roasting pan and fill roasting pan with enough hot water to come halfway up the sides of the baking dish. Bake for 30-40 minutes, or until the pudding is set and the top is golden brown. Serve hot or warm.

Too Much of a Good Thing

What do you do when you have too many or too much of a good thing? This is a question that comes up a lot when you subscribe to a CSA or food shares program. To many, part of the fun of subscribing to such a program is wondering what delicious bounty will be delivered each week. And it is guaranteed that some weeks boxes will be laden with root vegetables, grains, and greens. Greens can easily be made into chips (see kale chip recipe) or chopped and used on pizza, in soup, or stirred into pasta. Cook pasta in chicken or vegetable broth, and as the pasta cooks, add a large mound of kale, chard, or other hearty leafy green. Stir together with the pasta until they are cooked. Drain off most of the broth, leaving a little in the pot. Stir in grated Parmesan cheese and mix with the hot pasta. Serve immediately for a delicious, silky-tasting main or side dish.

Storing Foods

Grains and beans can both be cooked ahead and refrigerated or frozen. One very easy method for cooking beans, grains, and rice is to boil them in enough water to cover them by about 3 inches. Beans do not need to be soaked in advance, although you may do so if you like. Put your beans or grains into a large pot, add the water, and bring it to a boil. If you are cooking beans, do not salt the water until later, but for grains or rice, you may add salt if you like. Reduce the heat to a simmer and cook until done. You may need to add more water to make sure the beans or grains are always covered by several inches. When they are cooked, drain the water and store the beans or grains in the refrigerator to use within the week, or store in the freezer to use over the next few months. You could also save beans with some of their cooking liquid if you want to use them in chili or soup.

Root vegetables keep for a long time, especially if you store them properly. One ingenious trick is to put a layer of insulation (sawdust, moistened peat moss, or sand) in a wood or cardboard box in the basement (making sure it is raised off the floor a little so it doesn't get damp—try resting it on two by fours). Add a layer of root vegetables (beets, potatoes, carrots, parsnips, turnips, etc.) then cover those with more insulation—about ¼ inch. Keep layering the vegetables and the insulation until the box is full or you run out of vegetables.

Roasted root vegetables have become a Thanksgiving staple in our homes, and for good reason: they are easy and satisfying, and the leftovers can be made into lots of great dishes like soup, hash, or even a sandwich filling (just add a little cheese of your choice and maybe some greens—great as a pressed panini).

Quick Pickles and Other Ways to Preserve

The summer brings an abundance of fresh produce, and in mid-season, it seems like there will be no end to the quantity and variety of fruits and vegetables. But those summer months turn to fall and winter, and with that the absence of fresh produce. As long as you have preserved some of your bounty in advance you can eat summer vegetables and fruits in the winter.

Popular and simple methods for preserving foods include freezing, drying, canning, and pickling. To freeze vegetables like green beans, corn, tomatoes, okra, etc., blanch them first by washing and cutting them up into the desired size then boiling them for a few minutes until the color intensifies. Immediately drain the vegetables and plunge them in an ice water bath to stop the cooking process. When they have cooled, drain them and place them in freezer bags and store them in the freezer. It's a good idea to label the bag so you remember when you stored them. Fruits are best cut into pieces (for peaches or other large fruit) or left whole (for berries), sprinkled with a bit of ascorbic acid dissolved in water (available where you buy canning supplies). Spread the fruit on a baking sheet or other large tray and place in the freezer. When the fruit is frozen, transfer to airtight containers or freezer bags and label them with the date and contents.

You can dry fruits and vegetables in a food dehydrator or in the oven on low heat. Blanch the vegetable first, then heat the oven to 140 or 150°F. Place cut or sliced vegetables on baking sheets in the oven, making sure there is enough space between the oven racks for air to circulate. Keep the oven door open slightly to allow moist air to escape. Check the pans every 30 minutes, stirring vegetables and moving the trays from front to back, top to bottom, etc., to ensure even exposure to the heat and avoid actually cooking the vegetables (you're just trying to remove the water from them).

Fruits and certain vegetables can be made into butters, jams, or preserves, sorbet, granita, or ice cream, juices, or infusions.

Pickling and canning vegetables like green tomatoes, beets, cucumbers, beans, carrots, peppers, garlic, etc., take a little more effort and equipment than freezing or drying, but not that much. Once you have the proper equipment, you may never buy pickles from a store again. There are many good books and websites that detail the steps to canning and pickling, including Eugenia Bone's *Well Preserved*, in which she describes preserving foods in smaller batches that are less intimidating than the epic all-day canning fests so many people imagine. Many state school extension programs have advice on food preservation and safety, including the one at Mizzou: http://extension.missouri.edu/main/DisplayCategory.aspx?C=194.

Quick pickles are the easiest to make. This recipe is for cucumbers, but you could also use beets, cauliflower, beans, Brussels sprouts, hot peppers, or any number of summer vegetables. Experiment with the salt-vinegar ratio, but it is important to use vinegar that has 5 percent acidity. Some people like to cut the tartness with a little sugar or agave, which is fine.

Quick Pickles

¼ cup non-iodized salt (sea salt, kosher salt, or pickling salt)
1 cup apple cider vinegar (5% acidity)
8 cups water
1½ pounds cucumbers, thoroughly washed and dried
few sprigs fresh dill, washed and dried
whole peeled garlic cloves (optional)
dried red chili peppers (optional)
pickling spice (optional)

Wash and sterilize as many jars as you will need (you can boil them in a large pot or run them through the dishwasher). Mix the salt, apple cider vinegar, pickling spice (if using), and water and bring to a boil. Simmer for 5 minutes. Remove the brine from the heat and allow it to cool slightly. Arrange the cucumbers upright in a container large enough to hold the brine. Place the dill sprigs, garlic, and peppers amongst the cucumbers in the jars. The cucumbers should fit tightly and should come within ½-inch of the top of the container.

Fill the container with the brine to the top and tap on a flat surface to remove any possible air bubbles. Store in the refrigerator for several months (if they last that long!).

Another way to preserve and eat all those vegetables is to make giardiniera. This would be great served at a picnic or cocktail party.

Giardiniera

2 green bell peppers, diced
2 red bell peppers, diced
8 fresh jalapeno peppers, sliced
1 celery stalk, diced
1 medium carrot, diced
1 small onion, chopped
½ cup fresh cauliflower florets
½ cup salt
water to cover
1 clove garlic, finely chopped
1 Tablespoon dried oregano
1 teaspoon red pepper flakes
½ teaspoon black pepper
1 (5-ounce) jar pimento-stuffed green olives, chopped
1 cup white vinegar
1 cup olive oil

Place the green and red peppers, jalapenos, celery, carrots, onion, and cauliflower in a bowl. Stir in salt, and fill with enough cold water to cover. Place plastic wrap or aluminum foil over the bowl, and refrigerate overnight.

The next day, drain the salty water, and rinse the vegetables. Mix together the garlic, oregano, red pepper flakes, black pepper, and olives. Add vinegar and olive oil, and mix well. Combine with the vegetable mixture, cover, and refrigerate for two days before using.

Of course, another great way to preserve summer's bounty for use in the winter is to make sauces. Tomato sauce is probably the most common, but also consider red pepper sauce for a bit of a kick. This sauce recipe comes from YellowTree Farm.

Heirloom Tomato Sauce, YellowTree Farm

Yield: 3 to 4 quarts of tomato sauce

1 handful* fresh sage
1 handful fresh oregano
1 handful fresh thyme
1 handful fresh rosemary
1 handful fresh basil
1 handful fresh tarragon
1 handful fresh marjoram
3 whole cloves garlic
4 cups olive oil
7 to 10 pounds heirloom tomatoes
2 Tablespoons table salt
2 Tablespoons minced fresh garlic
ground white pepper

*1 handful equals about 1 cup. The herbs should not be chopped up, so using a measuring cup is difficult.

Make an herb-infused olive oil: In a small saucepan, combine sage, oregano, thyme, rosemary, basil, tarragon, marjoram, whole garlic cloves, and olive oil. Place over low heat for at least 1 hour, longer for a more intense herb infusion. Stir occasionally, and be sure oil does not boil. Remove from heat; pour through a strainer. Discard solids.

Wash and core tomatoes. (Chef's hint: Core tomatoes with a metal decorating tip designed to be used with a pastry bag.) Cut tomatoes in half, place in a large pot, and add salt, minced garlic, and white pepper to taste.

Bring to a simmer over medium heat. Cook about 30 minutes, stirring frequently, until tomatoes disintegrate.

Pour 2 cups of the simmered tomato mixture into a blender, and blend on high until smooth. Reduce speed to low and slowly add a drizzle of the herb-infused olive oil. Stop blending and adding oil when the mixture reaches near the top of the blender. Repeat with remaining simmered tomatoes and olive oil. (Any remaining infused oil can be refrigerated and used later to add a fragrant, herbal element to any dish that calls for olive oil.)

Equipment

Throughout this chapter, we have mentioned **equipment** needed (or recommended) to make these recipes. Below is a list of useful equipment:

- immersion blender
- pressure cooker
- slow cooker/crockpot
- large pot for boiling jars
- pot rack for placing jars in the pot
- jar tongs
- jar funnel
- canning jars, lids, and bands
- cheesecloth
- pizza stone

We hope we have left you with some ideas for using all the wonderful foods you can find throughout the state, and if you have thought about joining a food shares program, these tips may push you toward signing up for one!

Finding Missouri Products

There are lots of vendors, markets, and restaurants in Missouri
that carry local products, and the list keeps growing. Because that number is always
in flux, this book is not meant to be an exhaustive guide, but an introduction
to the bounty available in Missouri. That said, we have compiled a list of some
resources—a lot of them ones our farmers told us about—to help you locate
local products across the state and/or within specific regions in Missouri. Some
of the markets mentioned in the farm profiles go by different names, so this list
is not an exact match, and we have added several dozen additional markets that
we discovered or already knew about. Also, contact names and other information
are subject to change, especially farmers' markets, so if you plan to visit, check the
Internet first for the latest information.

Many markets and restaurants are getting onboard with selling and serving
local foods. However, the number of local products carried or used by the markets
and restaurants may vary; some use only one or two local products while others use
much more. When in doubt, ask the store manager or server. But keep your eyes

open for new places—it seems like they pop up all the time! One thing to note: more and more local and national supermarket chains are carrying local products to meet customer demand, so first, check your local grocery store, and second, if you want them to carry local products, let the store manager know!

There are several good websites that list resources in the state, and we'll start with some of those, but be warned: some websites are updated more frequently than others, so it's probably a good idea to call ahead to any business you plan to visit, especially if you are making a specific trip. Also remember that some of the farmers featured in this book sell from farm stands either on their farms or in their communities, so check the farm profiles for that information. Finally, many farmers' markets and other businesses listed here have or are creating Facebook pages, so please check if you are active on Facebook.

Now, on to the lists!

Websites

Local Harvest: www.localharvest.org (localharvest is a national organization dedicated to eating locally and sustainably. It has many resources listed by state. Please note: the national organization and the business in St. Louis are not affiliated.)

Missouri Farmers' Markets: www.care2.com/farmersmarket/search/state/MO (alphabetical list of Missouri farmers' markets)

University of Missouri School of Agriculture: www.agebb.missouri.edu/fmktdir/view.asp (From the University of Missouri extension program: farmers' markets listed by county)

Food Circles: www.foodcircles.missouri.edu/sources.htm (This is a general website with tons of great information about local food circles, markets, retail outlets, and more)

Missouri Department of Tourism: www.agrimissouri.com/mo-travel/ (This website from the Missouri Department of Tourism has a map with markets, farm stands, restaurants, and more)

Missouri Department of Agriculture: www.mda.mo.gov/connect/buyinglocal.pdf (This Missouri Department of Agriculture site includes great resources for markets, CSAs, restaurants, retail, etc.)

Slow Foods St. Louis: www.slowfoodstl.org/where-to/ (This site includes shopping and dining recommendations from Slow Foods St. Louis—local to St. Louis area. There are Slow Foods chapters in several cities in Missouri. Check www.slowfoodusa.org/index.php/local_chapters/ for local chapters.)

Chain Grocery Stores in Missouri That Carry Local Products

Big V Country Mart
C&R
Hy-Vee
IGA
Paul's Supermarkets
Prengers Foods

Price Chopper
Schnucks
Straub's
Summer-Fresh
Town & Country Stores
Whole Foods

Stores and Markets, CSAs, and Restaurants by Region

Northwest Region

Stores and Markets

Bethany Farmers' Market
Tuesdays, 4:00-6:00 p.m.; Fridays, 10:00 a.m.
May-October
Contact: Donald G. Terry
38582 E. 330th Ave.
Gilman City, MO 64642
660-876-5303

Caldwell County Farmers' Market
Saturdays, 8:00 a.m.-Noon
May-October
Contact: Betty Motsinger

3629 Northeast State Route U
Hamilton, MO 64644
motsing@cameron.net
816-583-4898

Chillicothe Farmers' Market
First Saturday in May through the last Saturday in October, rain or shine.
Sales begin strictly with the ringing of the bell at 8:00 a.m.
Contact: Beth Weidner
12947 CR 231
Tina, MO 64682
bweeds@greenhills.net
660-646-4050

Homestead Co-Op of Maryville

1730 N. Clayton Ave.
Maryville, MO 64468-1485
660-582-4455

Jamesport Farmers' Market

Mondays, Wednesdays, and Saturdays,
10:00 a.m.-5:00 p.m.
April-October
Contact: Joe C. Gingerich
25573 State Hwy. 190
Jamesport, MO 64648
660-684-6352

Lathrop Farmers' Market

Saturdays, 8:00 a.m.-2:00 p.m.
First Saturday in May-First Saturday in
November
Contact: Lori Barringer
3795 Breckenridge Rd.
Turney, MO 64493
gene@cameron.net
816-664-3334

Mercer County Farmers' Market

Saturdays, 7:30-10:30 a.m.
May-October
Contact: Gwen Coppick
Sub 5 Lot 13,
Atlantic Ave., Lake Marie
Mercer, MO 64661
660-382-4384

Nodaway County Farmers' Market

Mary Mart Shopping Center
1416 South Main St.
Maryville, MO 64468
Contact: Eddie Niewald
660-582-7621

June-October
Monday & Wednesday, 7:00 a.m.-Noon

Nodaway County Farmers' Market

Wednesdays and Saturdays, 7:00 a.m.-
Noon
June-October
Contact: Connie Callow
40474 Icon Rd.
Barnard, MO 64423
doncon@grm.net
660-652-4424

Parkville Missouri Farmers' Market

127 S. Main St.
Parkville, MO 64152
816-330-3279
www.parkvillefarmersmarket.com

Parkville Farmers' Market

English Landing Park
Hwy. 9
Parkville, MO 64152
Contact: Ida Lake
816-450-8810
OPEN-AIR/SEASONAL
May-September
Wednesday, 3:00-6:00 p.m.; Saturday, 6:00
a.m.-sellout

Pony Express Farmers' Market

Wednesdays and Saturdays, 7:00 a.m.-1:00
p.m. or sellout, rain or shine
East Ridge Village Shopping Center
Contact: Sandra Justice
St. Joseph, MO 64506
hdpeek@centurytel.net
www.ponyexpressfarmersmarket.com
816-617-2086

Tarkio Farmers' Market
> Fridays, 7:30-10:00 a.m.
> June-October
> Contact: Wendell L. Johnson
> 13321 V Ave.
> Westboro, MO 64498
> wjohnson@heartland.net
> 660-984-5518

Trenton Farmers' Market
> Fridays, 8:00-10:00 a.m.
> May-October
> Contact: Gerry Robbins
> 680 West Hwy. 6
> Trenton, MO 64683
> 660-359-5104

Yoder's Discount Grocery
> 20340 State Hwy. 190
> Jamesport, MO 64648
> 660-684-6082

Restaurants

The Klub
> 1710 Nebraska St.
> Mound City, MO 64470-1611
> 660-442-4043
> theklubmoundcity.com

Northeast Region

Stores and Markets

Bowling Green Farmers' and Artists' Market
> Fridays 3:00-7:00 p.m.
> Last Friday in May thru the 2nd week
> in October
> Contact: Sarrah Patton
> P.O. Box 5
> Bowling Green, MO 63334
> bgfam@ymail.com
> 573-213-3183

Bratcher's Market
> 301 S. Morley
> Moberly, MO 65270
> 660-263-7790; 660-263-7128
> www.bratchersmarket.com

Brookfield Farmers' Market
> Saturdays, 8:00 a.m.-Noon
> May-October
> Contact: Fran Graff, Brookfield
> Chamber of Commerce
> 300 N. Main St.
> Brookfield, MO 64628
> chamber@brookfieldmochamber.com
> www.brookfieldmochamber.com/
> farmersmarket.htm
> 660-258-7255

Clark Produce Auction LLC
> April: Fridays
> May-September: Tuesdays and Fridays
> October: Fridays
> All auctions start at 10:30 a.m.
> Contact: Elmer Gingerich or Leo
> Kempf

1966 Hwy. Y
Clark, MO 65243
agebb.missouri.edu/hort/auction/clark.
    htm
660-264-4555 or 660-261-4553

Countryside Market
15971 U.S. Hwy. 63
Kirksville, MO 63501-6908
888-587-1566

Danjo Country Store
1210 Private Rd. 2717
Moberly, MO 65270
660-263-1043 or 573-823-5452
danjofarms.com

The Downtown Grocery Store
111 South Franklin St.
Kirksville, MO 63501
660-627-5655

Hannibal Farmers' Market
Tuesday, 3:00-7:00 p.m.; Saturday, 8:00
    a.m.-Noon
May-September
Contact: Nan Poage-Prater
14491 Hwy. H
Hannibal, MO 63401
nanapoage@onemain.com
573-221-2640

Kirksville Kiwanis Farmers' Market
Saturdays, 7:00 a.m.-Noon
May-October
Contact: Ben and Brad Beard
120 East Washington
Kirksville, MO 63501
660-665-1928

Louisiana Farmers' Market
Saturday 7:00 a.m.-Noon
May through the end of October
Contact: Karen Stoeckley
Louisiana Chamber of Commerce
202 S. Third St.
Louisiana, MO 63353
573-754-3787

MABCC Farmers' Market
Thursdays, 3:00-7:00 p.m.
June-September
Contact: Mary Ann Schmitt
109 N. Main St.
Marceline, MO 64658
info@marcelinemarket.com
www.marcelinemarket.com
660-376-3330

Moberly Farmers' Market
Thursdays, 3:00-7:00 p.m.
May-October
Contact: Dan Nelson
1210 Private Rd. 2717
Moberly, MO 65270
moberlyfarmersmarket@gmail.com
573-823-5452

Monroe County Farmers' Market
Saturdays, 9:00 a.m.-Noon
May-October
Contact: Julie Ensor
24036 Monroe Rd. 217
Holliday, MO 65258
660-266-3465

Putnam County Farmers' Market
Saturdays, 7:00-11:00 a.m.
May-October
Contact: Leta Torrey
14747 State Hwy. 129
Unionville, MO 63565
660-947-2067

Rutledge Farmers' Market
Saturdays, 9:00 a.m.-Noon
June-September
Contact: Alyson Ewald
7 Smith Rd.
Rutledge, MO 63563
alyson@ic.org
660-883-5529

Schuyler County Farmers' Market
Saturdays, 8:00 a.m.-2:00 p.m.
May-mid-October
Contact: Darla Campbell
P.O. Box 310
Lancaster, MO 63548
CampbellD@missouri.edu
660-457-3469

Scotland County Farmers' Market
Tuesday 3:00-6:00 p.m.
May-September
Contact: Gigi Wahba
Rt 1 Box 155
Rutledge, MO 63563
gigi@sandhillfarm.org
660-883-5543

Southside Farmers' Market
Saturdays 8:00 a.m.-Noon
May-October

Contact: Mollie Gilliland
P.O. Box 306
Macon, MO 63552
mollieg@centurytel.net
660-385-5781 ext. 21

Zimmerman's Store
Main State Hwy. M
Rutledge, MO 63563
660-883-5766

CSAs

**Danjo Farms, Moberly CSA
(danjofarms.com)**
1210 Private Rd. 2717
Moberly, MO 65270
660-263-1043 or 573-823-5452

Restaurants

Bubba's Burger Bar and Egg Emporium
213 N. 5th St.
Moberly, MO 65270-1501
660-651-8200

Clarksville Station Restaurant
901 S. Hwy. 79
Clarksville, MO 63336
573-242-3838
www.overlookfarmmo.com/the-fork

Costa Rican Café Company
107 W. Washington
Kirksville, MO 63501
660-988-6861

The Eagle's Nest Winery, Inn & Bistro
  221 Georgia St.
  Louisiana, MO 63353
  573-754-9888
  www.theeaglesnest-louisiana.com/index.
    htm

Ice House
  1730 S. Morley St.
  Moberly, MO 65270
  660-263-8648

Central Region

Stores and Markets

Bagnell Dam Farmers' Market
  Contact: Jocelyn White
  1310 Proctor Dr.
  Osage Beach, MO 65065

Better Lives Today Farmers' Market
  Saturday 8 a.m.-Noon
  May-August
  Contact: Florence Jarchow
  P.O. Box 496
  Richland, MO 65556
  flojarchow@gmail.com
  betterlivestoday.org/3.html
  573-765-2012

Blue Springs Downtown Farmers' Market
  Downtown Blue Springs
  11th & Main streets
  Blue Springs, MO 64016
  Contact: Mike Lundquist
  816-650-9474
  OPEN-AIR/SEASONAL
  May 6-October 28
  Tuesday & Saturday, 7:00 a.m.-Noon

Boone County Farmers' Market
  Wednesdays, 4:00-6:00 p.m.; Saturdays, 8:00 a.m.-Noon
  Saturdays: April-October; Wednesdays: June-September
  Contact: Kevin Martz, Treasurer
  6789 E. Palmer Rd.
  Columbia, MO 65202
  boonecou@boonecountyfarmers.com
  www.boonecountyfarmers.com
  573-474-0405

Boonslick Farmers' Market
  Every day, 8 a.m.-sellout; Primary days are Friday and Saturday
  April through October
  Contact: Gene Walther
  17524 Scenic Dr.
  Boonville, MO 65233
  settlers@iland.net
  660-882-3125

Bourbon Farmers' Market
  Tuesdays, Thursdays, and Fridays 7:00 a.m.-5:00 p.m.
  May-September
  Contact: Robert Gargus
  P.O. Box 76
  Bourbon, MO 65441
  rgargus@centruytel.net
  573-732-5894

CDR Naturals

363 E. Pine St.
Bourbon, MO 65441
573-732-5900
cdrnaturals.com

Cabool Area Farmers' Market

Wednesdays, 11:00 a.m.-4:30 p.m.
April-October
Contact: Deborah French
2575 Limestone Dr.
Mountain Grove, MO 65711
gpicker@centurytel.net
caboolfarmersmarket.wordpress.com
417-926-4226

Clovers Natural Foods

802 Business Loop 70E
Columbia, MO 65201
573-449-1650

Clovers Natural Market

2100 Chapel Plaza Court
Columbia, MO 65203
573-445-0990
www.cloversnaturalmarket.com

Cole County Farmers' Market

Tuesdays and Fridays, 4:00-6:00 p.m.;
Saturdays, 2:00-4:00 p.m.
April 14-October
Contact: James Hohman
43422 Hobby Horse Rd.
Russellville, MO 65074
hohman2@hotmail.com
573-392-3088

Columbia Farmers' Market, Columbia South, MU, and Winter Farmers' Markets

Contact: Caroline Todd, Market
Manager
P.O. Box 10012
Columbia, MO 65205
columbia.farmers.market@yahoo.com
www.columbiafarmersmarket.org
573-823-6889

Coyote Market Farm & Home

Thursdays, 4:00-7:00 p.m.
April-mid-October
Contact: Zach Rippeto
13301 South Bob Veach Rd.
Ashland, MO 65010
zrippeto@earthlink.net
573-489-0928

Farmers Alliance of Rural Missouri (FARM)

Wednesdays, 3:00-6:00 p.m.;
Saturdays, 7:00 a.m.-Noon
May-September
Contact: Sandy Nelson
761 Rodeo Rd.
Camdenton, MO 65020
573-873-4038 daytime or 573-346-3346

Farmers Alliance of Rural Missouri (FARM)

May-September
Contact: Sandy Nelson
761 Rodeo Rd.
Camdenton, MO 65020
573-873-4038 daytime or 573-346-3346

Farmers' Market of Laclede County

Saturdays 8:00 a.m.-Noon
May-October
Contact: Linda Bethurem
P.O. Box 573
Lebanon, MO 65536
anewlife06@netzero.net
417-531-1365

Fayette Farmers' Market

Tuesdays, 4:00-7:00 p.m.
May-October
Contact: Cathy Johnmeyer
3030 Hwy. 240
Fayette, MO 65248
fayettefarmersmarket@gmail.com
660-248-3791

Foods for Health

707 S. Bishop
Rolla, MO 65401
573-364-7860
foodsfor@embarqmail.com

Fulton Farmers' Market

Wednesdays, 3:30-6:00 p.m.; Saturdays,
9:00 a.m.-Noon
May-October
Contact: Charles Bland
1203 Bradley
Fulton, MO 65251
charlie54@charter.net
573-590-1817

Gordon's Orchard

P.O. Box 394
Osceola, MO 64776
417-646-8889

Hallsville Farmers' Market

Tuesdays, 4:00-6:00 p.m.
Saturdays, 2:00-6:00 p.m.
May 2-October 10
Contact: Christa Smith or Brian
Rickard
P.O. Box 284
Hallsville, MO 65255
smithchrista@umsystem.edu;
celtic_wyndes_farm@yahoo.com
573-881-6205 or 573-289-5908

Hartville Farmers' Market

Thursdays, 7:30-11:00 a.m.
Saturdays, 7:00 a.m.-Noon
May-September
Contact: Cody & Dawnnell Holmes
6156 Curtner Rd.
Norwood, MO 65717
cdholmes@hughes.net
417-259-CHKN (2456)

Hermann Farmers' Market

Wednesdays and Saturdays, 8:00 a.m.-?
May-October
Contact: Janet Rodgers
208 East First St.
Hermann, MO 65041
573-486-2121 ext. 4000

J & T Country Store

7706 N. State Hwy. 7
Roach, MO 65787-8079
573-347-3500

I-70 Farmers' Market

Mondays, 4:30-6:30 p.m.
late May-October
Saturdays, 9:00 a.m.-1:00 p.m.

June–September
Contact: Cathy Geary
14796 Burr Oak Rd.
Odessa, MO 64706
mom81549@yahoo.com
816-263-1914

Lafayette County Farmers' Market
Thursdays, 4:30-7:00 p.m.
mid-May through mid-August
Contact: Dale Klussman
600 Main St.
Concordia, MO 64020
concordiaadmin@galaxycable.net

Lafayette County Farmers' Market
Tuesdays, 4:30-7:00 p.m.
mid-April through mid-September
Contact: Ryan Cole
15 E. 20th St.
P.O. Box 675
Higginsville, MO 64037
jcole@ctcis.net
www.higginsvillechamber.org/market.
   aspx
660-238-6651

Lafayette County Farmers' Market
Wednesdays, 4:30-7:00 p.m.
May through August
1211 Main St.
Lexington, MO 64067
www.visitlexingtonmo.com

Lebanon Farmers' Market
Wednesdays 2:30-6:30 p.m.
Saturdays 7:30 a.m.-1:00 p.m.
April through October

Contact: Kate Bolden
13052 Hwy. NN
Eldridge, MO 65463
417-426-5690

Market on the Square: A Farmers' Market
Saturdays 8:00 a.m.-Noon Memorial
   Day-Labor Day
Set-up begins at 6:30 a.m., and vendors
   need to bring their own tables,
   canopies, etc.
Contact: Amy Crump and Kathy
   Fairchild
Marshall, MO 65340
mmotssc@gmail.com
660-886-3392 or 660-886-2233

Mexico Area Farmers' Market
Saturdays, 8:00-11:00 a.m., May-
   October
Wednesdays, 4:00-6:00 p.m., mid-July-
   August
Contact: Sue Caine
100 West Jackson
Mexico, MO 65265
scaine@mexico-chamber.org
www.mexico-chamber.org
800-581-2765

Mountain Grove Farmers' Market
Tuesdays and Thursdays, 2:00-6:00
   p.m.; Saturdays, 7:00 a.m.-Noon
May-October
Contact: Bob Long
2299 Stone Ridge Dr.
Mountain Grove, MO 65711
417-926-7813

Nature Girls

2100 N. Bishop Ave.
Rolla, MO 65401
573-341-1919
naturegirlshealthfood@gmail.com

Osceola Cheese Company

3700 NE Hwy. 13
Osceola, MO 64776
417-646-8131 or 417-646-2396
Open seven days a week, year round
info@osceolacheese.com
www.osceolacheese.com

Peculiar Farmers' & Artisans' Market

Saturdays, 7:30 a.m.-Noon
May-October
Contact: Doris Sherrick
10807 E. 205th St.
Peculiar, MO 64078
info@peculiarmarket.com
www.peculiarmarket.com
816-779-6708

Prairie Home General Store in Prairie Home

413 Hwy. Dr.
Prairie Home, MO 65068
660-841-5252
prairiehomegeneralstore@yahoo.com

Rasa Orchards

19510 Garr Rd.
Lexington, MO 64067-8239
660-259-2938

Rolla Farmers' Market

Tuesdays and Saturdays, 7:00 a.m.-Noon
May-October
Contact: Laura Weiss
Rolla, MO 65401
573-364-7855

Root Cellar

1023 E. Walnut St.
Columbia, MO 65201
573-443-5055

Russellville Farmers' Market

Saturdays, 9:00 a.m.-Noon
Contact: Jeanne Salmons
P.O. Box 129
Russellville, MO 65074
573-782-4682

SACBA Farmers' Market

Tuesdays, 3:00-6:00 p.m.; Saturdays, 7:30 a.m.-Noon
May-September
Contact: Chris Mathes
P.O. Box 732
Salem, MO 65560
sacba2@salemmo.com
573-247-3974

Schreiman Orchards

U.S. Hwy. 24
Waverly, MO 64096
SchreimanOrchards@hotmail.com
660-493-2477

St. James Farmers' Market

Fridays, 7:00 a.m.-Noon; Saturdays,
7:00 a.m.-Noon
May-October
Contact: Jamie Hunt, Tourism Director,
City of St. James
100 State Route B
St. James, MO 65559
director.tic@centurytel.net
www.stjamesmissouri.org
573-265-3899

Sedalia Area Farmers' Market

Saturdays, 9:00 a.m.-1:00 p.m.;
Tuesdays 3:00-6:00 p.m.
May-October
Contact: Beverly Rollings
c/o Sedalia Area Chamber of
Commerce
600 E. Third
Sedalia, MO 65301
info@sedaliaareafarmersmarket.com
www.sedaliaareafarmersmarket.com
660-826-2222

Sibley Orchard

3717 N. Buckner Tarsney Rd.
Sibley, MO 64088
816-650-5535
www.sibleyorchards.com

Slater/Saline Farmers' Market

Tuesdays and Fridays, 2:30-5:00 p.m.
Contact: Geary Norris
P.O. Box 12
Slater, MO 65349
gearynor@yahoo.com
660-529-2171

Templeton's Orchard

21940 Hodge Rd.
Dover, MO 64022
660-259-3838

Thursday Nite Farmers' Market

Thursdays, 5:00-8:30 p.m.
Mid-July-Late October
Contact: Marcia Cotton
411 Taylor Lane
Belton, MO 64012

Versailles Area Farmers' Market

Thursdays, 3:00-7:00 p.m.
Starting May
Contact: Jim Kykzeul
P.O. Box 256
Versailles, MO 65084
tulipfieldsllc@yahoo.com
573-378-4401 or 573-378-0303

Warsaw Farmers' Market

Saturdays, 7:00 a.m.-Noon
May-October
(Second Saturday in May thru last
Saturday in October)
Contact: Connie Mefford
1551 Commercial St.
Warsaw, MO 65355
meffordc@missouri.edu
www.extension.missouri.edu/benton
660-438-5012

CSAs

Pierpont Farms

8810 S. Route N
Columbia, MO 65203
573-499-9851; 573-356-0351; 573-
356-0352

Seven Gables Farm
4487 Elder Rd.
Villa Ridge, MO 63089
636-451-5745
timothyortmann@yahoo.com
www.sevengablesfarmorganic.com

Restaurants

Abigail's
206 Central St.
Rocheport, MO 65279
573-698-3000
www.abigails-restaurant.com

Broadway Brewery
6 E. Broadway
Columbia, MO 65201
573-443-5054
www.broadwaybrewery.com

Café Berlin
220 N. 10th at Park
Columbia, MO 65201
573-441-0400
www.cafeberlincomo.com

Cherry Street Wine Seller and Bistro
505 Cherry St.
Columbia, MO 65201-4242
573-442-7281
www.winecellarbistro.com

Glenn's Café
Main and High St. (at the Frederick
    Hotel)
Boonville, MO 65233
660-882-9191
www.glennscafe.com

Les Bourgeois Winery and Bistro
14020 W. Hwy. BB
Rocheport, MO 65279
573.698.2133
www.missouriwine.com

The Main Squeeze
28 S. Ninth St.
Columbia, MO 65201
573-817-5616
www.main-squeeze.com

Red and Moe's
21 N. 9th St.
Columbia, MO 65201
573-777-8654
www.redandmoe.com

Sycamore
800 E. Broadway
Columbia, MO 65201
573-874-8090
sycamore.restaurant@gmail.com
sycamorerestaurant.com

Uprise Bakery
10 Hitt St.
Columbia, MO 65201-5014
573-256-2265
www.uprisebakery.com

St. Louis Region

Stores and Markets

Baumann's Fine Meats
8829 Manchester Rd.
St. Louis, MO 63144
314-968-3080
sales@baumannsfinemeats.com
www.baumannsfinemeats.com

Byrnes Mill Farmers' Market
Alternating Fridays, May-October
3:00-7:30 p.m.
Contact: Susan Gibson
3751 South Lakeshore Drive
Byrnes Mill, MO 63051
moonvalleyvista@charter.net
www.byrnesmill.org
636-677-0514

Carondelet Farmers' Market
Saturdays 8:00 a.m.-Noon
June-October
Contact: Sister Mary Ann Nestel
6408 Michigan Ave.
St. Louis, MO 63111
nestelcsj@aol.com
314-752-6339

Chandler Hill Farmers' Market
596 Defiance Rd.
Defiance, MO 63341
May-October
On the grounds of Chandler Hill
    Vineyards in Defiance, MO
Sundays only Noon-4 p.m.

Contact Information: Leigh Sweet
www.chandlerhillvineyards.com
636-798-2675

Clayton Farmers' Market
Saturdays, 8:30 a.m.-Noon
May-October
Contact: Trip Straub
15830 Fountain Plaza
Ellisville, MO 63017
trip@straubs.com
www.claytonfarmersmarket.com
636-779-8500 ext 246 or cell: 314-566-
    6011

Connie's Produce & Plants
1257 Saint Peters Cottleville Rd.
St. Peters, MO 63376
636-498-2500

Cornerstone Nutrition, Inc.
17701 Edison Ave. #102
Chesterfield, MO 63005
636-537-5858

Crown Valley Farmers Market and Winery
7 days a week 8:00 a.m.-3:30 p.m.
Open until 5 on Fri. & Sat. in the fall
Contact: Sarah Krannig
23589 State Rt
Ste. Genevieve, MO 63670
skrannig@crownvalleywinery.com
www.crownvalleywinery.com
573-760-8876

Crystal City Farmers' Market

Wednesdays, 4:00-8:00 p.m.
May-October
Contact: Ben DeClue
200 Taylor Ave.
Crystal City, MO 63019
ccfarmersmarket@gmail.com
www.crystalcityfarmersmarket.blogspot.
   com
636-937-0288 or 314-630-0280

Delmar Food and Farm Market

Contact: Sandra Zak
4437 Laclede Ave
St. Louis, MO 63108
4100@charter.net
314-534-6166

DeSoto Farmers' Market

Saturdays, May-October
8:00 a.m.-Noon
Contact: Debby Campbell
DeSoto, MO
buyfreshlocal@gmail.com
www.buyfreshlocal.blogspot.com
636-586-4570

Earth Mother Foods

220 E. Harrison St.
Farmington, MO 63640
573-756-7852

Ellisville Farmers' Market

Thursdays, 4:00-7:00 p.m.
May-October
Contact: René Sackett
225 Kiefer Creek Rd.
Ellisville, MO 63021

renewhatsup@yahoo.com
ellisvillefarmersmarket.org
314-435-9445

Farmington Farmers' Market

Wednesdays 2:00-5:00 p.m.
May-October;
Saturdays, 7:00-11:00 a.m.
April-October
Contact: Ginny Smith
15 Winchester Rd.
Farmington, MO 63640
vsmith@wildblue.net; ozora@brick.net
573-756-2284

Ferguson Farmers' Market

Saturdays, 8:00 a.m.-Noon
May-end of October
Contact: Kathleen Noelker
20 S. Florissant Rd.
Ferguson, MO 63135
knoelker@sbcglobal.net
www.fergusonfarmersmarket.com
314-324-4298

Foristell Farmers' Market

Saturdays, 9:00 a.m.-1:00 p.m.
June-October
Contact: Zell Setzer
1125 Dietrich Rd.
Foristell, MO 63348
admin@valleyfarms.info
www.valleyfarms.info/home.htm
636-463-1205

Freddie's Market

9052 Big Bend Blvd.
St. Louis, MO
314-968-1914

Frick's Market in Sullivan and Union

10 East Locust St.
Union, MO 63084-1893
636-583-2181

Garden Gate Shop at the Missouri Botanical Garden

4344 Shaw Blvd.
St. Louis, MO 63110
314-577-5137
www.gardengateshop.org

Good 4 You Nutrition

3940 Jeffco Blvd.
Arnold, MO 63010
636-467-2000

Greene's Country Store

8621 Hwy. N
Lake Saint Louis, MO 63367
636-561-6637
info@greenescountrystore.com
greenescountrystore.com

John's Butcher Shoppee

2608 Walton Rd.
St. Louis, MO 63114
314-423-8066
503 N. Mill St.
Festus, MO 63028
636-931-7776
johnsbutchershoppee.com

K & R Market in Marthasville

15971 State Hwy. 47
Marthasville, MO 63357
636-433-2584
www.KandRMarket.com

Kirkwood Farmers' Market

Monday-Friday 9:00 a.m.-6:00 p.m.
8:00 a.m.-5:00 p.m. Saturdays
April-September
Contact market for winter hours and
   days. Sunday hours vary by vendor.
Contact: Kori Thompson
130 E. Jefferson floor 2
Kirkwood, MO 63122
info@downtownkirkwood.com
www.downtownkirkwood.com
314-822-0084

Loaves and Fishes (L&F) in Washington

1035 Washington Sq.
Washington, MO 63090
636-239-2373
loavesandfishes@centurytel.net
www.lnfshop.com

Local Harvest Grocery

3108 Morgan Ford Rd.
St. Louis, MO 63116
314-865-5260
www.localharvestgrocery.com

Mannino's Market

5205 Hwy. North
Cottleville, MO 63338
636-441-7755
5023 Hwy. P
Flint Hill, MO 63346
636.332.3212
www.manninosmarket.com

Maplewood Farmers' Market

Wednesdays, 4:00-7:00 p.m.
April-October
Contact: Schlafly Bottleworks
7260 Southwest Blvd.
Maplewood, MO 63143
farmersmarket@schlafly.com
314-241-2337

Market in the Loop

Thursdays, Fridays, and Saturdays, 7:00
    a.m.-6:00 p.m.
Year-round
Contact: Dan Wald
8420 Delmar, Suite 406
St. Louis, MO 63124
rodanmgmt@aol.com
www.themarketintheloop.com
314-991-3300

Maude's Market

4219 Virginia Ave.
St. Louis, MO 63111
314-353-4219
www.MaudesMarket.com

The Natural Way (3 locations)

8110 Big Bend Blvd.
St. Louis, MO 63119
314-961-3541
12345 Olive Blvd.
St. Louis, MO 63141
314-878-3001
468 Old Smizer Mill Rd. (Hwy. 141
    and Gravois)
Fenton, MO 63026
636-343-4343
www.thenatway.com

New Haven Farmers' Market

Thursdays, 4:00 p.m.-to dusk, rain or shine
April-September
If there is inclement weather, the market
    is held inside the Riverfront Cultural
    Society.
Contact: Janelle Hoffmann
P.O. Box 149
New Haven, MO 63068
janelle@riverfrontsociety.com
www.riverfrontsociety.com
573-237-5100

North City Farmers' Market

Saturdays, 9:00 a.m.-Noon
June to October
Contact: Julia Weese-Young
2800 N. 14th St.
St. Louis, MO 63107
julia@northcityfarmersmarket.org
www.northcityfarmersmarket.blogspot.com
314-241-5031

Nutrition Stop

4101-K Mexico Rd.
St. Peters, MO 63376
636-928-7550

O'Fallon Farmers' & Artists' Market

900 TR Hughes Blvd.
O'Fallon, MO 63366
2011 Season: Every Saturday in mid-
    April-mid-October
8:00 a.m.-Noon
Contact: Wendy Glidden
P.O. Box 514
O'Fallon, MO 63366
ofallonfarmersmarket@gmail.com
636-293-1256

Overland Farmers' Market
Saturdays May-October
Contact: Michael Oakes
P.O. Box 142728
Overland, MO 63114
moakes-jenahrealty@sbcglobal.net
overlandfarmersmarket.com
314-769-6360

Planet Health
5 Clarkson Rd.
Ellisville, MO 63011
636-527-8888

River Hills Farmers' Market-Silex
Second and Fourth Saturdays, 7:00
a.m.-Noon
Contact: Paul Harter
1010 S. Muldrow St.
Mexico, MO 65265
pbr4320@sbcglobal.net
573-721-6223 or 573-384-5859

River Hills Farmers' Market—Troy
First and Third Saturdays, 8:30 a.m.-
1:00 p.m.
Contact: Paul Harter
1010 S. Muldrow St.
Mexico, MO 65265
pbr4320@sbcglobal.net
573-721-6223 or 573-384-5859

Route 66 Farmers' Market
7 days a week 8:00 a.m. -Noon
May-October
Contact: Terry Triphahn
920 Plaza Dr., Suite F
St. Clair, MO 63077
chamber@stclairmo.com
636-629-1889

Sappington Farmers' Market
8400 Watson Rd.
St. Louis, MO 63119
314-843-7848

St. Charles Lions Club Farmers' Market
Saturdays, 7:00 a.m.-Noon
May-October
Contact: Gerry Shatro
907 Lindenwood
St. Charles, MO 63301
636-723-2412

Ste. Genevieve Farmers' Market
Saturdays, 7:00 a.m.-Noon
May-October
Contact: Jim Bruckerhoff
9951 N. Hwy. 61
St. Mary, MO 63673
573-543-2562

St. Louis Community Farmers' Market
Second Saturday of the month, 9:00 a.m.-
1:00 p.m.
November-April
Contact: Michael McLellan
4021 Wyoming St.
St. Louis, MO 63116
stlcfm@gmail.com
314-856-5557

Soulard Farmers' Market
Wednesdays through Fridays, 8:00 a.m.-
5:00 p.m.; Saturdays, 6:00 a.m.-5:00 p.m.
Year-round
730 Carroll St.
St. Louis, MO 63104
market@stlouis.missouri.org
www.soulardmarket.com
314-622-4180

South Hampton Farmers' Market
Saturdays, 8:00 a.m.-1:00 p.m.
May-October
Contact: Maria Gianino
7526 Big Bend Ave.
St. Louis, MO 63119
sohafarmersmarket@yahoo.com
314-647-4635

T-Bones Natural Meats
121 O'Fallon Commons Dr.
O'Fallon, MO 63368
636-272-0422
www.tbonesstore.com

Tower Grove Farmers' Market
Saturdays, 8:30 a.m. to 12:30 p.m.
May-October
Contact: Patrick Horine
3877 Connecticut
St. Louis, MO 63116
contact@tgmarket.org
www.tgmarket.org
314-772-3899

Union Farmers' Market
Wednesdays 3:30-5:30 p.m.
Saturdays 6:00-11:00 a.m.
Contact: Joseph A. Graves
500 E. Locust St.
Union, MO 63084
www.unionmissouri.org/farmersmarket
636-583-3600

Warren County Farmers' Market
Thursdays, 4:00-6:30 p.m.
May-October
Contact: Irv Huser
17736 Keller Dr.

Wright City, MO 63390
636-456-3066

Warrenton Farmers' Market
Saturdays, 8:00-11:00 a.m.
July-September
Contact: Lyndsay Carson
200 West Booneslick
Warrenton, MO 63383
specialevents@warrenton-mo.org
www.warrenton-mo.org
636-456-3535

Warson Woods Farmers' Market
Tuesdays, 3:00-7:00 p.m.
May-October
Contact: Sally Scott
10001 Manchester Rd.
Warson Woods, MO 63122
emporium.stl@sbcglobal.net
314-909-0100

Washington Farmers' Market
Saturdays, 8:00-2:00 p.m.
April-October
Wednesdays, 3:00-6:00 p.m.
Contact market for winter hours and days.
Contact: Amanda Griesheimer
317 West Main St.
Washington, MO 63090
agriesheimer@washmo.org
www.washmo.org
636-239-2715 ext. 106

Washington County Farmers' Market—Health Department
Wednesdays, 7:30 a.m.-2:00 p.m.
July-October
Contact: Shawnee Douglas

310 Cedar Dr.
Potosi, MO 63664
573-438-2164

Washington County Farmers' Market—Courthouse

Saturdays, 7:30 a.m.-Noon
June-October
Contact: Shawnee Douglas
310 Cedar Dr.
Potosi, MO 63664
573-438-2164

Webster Groves Farmers' Market

May-October
Contact: Angela Foley
#4 E. Lockwood Ave.
Webster Groves, MO 63119
info@webstergrovesfarmersmarket.com
www.webstergrovesfarmersmarket.com
314-963-5696 x888

Wildwood Farmers' Market

Saturdays, 8:00 a.m.-1:30 p.m.
May-October
Contact: Glenn Gaehle
18538 Hardt Rd.
Glencoe, MO 63038
wildwoodfarmersmarket@gmail.com
www.wildwoodfarmersmarket.com
314-486-2562

Wine and Cheese Place (4 locations)

7435 Forsyth Blvd.
Clayton MO, 63105
314-727-8788
9755 Manchester Rd.
Rock Hill MO, 63119

314-962-8150
14748 Clayton Rd.
Ballwin, MO 63011
636-227-9001
457 North New Ballas Rd.
Creve Coeur, MO 63141
314-989-0020
wineandcheeseplace.com

CSAs

Dry Dock, Silex

29 Silex Elevator Rd.
Silex, MO 63377
573-384-5859

Earth Dance Farms

302 Thoroughman Ave.
St. Louis, MO 63135
314-521-1006
earthdancefarms@gmail.com
www.earthdancefarms.org

Fair Shares

www.fairshares.org/front

Local Harvest

3108 Morgan Ford Rd.
St. Louis, MO 63116
314-865-5260
www.localharvestgrocery.com

Maude's Market

4219 Virginia Ave.
St. Louis, MO 63111
314-353-4219
www.MaudesMarket.com

Rutherford Farms
741 Hwy. TT
Silex, MO 63377
636-279-5350

Restaurants

360 St. Louis
1 South Broadway
St. Louis, MO 63102
314-241-8439
www.360-stl.com

Acero
7266 Manchester Rd.
St. Louis, MO 63143
314-644-1790
www.fialafood.com

Almonds
8127 Maryland Ave.
Clayton, MO 63105
314-725-1019
www.almondsrestaurant.com

Annie Gunn's
16806 Chesterfield Airport Rd.
Chesterfield, MO 63005
636-532-3314
www.anniegunns.com

Atlas Restaurant
5513 Pershing Ave.
St. Louis, MO 63112
314-367-6800
www.atlasrestaurantstl.com

BC's Kitchen
11 Meadow Circle Dr.
Lake St. Louis, MO 63367
636-542-9090
www.billcardwell.com

Big Sky Café
47 S. Old Orchard Ave.
St. Louis, MO 63119
314-962-5757
www.bigskycafe.net

Bixby's at the Missouri History Museum
5700 Lindell Blvd.
St Louis, MO 63112
314-361-7313
www.bixbys-mohistory.com/index.php

Blood and Sand
1500 St. Charles St.
St. Louis, MO 63103
314-241-7263
www.bloodandsandstl.com

Bon Appetit Dining Services
Washington University Dining Services
St. Louis, MO

Bottleworks
7260 Southwest Ave.
St. Louis, MO 63143
314-241-2337
www.schlafly.com

Brasserie by Niche
4580 Laclede Ave.
St. Louis, MO 63108
314-454-0600
www.brasseriebyniche.com

Café Osage
4605 Olive St.
St. Louis, MO 63108
314-454-6868
www.bowoodfarms.com

Café Provencal
427 S. Kirkwood Rd.
St. Louis, MO 63122
314-822-5440
www.cafeprovencal.com

Cardwell's at the Plaza
97 Plaza Frontenac
St. Louis, MO 63131
314-997-8885
www.cardwellsattheplaza.com

Cielo
Four Seasons Hotel
999 N. 2nd St.
St. Louis, MO 63102
314-881-5800
www.cielostlouis.com

Cowan's Restaurant
114 Elm St.
Washington, MO 63090
636-239-3213
www.cowansrestaurant.com

The Crossing
7823 Forsyth Blvd.
Clayton, MO 63105
314-721-7375
www.fialafood.com

Dressel's Pub
419 N. Euclid Ave.
St. Louis, MO 63108
314-361-1060
www.dresselspublichouse.com

Eclipse at the Moon Rise Hotel
6177 Delmar Blvd.
St. Louis, MO 63112
314-726-2222
www.eclipsestlouis.com

Farmhaus
3257 Ivanhoe Ave.
St. Louis, MO 63139
314-647-3800
www.farmhausrestaurant.com

Five Bistro
5100 Daggett Ave.
St. Louis, MO 63110
314-773-5553
www.fivebistro.com

Foundation Grounds
7298 Manchester Rd.
Maplewood, MO 63143
314-601-3588
www.foundationgrounds.com

Franco

1535 South Eighth St.
St. Louis, MO 63104
314-436-2500
www.eatatfranco.com

Fresh Gatherings @ St. Louis University

Grand & Park, School of Allied Health
   Professions
St Louis, MO 63108
314-977-1154

Harvest

1059 South Big Bend
St. Louis, MO 63117
314-645-3522
www.harveststlouis.com

I Fratellini

7624 Wydown Blvd.
St. Louis, MO 63105
314-727-7901

La Dolce Via Bakery & Cafe

4470 Arco Ave.
St. Louis, MO 63110
314-534-1699
www.ladolceviabakery.com

Latitude 26

6407 Clayton Ave.
St. Louis, MO 63139
314-932-5600
www.latitude26texmex.com

Liluma

238 N. Euclid at Maryland
St. Louis, MO 63108
314-361-7771
www.fialafood.com

Local Harvest Café

3137 Morgan Ford Rd.
St. Louis, MO 63116
314-772-8815
www.localharvestcafe.com

Lucas Park Grille

1234 Washington Ave.
St. Louis, MO 63103
314-241-7770
www.lucasparkgrille.com

Mad Tomato

8000 Carondelet
St. Louis, MO 63105
314-932-5733
www.madtomatostl.com

McCormick & Schmick's

17 West County Center
Des Peres, MO 63131
314-835-1300
www.mccormickandschmicks.com

Mike Shannon's

620 Market St.
St. Louis, MO 63101
314-421-1540
www.ShannonSteak.com

Mosaic
1001 Washington Ave.
St. Louis, MO 63101
314-621-6001
www.mosaicrestaurants.com

Mud House
2101 Cherokee St.
St. Louis, MO 63139
314-772-8815
www.mudhousecoffee.com

Niche Restaurant
7734 Forsyth
Clayton, MO 63105
314-773-7755
www.nichestlouis.com

Onesto Pizza
5401 Finkman St.
St. Louis, MO 63109
314-802-8883
www.onestopizza.com

Prime 1000
1000 Washington Ave.
St. Louis, MO 63101
314-241-1000
www.prime1000.com

PW Pizza
2017 Chouteau Ave.
St. Louis, MO 63103
314-241-7799
www.pwpizza.com

St. Louis Racquet Club
476 N. Kingshighway Blvd.
St. Louis, MO 63108-1296
314-361-2100

Range
920 Olive St.
St. Louis, MO 63101
314-241-8121
www.baileysrange.com

Robust Wine Bar Cafe
227 W. Lockwood
Webster Groves, MO 63119
314-963-0033
www.robustwinebar.com

Salt
4356 Lindell Blvd.
St. Louis, MO 63108
314-932-5787
www.enjoysalt.com

Salume Beddu
3467 Hampton Ave.
St. Louis, MO 63139
314-353-3100
www.salumebeddu.com

Scottish Arms
8 S. Sarah St.
St. Louis, MO 63108
314-535-0551
www.thescottisharms.com

Shaved Duck

2900 Virginia Ave.
St. Louis, MO 63118
314-776-1407
www.theshavedduck.com

Sidney Street Café

2000 Sidney St.
St. Louis, MO 63118
314-771-5777
www.sidneystreetcafe.com

Sqwires

1415 S. 18th St.
St. Louis, MO 63104
314-865-3522
www.sqwires.com

Stellina Pasta

3342 Watson Rd.
St. Louis, MO 63139
314-256-1600
www.stellinapasta.com

Sub Zero Vodka Bar

308 N. Euclid Ave.
St. Louis, MO 63108
314-367-1200
www.subzerovodkabar.com

Taste

4582 Laclede Ave.
St. Louis, MO 63108
314-361-1200
www.tastebarstl.com

Todd's Canteen

5642 Gravois Rd.
House Springs, MO 63051
636-285-7522

Train Wreck Saloon (2 locations)

9243 Manchester Rd.
St. Louis, MO 63144
314-962-8148
314 Westport Plz.
St. Louis, MO 63146
314-434-7222
www.trainwrecksaloon.com

Truffles in Ladue

9202 Clayton Rd.
St. Louis, MO 63124
314-621-1996
www.trufflesinladue.com

Winslow's Home

7213 Delmar Blvd.
St. Louis, MO 63130
314-725-7559
www.winslowshome.com

Yia-Yia's Euro Café

15601 Olive Blvd.
Chesterfield, MO 63017
636-537-9991
www.yiayias.com/stl

Kansas City Region

Stores and Markets

Antoine's Seed and Supplies
1000 S. Crysler Ave.
Independence, MO 64052
orders@antoineseed.com
www.independencefarmersmarket.com
816-252-8860

BADSEED Funky Friday Night Farmers' Market
Fridays, 4:30-9:00 p.m.
May-November
Contact the market for winter hours.
Contact: Brooke Salvaggio
1909 McGee
Kansas City, MO 64108
badseedfarm@hotmail.com
www.badseedfarm.com
913-522-3458

Bannister Federal Complex Farmers' Market
Tuesdays, 10:30 a.m.-1:30 p.m.
June-September
Contact: Debbie Crow
6501 Beacon Drive
Kansas City, MO 64133
deborah.crow@kcc.usda.gov
816-926-3039

The Better Cheddar
604 W. 48th St.
Kansas City, MO 64112
816-561-8204
www.thebettercheddar.com

Blue Springs Farmers' Market
Saturdays 7:00 a.m.-Noon
May-October
Contact: Chris Williams
412 East Mason
Odessa, MO 64076
bluespringsfarmersmarket@yahoo.com
www.bluespringsfarmersmarket.com
816-230-0007

Briarcliff Farmers' Market
Thursdays, 3:00-7:00 p.m.
May-September
Contact: Kasey Rausch
4175 Mulberry Dr.
Kansas City, MO 64116
kaseyr@greenacres.com
www.briarcliffvillagekc.com
816-746-0010 ext. 206

Cass County Farmers' Market
Wednesdays, 3:00-6:00 p.m.; Saturdays, 7:30 a.m.-Noon
May-October
2601 Cantrell
Harrisonville, MO 64701
www.cassfarmers.com
816-726-5213

Cellar Rat Wine Merchants
1701 Baltimore
Kansas City, MO 64108
816-221-9463
www.cellarratwine.com

Chilhowee Main Street Farmers' Market

Saturdays, 8:00 a.m.-Noon

May-November

Contact: Melody Robinson

P.O. Box 183

Chilhowee, MO 64733

cityofchilhowee@centurylink.net

mainstreetfarmersmarket.webs.com

660-678-3738

Clinton Farmers' Market

Tuesdays, 2:00 p.m.-sellout; Saturdays,
7:00 a.m.-sellout

April-October

Contact: Jennifer Shadwick

100 W. Jefferson

Clinton, MO 64735

fizzicians@hotmail.com

660-885-4700

Consentino's Market (2 locations)

10 E. 13th St.

Kansas City, MO 64106

816-595-0050

14 W. 62nd Ter.

Kansas City, MO 64113

816-523-3700

www.cosentinos.com

Downtown Lee's Summit Farmers' Market

Wednesdays and Saturdays, 7:00 a.m.-
sellout

April-November

Contact: Stacy Brandt

226 SE Douglas, Ste. #203

P.O. Box 1688

Lee's Summit, MO 64063

events@downtownls.org

www.downtownls.org

816-246-6598

The Farmers' Community Market at Brookside

Saturdays, 8:00 a.m.-1:00 p.m.

Starting April

Contact: Tim Walters

P.O. Box 7088

Kansas City, MO 64113

information@farmerscommunitymarket.
com

www.farmerscommunitymarket.com

816-719-0469

Gladstone Farmers' Market

Wednesdays 2:00-6:00 p.m.

May-September

Contact: Becky Jarrett

7010 N. Holmes

Gladstone, MO 64118

beckyj@gladstone.mo.us

www.facebook.com/pages/Gladstone-
Farmers-Market/107406389284555

816-436-2200

Golden Valley Produce & Craft Market

Tues., 1:00-5:30 p.m.; May-Oct.; Sat.,
8:00 a.m.-Noon; May and Oct. only

Saturdays, 7:00 a.m.-Noon; June-
September

Contact: Dennis Winkler

549 NE 251st Rd.

Clinton, MO 64735

sue.stropes@gmail.com

660-351-4757 or 816-405-9545

Grand Court Four Seasons Farmers' Market

Saturdays, all year
Contact: Tena Bellovich
10530 Askew Ave.
Kansas City, MO 64137
bellovicht@umkc.edu

Grandview Farmers' Market

Saturdays 7:00 a.m.-sellout
June-October
Contact: Johnna Clark
13705 Norby Rd.
Grandview, MO 64030
816-405-5561

Green Acres Market

4175 N. Mulberry Dr.
Kansas City, MO 64116
816-746-0010
www.greenacres.com

Hartman's Heritage Community Market

Tuesdays, 3:00-7:00 p.m. & Sundays,
10:00 a.m.-2:00 p.m.
June-September
Contact: Joe Antoine
1000 S. Crysler Avenue
Independence, MO 64052
816-252-8860
orders@antoineseed.com
www.independencefarmersmarket.com

Historic Downtown Liberty Farmers' Market

Saturdays, 7:00 a.m.-Noon
May-October
Contact: Patrick McDowell
Liberty's Courthouse Square
(Franklin, Main, Kansas, and Water
streets)
Liberty, MO 64068
www.historicdowntownliberty.org
816-781-3575

Holden Farmers' Market

Saturdays, 7:00 a.m.-Noon or sellout
June-September
Contact: Jo Ann Nolan
1551 SW 25th Rd.
Kingsville, MO 64061
info@holdenmarket.com
www.holdenmarket.com
816-597-3353

Kansas City City Market

Summer Hours—March-October;
Saturdays 6:00 a.m.-3:00 p.m.,
Sundays 8:00 a.m.-3:00 p.m.,
Wednesdays 10:00 a.m.-2:00 p.m.
Winter Hours—November-March;
Saturdays 7:00 a.m.-3:00 p.m.,
Sundays 7:00 a.m.-3:00 p.m.,
Wednesdays 8:00 a.m.-2:00 p.m.
(City Market special events may require
an early closing.)
Contact: Deb Connors
20 East Fifth St., Suite 201
Kansas City, MO 64106
dconnors@cwbkc.com
www.thecitymarket.org
816-842-1271

KC Organics and Natural Market

Saturdays, 8:00 a.m.-12:30 p.m.
May-mid-October
(Contact market for winter hours and
     days.)
Contact: Peter Stauffer
5725 McGee
Kansas City, MO 64113
kcorganics@yahoo.com
www.kcorganics.com
816-444-FOOD (3663)

Independence Farmers' & Craft Market

During May farmers are there on
     Saturdays, 5:00 a.m.-1:00 p.m.
During June-October crafters and
     farmers are there on Saturdays and
     Wednesdays, 5:00 a.m.-1:00 p.m.
Contact: Joe Antoine
Antoine's Seed and Supplies
1000 S. Crysler Ave.
Independence, MO 64052
orders@antoineseed.com
www.independencefarmersmarket.com
816-252-8860

Lawson Farmers' Market

Thursdays 4:00-7:00 p.m.
1st Thursday in May through October
Contact: Chrissy Craig
19502 N. U.S. 69
Lawson, MO 64062
lawsonfarmersmarket@yahoo.com
816-296-1232

Liberty Wednesday Farmers' Market

Wednesdays, 7:00 a.m.-Noon
May-October
Contact: Clara Hanks

4850 SW Middle Rd.
Plattsburg, MO 64477
williamslhanks482@centurytel.net
816-930-2175

Martin City Farm and Outdoor Market

Saturdays 9:00 a.m.-1:00 p.m.
May-October
Contact: Tami Bourquin
11936 W. 119th St., Suite 189
Overland Park, KS 66213
tami@generationrelevant.com
913-317-6363

Nature's Market

551 SE Melody Ln.
Lees Summit, MO 64063
816-525-2625

Nature's Own

4301 Main
Kansas City, MO 64111
816-997-9420

Nature's Pantry

19019 E. 48th St. S.
Independence, MO 64055
816-478-1990
www.pantry.biz

North Kansas City Farmers' Market

Open 7:00 a.m.-1:00 p.m. Fridays
May-October
Contact: Rick Groves
406 Armour Rd.
North Kansas City, MO 64116
richard@nkcbusinesscouncil.com
816-472-7700 or 816-345-9339

Paradise Locker Meats
405 W. Birch St.,
Trimble, MO 64492
816-370-6328
Paradisemeats.com

Parkville Farmers' Market
Wednesdays, 2:00-5:00 p.m., June 10-rest
of season; Saturdays, 7:00 a.m.-sellout
April-October
Contact: Shelley Oberdiek
24440 Oberdiek Lane
Platte City, MO 64079
soberdiek@yahoo.com
816-330-3279

Patricia's Foods
1212 W. U.S. Hwy. 40
Odessa, MO 64076
816-633-4700

Platte City Farmers' Market
Wednesday, 4:00-7:00 p.m.; Saturday
mornings beginning at 7 a.m.
May-September
Contact: Mary Anne Brooks
P.O. Box 2305
Platte City, MO 64079
mbrooks826@kc.rr.com
www.plattecitymo.com
816-858-5306

Raymore's Original Town Farmers' Market
Tuesdays 4:00-8:00 p.m.
June-October
Contact: Janet Snook
1021 S. Madison (Parks and Rec Office)

Raymore, MO 64083
816-322-2791

Raytown City Center Market
Saturdays, 7:00 a.m.-sellout
June-November
Contact: Graham Cummings
10012 E. 63rd St.
Raytown, MO 64133
gcummings@kc.rr.com
816-590-6817

Rosedale Farmers' Market
340 Southwest Blvd.
Kansas City, KS 66103
913-645-7826
www.rosedalefarmersmarket.com

South Kansas City's Farmers' Market
Saturdays and Sundays, 9:00 a.m.-3:00
p.m.
June-November
Contact: Wardell Williams
2917 E. 29th St.
Kansas City, MO 64128
skcmofm@gmail.com
816-507-4796

The Sunday Market, Unity Temple the Plaza
1st and 3rd Sundays of each month,
9:00 a.m.-1:00 p.m.
Contact: Greg Clootz
707 W. 47th St.
Kansas City, MO 64112
sundayMarket@edenalley.com
www.edenalley.com

Troostwood Youth Garden Market

Saturdays, 8:00 a.m.-2:00 p.m.
May-October
Youth are providing fresh and healthy
    vegetables from A to Z.
Contact: Ericka Wright
5142 Paseo
Kansas City, MO 64110
troostwood@kcfoodcircle.org
816-444-5788
www.KCFoodCircle.org/growers/
    troostwood/

Troque Farms Store

31710 E. Oakland School Rd.
Buckner, MO 64016
816-215-9925
troquefarms.net, troquefarms@aol.com

Van Till Farms and Rayville Baking Co.

13986 Hwy. C
Rayville, MO 64084
816-776-2720
www.rayvillebaking.com

Waldo Farmers' Market

303 W. 79th St.
Kansas City, MO 64114
www.wholesomewaldowednesdays.org

Warrensburg Farmers' Market

Wednesdays, 4:30-6:30 p.m.
May-October
Saturdays, 7:00 a.m.-sellout, April–
    October
Contact: Jessica Rhodes
111 North Holden
Warrensburg, MO 64093
660-229-0899
wmainst@embarqmail.com
www.warrensburgmainstreet.com

Westport Plaza Farmers' Market

Wednesdays, 4:30-7:30 p.m.
May-October
Contact: David Bennett
Kansas City, MO
freelingd@yahoo.com
www.farmersmarketkc.org
913-432-4101

Zona Rosa Farmers' Market

Tuesdays, 4:00-8:00 p.m. or sellout
June-September
Contact: Brenda Noorbakhsh
8640 N. Dixson Ave.
Kansas City, MO 64153
bnoorbakhsh@steiner.com
www.zonarosa.com
816-587-8180

CSAs

Barham Cattle Company

Kearney, MO
816-628-4567; 816-365-2445
barhamcattleco@embarqmail.com

Door to Door Organics

110 E. 3rd St.
Kansas City, MO 64106
877-711-3636
kc.doortodoororganics.com

Heartland Organic World

1800 E. 231 St.
Cleveland, MO 64734
913-530-3277
www.heartlandorganicworld.com

Karbaumer Farm

Klaus and Lee Karbaumer

12200 Missouri Hwy. 92
Platte City, MO 64079
816-270-2177

Parker Farms Natural Meats
Richmond, MO 64085
816-470-FARM (3276)
parkerfarms@peoplepc.com
www.ParkerFarmsMeats.com

Restaurants

The American
200 E. 25th St.
Kansas City, MO 64108
816-545-8001
www.theamericanrestaurantkc.com

Blue Bird Bistro
1700 Summit
Kansas City, MO 64108
816-221-7559
www.bluebirdbistro.com

Blue Grotto
6324 Brookside Pl.
Kansas City, MO 64113
816-361-3473
www.bluegrottobrookside.com

Bluestem Restaurant
900 Westport Rd.
Kansas City, MO 64111
816-561-1101
www.bluestemkc.com

**Café Sebastienne
(at Kemper Art Museum)**
4420 Warwick Blvd.
Kansas City, MO 64111

816-561-7740
www.kemperart.org/cafe

Courthouse Exchange Restaurant
113 W. Lexington Ave.
Independence, MO 64050
816-252-0344
www.courthouseexchange.com

Eden Alley Café
707 W. 47th St.
(lower level of Unity Temple)
Kansas City, MO 64112
816-561-5415
www.edenalley.com

Farmhouse
300 Delaware St.
Kansas City, MO 64105
816-569-6032
www.eatatthefarmhouse.com

Grünauer
101 W. 22nd St.
Kansas City, MO 64108
816-283-3234
www.grunauerkc.com

Julian
6227 Brookside Plz.
Kansas City, MO 64113
816-214-8454
www.juliankc.com

Justus Drug Store (a Restaurant)
106 W Main St.
Smithville, MO 64089
816-532-2300
www.drugstorerestaurant.com

Le Fou Frog
400 E. 5th St.
Kansas City, MO 64106
816-474-6060
www.lefoufrog.com

Lidias
101 W. 22nd St.
Kansas City, MO 64108
816-221-3722
www.lidias-kc.com

The Majestic Restaurant
931 Broadway
Kansas City, MO 64105
816-221-1888
www.majestickc.com

Michael Smith's Restaurant
1900 Main St.
Kansas City, MO 64108
816-842-2202
www.michaelsmithkc.com

Rieger Hotel Grill and Exchange
1924 Main St.
Kansas City, MO 64108

816-471-2177
theriegerkc.com

Room 39
1719 W. 39th St.
Kansas City, MO 64111
816-753-3939
www.rm39.com

Starker's Restaurant
201 W. 47th St.
Kansas City, MO 64112
816-753-3565
www.starkersrestaurant.com

Westside Local
1663 Summit St.
Kansas City, MO 64108
816-997-9089
www.thewestsidelocal.com

You Say Tomato
2801 Holmes
Kansas City, MO 64109
816-756-5097
www.ystkc.com

Southwest Region
Stores and Markets

Aurora Local Farmers' Market
Wednesdays, 11:00 a.m.-sellout
Saturdays, 8:00 a.m.-Noon
May-October
Contact: Trish Matheny

19107 Lawrence 1202
Aurora, MO 65605
mathenytrish@yahoo.com
417-236-5101

Aurora Open Farmers' Market

Wednesdays, Noon-sellout
Saturdays, 7:00 a.m.-Noon
May-October
Contact: Bobby Garoutte
18093 Lawrence 2175
Aurora, MO 65605
417-678-0152

Ava Growers' Market

Saturdays, 7:00 a.m.-Noon
April-October
Contact: Arnold (Arne) Ahlstadt
Rt. 2, Box 503
Norwood, MO 65717
417-746-4006

B2B (Back to Basics) Farmers' Market

4:00-7:00 p.m. Tuesdays; 8:00 a.m.-
Noon Saturdays
Contact: Robin Killion
P.O. Box 85
Anderson, MO 64831
robin_killion@yahoo.com
417-845-0170

Branson Farmers' Market

Saturdays, 7:00 a.m.-Noon May
9-October
Contact: Angela Walker
events@downtownbranson.org
417-334-1548

Buckner's Orchard

10446 State Route 76
Reeds Spring, MO 65737
417-272-3429

Buffalo Farmers' Market

Tuesdays April-November
Starting June, first Saturdays of each
month
Tuesdays 3:00-7:00 p.m., Saturdays
10:00 a.m.-3:00 p.m. (events planned
each Saturday)
Contact: Faith Cannon
1011 W. McDaniel St.
Buffalo, MO 65622
bachfamilies@yahoo.com
417-345-4487 or 417-459-5014

C-Street Market (Commercial Street Market)

Tuesday evenings, 4:00-7:00 p.m.
Saturday mornings, 8:00 a.m.-Noon
April-October
Contact: Carolyn Elder
201 E. Commercial
Springfield, MO 65803
www.itsalldowntown.com/cstreet
417-343-4073

Carthage Farmers' Market

Wednesdays and Saturdays, 7:00 a.m.-
sellout
April-October
Contact: Ray Mathis
119 E. 3rd
Carthage, MO 64836
417-358-3579

Christian County Farmers' Market

1530 W. Jackson
Ozark, MO 65721
417-582-6246

Crab Shack Seafood Market
409 Northview Rd., Suite 1
Nixa, MO 65714
417-724-2234

Crane Creek Market "Arts and Crops"
Saturdays 8:00 a.m.-1:00 p.m.
July-October
Contact: Margie Williams
P.O. Box 317
Crane, MO 65633
417-723-5563

Dora Farmers' Market
Beginning mid-April
Saturday 8:00 a.m.-Noon
Contact: Leslie Collins
Route 1, Box 1685
Sycamore, MO 65760
lesliecolin@gmail.com
417-261-2242

Down to Earth Foods
1952 E. Grand St.
Springfield, MO 65804
417-501-1054
www.D2EFoods.com

Eastland Farmers' Market
Wednesdays-Saturdays, morning session
8:00 a.m.-1:00 p.m., afternoon
session 1:00-6:00 p.m.
Year-round beginning May 1, 2010
Contact: Mike McCamish
8071 E. Farm Rd. 148
Rogersville, MO 65742
m.mccamish@sbcglobal.net
Office: 417-862-1034; cell: 417-224-
5691

El Dorado Springs Farmers' Market
7:00-11:00 a.m. Saturdays
May-October
El Dorado Springs, MO 64744
417-876-3532 or 417-321-2000

Fair Grove Farmers' Market
Wednesdays, 3:30-7:00 p.m.
April-October
Contact: Debra VanBenthusen
8984 E. Farm Rd. 10
Fair Grove, MO 65648
debsgourds@yahoo.com
www.fairgrovefarmersmarket.com
417-459-9734

Farmers' Market in Fanning
Saturdays, 9:00 a.m.-Noon
Starting June, through season as available
Contact: Faye Howard or Joe Stubblefield
405 N. Park Ave.
Cuba, MO 65453
faye2838@centurytel.net
Faye: 573-885-2220 or Joe: 573-885-
7343

Farmers' Market of the Ozarks
Republic Rd.
Springfield, MO 65807
Matt O'Reilly: matt@dynamicearth.
net or Lane McConnell: Lane.
McConnell1390@gmail.com
573-489-0373

Forsyth Farmers' Market
Tuesdays, Thursdays, and Saturdays
7:00-10:00 a.m.
Contact: Brian Atchley
14974 U.S. Hwy. 160, Suite 4

Forsyth, MO 65653
trilakeorchards@yahoo.com
417-230-3188

Friday Night Market
Fridays, 6:00-9:00 p.m.; May-October
Contact: Rusty Worley
304 W. McDaniel
Springfield, MO 65806
rusty@itsalldowntown.com
417-831-6200

Galena Farmers' & Crafters Market
Fridays and Saturdays 8:00 a.m.-2:00
    p.m.
May-September
Contact: Paula Stewart
1074 Abesville
Galena, MO 65656
lstewartp@centurytel.net
417-357-6591

Garden Sass Farmers' Market
Tuesday 7:00-11:00 a.m. or Friday 7:00-
    11:00 a.m. and 3:00-7:00 p.m.
May to first frost
Contact: John Potter
P.O. Box 127
Wheaton, MO 64874
gardensass@potterfarm.com
www.gardensass.9f.com/index.html
417-489-6971

Greater Polk County Farmers' Market (merged with B.C.B.A. [Bolivar] Farmers' Market)
Tuesdays, 3:30-7:00 p.m. and Saturdays
    7:30-11:00 a.m. through Labor Day
    weekend. After Labor Day hours are

Saturday only 7:30-11:00 a.m.
April-October
Contact: Jim Gulick
P.O. Box 662
Bolivar, MO 65613
berrypatch1@windstream.net
417-777-4586

Greater Springfield Farmers' Market
Tuesdays, Thursdays, Saturdays, 8:30 a.m.
April-October
Contact: Don Bauers
1173 S. Maryland
Springfield, MO 65807
realmccoyfille1@yahoo.com
www.springfieldfarmersmarket.com
417-267-2371

Harter House Quality Meats
Various locations in and around
    Springfield, MO
www.harterhouse.com

Heather Hill Farms
5255 N. 17th St.
Ozark, MO 65721
417-581-7665

Homegrown Food
601 S. Pickwick
Springfield, MO 65804
417-868-7004
www.homegrownfoodstore.com

Hörmann Meat Company
690 Red Top Rd.
Fair Grove MO 65648
417-759-2027
sales@horrmannmeat.com

Jean's Healthway
110 W. Public Sq.
Ava, MO 65608
417-683-3026

Joplin Farmers' Market
Wednesdays and Saturdays, 9:00 a.m.-
2:00 p.m.
Contact: Beth Peacock
212 W. 8th St.
Joplin, MO 64801
bpeacock@joplinmo.org
417-623-3254

MaMa Jean's Natural Market
1727 S. Campbell
Springfield, MO
417-831-5229
1110 E. Republic St.
Springfield, MO 65807
415-881-5326
mamajeansmarket.com

Marshfield Farmers' Market
Fridays, 3:00-7:00 p.m.; May-October
Contact: Sue DeWitt
503 Macedonia Rd.
Niangua, MO 65713
jsdewitt@centurytel.net
417-473-6910

Monett Farmers' Market
Saturdays, 7:00 a.m.-Noon
May-October
Contact: May Xee Xiong
7758 FR 2112
Purdy, MO 65734
mycwiong@gmail.com
417-342-0812

Mount Vernon Farmers' Market
Saturdays, 7:00 a.m.-Noon
April-mid-October
Contact: Norma Grunwald
12885 Lawrence 2155
Mt. Vernon, MO 65712
daturanorma@aol.com
417-466-3029

Mountain Grove Farmers' Market
On the Square
Mountain Grove, MO 65711
417-926-4226

The Neosho Farmers' Market
Saturdays 8:00 a.m.-1:00 p.m. or sellout
May-October
Contact: Mary Horine or Craig Jones
203 E. Main
Neosho, MO 64850
tahoe_mary@hotmail.com;
cjones@neoshomo.org
417-451-8050

**Nevada/Vernon County Market
Square Days**
Saturdays, 8:00 a.m.-Noon, May-
October; Wednesdays, 5:30-7:00
p.m., June-October
Contact: Janet Wray and Leslie Carroll-
Bartlett
225 W. Austin, Suite 200
Nevada, MO 64772
janetwray@sbcglobal.net;
carroll-bartlettl@lmissouri.edu
417-448-1212

New Life Natural Foods
451 S. Springfield Ave.
Bolivar, MO 65613
417-326-5701
www.newlifenatural.com

Newton County Farmers' Market
Mondays-Saturdays, 7:00 a.m.-1:00 p.m.
May-Fall
Contact: Rosalie Garner
P.O. Box 96
Stark City, MO 64866
woofy@mo-net.com
417-638-5453

Nixa Area Farmers' Market
Tuesdays and Thursdays, 3:00-7:00 p.m.,
June-November 5
Saturday, 7:00 a.m.-3:00 p.m. April-
November
Contact: Roy King
2055 S Stewart Ste D
Springfield, MO 65804
nafm@rking.com
www.nixachamber.com
417-881-1300

Old #1 General Store
8890 Hwy. M
Huggins, MO 65484-9217
417-926-1695

Ozark Farmers' Market
Monday-Saturday, 9:00 a.m.-6:00 p.m.
Contact: Patricia Donaldson
Rt. 2 Box 2747
Alton, MO 65606
mes@ortrackm.missouri.org
417-778-7062

Ozark Square Farmers' Market
Thursdays, 5:00 p.m.-sellout, April
16-October 15
Contact: Robert Snook
P.O. Box 1327
Ozark, MO 65721
rsnook@ozarkmainstreet.org
www.ozarkmainstreet.org
417-582-6246

Parkcrest Health Food Store
3853 S. Campbell Ave.
Springfield, MO 65807
417-889-9595

Pierce City Farmers' Market
Saturdays 8 a.m.-Noon
June-October
Contact: Polly McCrillis
100 W. Commercial St. Suite A
Pierce City, MO 65723
mosweetP@gmail.com
417-669-5146

Price Cutters Bistro Market
401 S. Ave.
Springfield, MO 65806
417-869-1840
www.bistromarket.net

Porter's Supermarket
209 Cortney Ln.
Crane, MO 65633
417-723-5700

Republic Farmers' Market

Thursdays at 5 p.m.
May–October
Contact: Mike Wilson
984 West Dade 2
Jerico Springs, MO 64756
417-682-4052

Richards Supermarket

410 W. U.S. Hwy. 60
Mountain View, MO 65548
417-934-2401

Rockaway Beach Farmers' Market

Saturdays, 8:00 a.m.–2:00 p.m.
April–October
Contact: Tom Nowacki or Sue Riggs
    (alternate)
P.O. Box 463
Rockaway Beach, MO 65740
thomass_n@yahoo.com
beachhousecafe@centurytel.net
417-546-2744

Seymour Farmers' Market

Saturdays, 8:00 a.m.–sellout
mid–May–October
Contact: Dorothy King
828 W. Thoroughfare St.
Seymour, MO 65746
417-935-2478

Shetler's Discount Grocery

200 Industrial Park
Cabool, MO 65689-9316
866-903-4193
shetlersdiscount@gmail.com

Southwest Farmers' Market

Wednesday evenings, 3:00–7:00 p.m. and
    Saturday mornings, 8:30 a.m.–12:30 p.m.
Contact: Ray Hackett
25 Arrowhead Trl.
Buffalo, MO 65622
KanHackitRR@aol.com
417-759-2483

Stockton Farmers' Market and Artisan Fair

Saturdays, 9:00 a.m.–Noon
year-round
Contact: Nikki Simmons Zitting
18150 E. 752nd Rd.
Humansville, MO 65674
stocktonmarket@nikkisimmons.com
417-276-3730

Strafford Route 66 Farmers' Market

Saturdays 8:30 a.m.–Noon
July–September
P.O. Box 21
Strafford, MO 65757
417-880-1235

Taste of Missouri

9308 Hwy. 76
Branson West, MO 65737
417-942-3243
tasteofmissouri@atasteofmissouri.com

Tenth St. Community Farmers' Market

Wednesdays 3:00–6:00 p.m.; Saturdays
    8:00 a.m.–1:00 p.m.
mid–April–late November
Contact: Janet Dermott
801 E. 12th St.
Lamar, MO 64759
417-682-3579

Webb City Farmers' Market

Tuesdays and Fridays, 11:00 a.m.-3:00
   p.m., May-October
Saturdays, 9:00 a.m.-Noon, June-
   September
11:00 a.m.-2:00 p.m., First and Third
   Fridays in November-April
Contact: Eileen Nichols
One South Main St.
Webb City, MO 64870
eileennichols@sbcglobal.net
www.localharvest.org/farmers-markets/
   M3615
417-483-8139

Well-Fed Neighbor

1925 E. Bennett
Springfield, MO 65804
417-799-3305
ruellchappell@gmail.com

Wilson's Creek Farmers' Market

Friday evening, 4:30 p.m.-sellout
May 1-October 30
Contact: Shannon McKaig-Buffington
5434 S. Tower Dr.
Battlefield, MO 65619
shannon@jabuffington.com
417-881-4138

Woody's Market in Highlandville

3208 W. State Hwy O
Highlandville, MO 65669
417-443-0275
Sarah@WoodysRocks.com
www.WoodysRocks.com

CSAs

Homegrown Food

601 S. Pickwick
Springfield, MO 65804
417-868-7004
www.homegrownfoodstore.com

Millsap Farms

6593 N. Emu Ln.
Springfield, MO 65803
Curtis 417-839-0847;
Sarah 417-773-1989
millsapfarms.wordpress.com
cmillsap1@yahoo.com

Seasons Harvest Eco-Farm

315 Diamond View
Sparta, MO 65753
417-634-5414
www.seasonsharvestecofarm.com

Restaurants

Big Momma's Coffee Bar

217 E. Commercial St.
Springfield, MO 65803
417-865-9911
www.bigmommascoffee.com

Candlestick Inn

127 Taney St.
Branson, MO 65616
417-334-3633

Chateau on the Lake

415 N. State Hwy. 265
Branson, MO 65616
888-333-5253

Common Ground Café
100 W. Hwy. 54
Weableau, MO 65774
417-428-0248
145 Main St.
Warsaw, MO 65355
660-438-2581

Farmers' Gastro Pub
431 S. Jefferson Ave.

Springfield, MO 65806
417-864-6994
www.farmersgastropub.com

Mudhouse/MudLounge
323 South Ave.
Springfield, MO 65806
417-832-1720
www.mudhousecoffee.com

Southeast Region

Stores and Markets

Arcadia Valley Farmers' Market
Saturdays 7:00 a.m.-Noon or sellout
June-October
Contact: Tony Harbison
P.O. Box 385
Ironton, MO 63650
573-546-3877

Begg's BerryWorld
190 County Highway 332
Benton, MO 63736-9131
573-545-3881

Bloomfield Farmers' Market
Thursdays, 4:00-6:00 p.m.
May-October
Contact: Lara Thorn
16383 State Hwy. AC
Bloomfield, MO 63825
cotton@ldd.net
573-568-3507

Bollinger County Farmers' Market
Saturdays, 8:00 a.m.-Noon
April-October
Contact: Barb Bailey
Route 4 Box 2925
Marble Hill, MO 63764
kntgbarb@macdialup.com
573-238-2143

Butler County Farmers' Market
Tuesday 1:00-7:00 p.m.
Saturday 8:00 a.m.-2:00 p.m. or until
    sold out
May-October
Contact: Carol Childress
3257 S. Westwood Blvd.
Poplar Bluff, MO 63901
www.sustainablecommunitiesozarks.org
573-712-5728

Cabool Farmers' Market
Gateway Park, Cedar and Main St.
Cabool, MO 65689
caboolfarmersmarket.wordpress.com

Cape Farmers' Market

Thursdays, 2:30-6:30 p.m.
May-October
Contact: Marilyn or Gene Peters
2707 Flora Hills
Cape Girardeau, MO 63701
mpeters_2001@yahoo.com
573-334-7676 or 573-579-0166

Cape Alternative Farmers' Market

Wednesdays, 8:00 a.m.-Noon
April-October
Contact: Octavia Scharenborg
187 Bighorn Ln.
Cape Girardeau, MO 63701
showmefreshfarm@yahoo.com
showmefreshfarm@sbcglobal.net
573-334-0287

Downtown Sikeston Farmers' Market

Saturdays, 8:00 a.m.-sellout
May-October
Contact: Kathy Medley
105 East Center
Sikeston, MO 63801
kmedley@sikeston.org
573-481-9967

Family Friendly Farm Store

834 State Hwy. V
Cape Girardeau, MO 63701
573-335-1622
www.familyfriendlyfarm.com/Store.html

Fruitland American Meats and Gourmet Butcher Shop

3006 State Hwy. FF
Jackson, MO 63755-7138
573-243-3107

Jackson Farmers' Market

Tuesdays 5:00-7:00 p.m.
May-September
Contact: Lance Green
101 Court St.
Jackson, MO 63755
info@jacksonfarmersmarket.org
www.jacksonfarmersmarket.org
573-866-2204

Jones Heritage Farm

5739 State Hwy. W
Jackson, MO 63755
573.332.PIGS (7447)
www.jonesheritagefarms.com

Kennett Community Farmers' Market

Saturdays from 7:00 a.m.-1:00 p.m.
May 7-October 22
Contact: Sara Graves
1601 1st St.
Kennett, MO 72454
sara@downtownkennett.org
573-888-7496

Mace's Supermarket

200 N. Franklin St.
Cuba, MO 65453
573-885-6223

Madison County Farmers' & Producers Saturday Market

Saturdays, 7:30 a.m.-1:30 p.m.
May-October
Contact: Donna Kranjec
320 N. Mine LaMotte
Fredericktown, MO 63645
madcofarmsupply@bigrivertel.net
573-783-5526

Madison County Farmers' Market

Open Thursdays 4:00-6:30 p.m.
May-October
Contact: Karen Yates
137 W Main
Fredericktown, MO 63645
Madisoncountyfarmersmarkets@yahoo.
    com
573-521-8691

Missouri Farmers' Market

Daily
June-late November
Contact: John Hutchinson
P.O. Box 1112
Caruthersville, MO 63830
573-333-0788

Mountain View Farmers' Market

Saturdays, 7:00 a.m.-Noon;
April-October
Contact: Earline Granier
HCR 3 Box 165B
Birch Tree, MO 65438
417-764-3724

Natural Health Organic Foods

135 S. Broadview St.
Cape Girardeau, MO 63703
573-339-0054
www.naturalhealthcape.com

Perryville Rozier's Food Center

217 N. Main St.
Perryville, MO 63775
573-547-6523
www.roziersgrocery.com

Pioneer Orchard's Market

2008 West Jackson Blvd.
Jackson, MO 63755
573-243-8476

Ripley County Farmers' Market

Saturday 8:00 a.m.-Noon
May-October
Contact: Tasha Miller
117 State St.
Doniphan, MO 63935
tasha@freshfarmcsa.com
www.freshfarmcsa.com
573-351-8988

Salem Farmers' Markets

200 S. Main St.
Salem, MO 65560
salemfarmersmarket.blogspot.com

Sikeston Downtown Farmers' Market

American Legion Park
E. Malone Ave. and N. New Madrid St.
Sikeston, MO 63801
573-481-9967

West Plains Farmers' Market

Wednesdays, 11:30 a.m.-4:00 p.m.;
    Saturdays, 7:00 a.m.-Noon
April-November
Contact: Laura Esterle
711 Washington Ave.
West Plains, MO 65775
dragon143@centurytel.net
417-293-8306

Willow Springs Farmers' Market
Wednesdays and Saturdays, 7:30-11:00 a.m.
June-October
Contact: Elizabeth Boyle, Marguerite Wehmer
2484 County Road 5430
Willow Springs, MO 65793
417-469-2454 or 417-469-3254

CSAs
Laughing Stalk Farmstead
1521 County Rd. 649
Cape Girardeau, MO 63701
573-576-0730
laughingstalkfarmstead@gmail.com
laughingstalkfarmstead.blogspot.com

Restaurants
Brick House Grill
1 S. Main
Salem, MO 65560
573-729-8500

Calix Coffee
818 Broadway St.
Cape Girardeau, MO 63701
573-803-1717
calixcoffee.com

Celebrations
615 Bellevue St.
Cape Girardeau, MO 63701
573-334-8330
www.celebrations-restaurant.com

BUYING CLUBS

In a typical buying club, farmers consolidate orders from a number of customers and deliver them to a central location, typically a customer's home. If you want to join a buying club in your area, contact the appropriate people below.

American Grassfed Beef (HC4 Box 253, Doniphan, MO 63935, 573-996-3716 or 866-255-5002, www.americangrassfedbeef.com) has a Monthly Buying Club that will ship orders to you automatically on a monthly basis. Buy eleven monthly orders and they will ship your order for free in the twelfth month.

Angel Acres Farm, LLC (1356 Hwy. D, Bland, MO 65014, 888-611-2167, sales@gallowaybeef.com, www.gallowaybeef.com). To join a buying club, contact Karen Mathis at 314-954-3017 for delivery dates and places.

Bechard Family Farm (13700 Athens Rd., Conway, MO 65632, 417-589-4152, www.bechardfarm.com; raw milk, yogurt, and cream, grass-fed and finished beef and lamb, pasture-raised chicken and turkeys, and pasture-raised eggs) offers pickups in Springfield, Missouri, on scheduled dates.

Greenwood Farms makes weekly deliveries to St. Louis and Rolla; visit their website for details: www.greenwoodfarms.com. They also sell some of their products through Fair Shares CSA in St. Louis. Visit the Fair Share website for contact information: www.fairshares.org.

Prairie Ridge Farms (Iowa) delivers to Des Moines, Iowa, and Kirksville, Missouri, during the winter months and during the summer months they are at the farmers' markets. To join their buying club, call them to receive their order forms and buying club dates.

Afterword

People don't just eat to live; they live to eat. They connect with friends over lunch, entertain at dinner, make snacks for their children's preschools, show respect for someone's loss at a church potluck.

Although our state is rich in agriculture, advertisers and agribusiness have coerced us into taking food shortcuts and abandoning our traditions. *Missouri Harvest* has offered us a lifeline. Maddie Earnest and Liz Fathman have helped us understand our fallen food habits and shared many ways to help us change. They have told of Missouri's food varieties, how to cook them, where to find them, and who grows them. For those accustomed to cruising the aisles of supermarkets on autopilot, the preceding pages can be used as a travel guide, one to help us slow down, discover our state, and once again enjoy the flavors of the Earth.

I teach teachers. One summer, I walked with a group to a nearby garden to discuss ways of bringing children closer to nature. "Would you like to try some fresh peas?" I asked as I pinched off a pod. They stood silently around the beds.

Only one student accepted. I was surprised and asked about their reluctance. "Those peas have touched dirt," one student offered. My heart sank. Was it possible that grown people did not realize that ALL food comes from dirt?

Dirt is soil. Thomas Jefferson said, "While the farmer holds the title to the land, actually it belongs to all the people because civilization itself rests upon the soil." It wasn't too long ago that Americans ate farm-fresh food from local producers. The milk in May, for better or for worse, had the flavor of onions; strawberries, piled high on a farmer's truck parked in the city neighborhood, came and went with June. Watermelons in July and August quenched a summer's thirst. Late fall and winter featured stews and root crops. Food was a celebration of seasons, cycles, family, and friends.

Somewhere during my childhood, the late 1950s and 1960s, it all changed. I remember the fanfare of our first TV dinner. In order to eat the over-packaged, over-salted, over-cooked, no-longer-fresh food, we had to have TV trays, the aluminum folding "let's-not-sit-together" individual tables. This dining novelty had been thrust into our middle-class home as validation of success, second only to a family night out at McDonald's. With the tables erected, and the TV dinners piping hot from the oven (no microwaves yet), we zoned out to the theme song of *Leave It to Beaver*, watching June Cleaver cook ham and sweet potatoes, while we chewed on dried-out chicken and leathery green beans.

Through the years, fast-paced lives have pulled us from the family table and plunged us into a sea of convenience foods. Some of my students have never cooked soup from scratch, think meals come from boxes, and their choice of produce lies wilting, chopped, and under lights in a supermarket delicatessen. On-the-run, maybe working two jobs, they dine in their cars or at their desks. They have grown used to the lure of salt, fat, and sugar; they feed fast foods to their kids. Many are sick with colds and allergies. But what can individuals do to improve this situation?

Earnest and Fathman have taken us for a ride through the Missouri terrain, selling the benefits of the Farm-to-Table Movement along the way. They have shown that finding great food can be a treasure hunt for taste and adventure, and they have invited us to return to a healthy, sustainable system of food production, distribution, and consumption. *Missouri Harvest* has helped us identify our responsibility in this social movement and has gently beckoned us to take action.

I am always in search of ways to help my students discover the beauty and richness of our Place. I have found that food is at the hub of this quest. Our food comes from our geography . . . the fertile river valleys, the clear Ozark streams, the expanses of glacial soil. Our Place defines who we are and what we eat. Our love of food creates our community, our civilization. The Farm-to-Table Movement offers us a way to celebrate our Place together, but only if we accept the challenge.

This book is timely, and I hope you will turn to this resource again and again in your search for quality local food. Because the next time I offer my students fresh peas from the garden, I would like to think there will be many reaching hands.

Lori Diefenbacher, EdS
Coord. Teacher Education for Sustainability
Webster University, School of Education
St. Louis, Missouri

Index

A & B Homecoming Beef, 126
Aharon's Heirlooms, 54
Alger Family Farm, 133
Alpine Dairy, 164
Altai Meadows, 109
Angel Acres, 110
Anne's Acres, 67
Auglaize Berry Patch, 82
Autumn Olive Farms LLC, 134
Baetje Farms, 153
Barham Cattle Company, 127
Bear Creek Farms, 39
Bechard Family Farms, 134
Bee Thankful Honey Co., 171
Bellews Creek Farm, 27
Benedict Builders Farm, 128
Berger Bluff, 28
Berry King Farm, 82
Berry Patch (Bolivar), The, 83

Berry Patch (Cleveland), The, 76
Big Bison Meat Company, 119
Binder's Hilltop Apple and Berry Farm, 63
Black Bell Acres, 139
Blackberry Lane Gardens, 83
Blackwell Family Produce, 54
Blazerfarmz, 62
Blue Heron Orchard, 64
Bob Finck, 182
Boondocks Farm, 98
Bosancu Honey, 180
Bountiful Acres, 102
Bowood Farms, 102
Braker Berry Farm, 84
Brandywine Farms, 90
Breezy Hill Farm, 128
Buttonwood Farms, 110
Byrd's Pecans, 189
Byron Miller, 174
Camp Branch Bee Ranch, 185
Campbell's Fresh Market, 47
Capps Chestnut Orchard, 177
Cardoza Blueberry Farm, 90
Cedar Ridge Honey Bees LLC, 170
Centennial Farms, 70
Chert Hollow Farm, 21
Circle B Ranch, 135
City Seeds Urban Farm, 28
Claverach Farm, 29
Clover Hill, 98
Cooper's Honey, 186
Crooked Lane Farm, 111
D & R Farms, 129
Danjo Farms, 16
Davis Farm, 103
Deep Mud Farms, 22
Delp Blackberry Farm, 84
Donald and Kay Tilman, 188
Drumm Farm Garden, 40
Dry Dock Farm, 30
Duncan's Berry Farm, 76
Earth Dance Farms, 31
Echigo Farms, 48

Eckenfels Farm, 120
Elderberry Life, 68
Engelhart Farm, 32
ESP (Environmentally Sound Products of Missouri), 32
Evans' Produce, 7
Evening Shade Organics, 48
Fadler Farm, 178
Fahrmeier Bros. Produce, 40
Family Friendly Farm, 161
Farmer's Larder, The, 120
Farrar Out Farms, 140
Fassnight Creek Farms, 49
Femme Osage Apiaries, 181
Finer Things from the Land of Milk and Honey, 182
First Fruits Orchard, 77
Five Oaks Honey and Christmas Tree Farm, 186
G's Orchard, 85
Gerald Auffert, 170
Goatsbeard Farm, 152
Golden Rule Meats, 130
Goods from the Woods, 194
Green Dirt Farm, 154
Green Hills Harvest, 150
Greenhill Vineyard and Farm, 91
Green Thumb Farm, 190
Green Valley Farm, 16
Haines Farms, 41
Hammons, 190
Hart Apiaries, 72
Harvest Hills Farms LLC, 8
Harvest Pride Farms, 17
Healing Hearts Farm, The, 8
Heartland Creamery, 151
Heartland Organic World, 41
Heritage Valley Tree Farm, 71
Hinkebein Hills, 140
Hollenbeck Honey Farms LLC, 174
Honey Heaven Bee-stro Café, 192
Houston's Home Grown, 112
Huckleberry Hollow, 72
International Institute Global Farm Initiative, 33
Ivan's Fig Farm, 33
J & T Country Store, 22

Janzow Farms, 141
JJR Family Farm, 112
John & Linda's Fruit and Berry Farm, 78
Jones Heritage Farm & Market, 142
K.C. Buffalo, 130
Karbaumer Farm, 42
King Hill Farms, Inc., 172
L & R Farm, 9
L'Osage Caviar Company, Inc., 114
Ladd's Family Farm, 122
Laughing Stalk Farmstead, 55
Lazy L. Elk Ranch, 104
Lazy Ox Farm, 56
Leeside Llamas and Organically Grown Produce, 17
Legacy Beef, 113
Lesher Family Farms, 10
Liberty Blueberry Farms, 73
Liberty Farm, 34
Lorenae Dairy, 156
Lost Branch Blueberry Farm, 65
Lost Creek Farm, 10
Maranatha Farm, 57
Martin Rice, 57
Max & Lula Drydale, 11
McKaskle Family Farms, 56
Meramec Bison Farm, 142
Meyer Farms & Apiary, 26
Meyer Hog Farm, 122
Miller Pecan Farms, Inc., 173
Miller's Honey Farm, 187
Millsap Farms, 50
Missouri Best Beef Co-Op, 143
Missouri Grass-Fed Beef, 144
Missouri Highland Farm, 68
Missouri Northern Pecan Growers, 192
Mo' Honey, 195
MSF Farm, 99
Muddy Creek Produce, 11
Mystic Foods USA, 12
Nature's Bounty Farm, 34
Nature's Choice Biodynamic Farm, 42
Neidholdt Pecan Farm, 173
Neuner Farms (Westphalia Vineyards), 114

Oak Ridge Goat Dairy, 162
Old Homestead, The, 123
Old Ott Farms, 13
On the Wind, 58
Overboe Farm, 51
Ozark Forest Mushrooms, 58
Ozark Mountain Creamery, 156
Ozark Mountain Orchard, 86
Ozark Natural Beef/Ozark Natural Pork, 136
Parker Farms Natural Meats, 131
Patchwork Family Farms, 115
Peach Tree Farm, The, 69
Pecans & More, LLC, 193
Persimmon Hill Berry Farm, 86
Pick and Pick, 70
Pierpont Farms, 23
Pisciotta Farms, 131
Platte Prairie Farm, 43
Possibility Alliance Farm & Sanctuary, The, 18
Prairie Birthday Farm LLC, 78
Price Family Farms, 124
Primmer Pasture Pork, 104
R & C Beefalo, 144
Rain Crow Ranch American Grass Fed Beef, 145
Rainbow Trout and Game Ranch, Inc., 136
Rains Natural Meats, 100
Red Brick Farm, 23
Red Ridge Farms, 43
Reisner Ranch, 115
Riverbluff Farm, 163
River Bluff Produce, 13
Robins Apiaries, 183
Rockin H Ranch, 137
Rocky Top Berry Farm, 87
Roger's Blueberry, 88
Root Deep Urban Farm, 44
RSK Farms, 132
Rutherford Farms, 124
Salad Garden, The, 24
Sandhill Farm, 175
Sassafras Valley Farm, 116
Sayersbrook Bison Ranch, 146
Scenery Hill Farm, 92

Schmuckers Vegetables, 19
Schreiman Orchards, 79
Schweizer Orchard, 62
Seasons Harvest Eco-Farm, 51
Seven Gables Farm, 184
Share-Life Farms, 25
Shatto Milk Company, 155
Shepherd Farms, 176
Shepherds Crook Dairy, 163
Shine Hollow Ranch, 52
Sho Me Garlic, 14
ShroomHeads Organic Farm, 44
Sibley Orchards & Cider Mill, 80
Simpsons Family Farm, 92
Singing Prairie Farm, 105
Sinking Creek Dairy, 152
Spring Hill Dairy, 158
St. Isidore Farm, 36
Stanton Brothers Eggs, 117
Stinger Honey, 184
Stoney Acres, 159
Strawberry Lane Farm, 14
Strumpler Farms, 35
Sugar Creek Piedmontese, 105
Sunflower Savannah, 35
Sunrise Farm, 19
Sunrise Pastures Farm, 100
Sunshine Valley Farms Orchards, 88
T.L. Baumann, 74
Terra Bella Farms, 23
Terrell Creek Farm, 160
Terry Spence, 106
Thierbach Orchards & Berry Farm, 74
Thies Farm, 36
Thompson Bees & Berries, 89
Thompson Premium Beef, 107
Three Girls and a Tractor, 37
Timberland Westside Community Orchard, 80
Todd Geisert Farms, 121
Trace Creek Blues, 93
Tri-Pointe Farm, 125
Troque Farms, 132
Troutdale Farms, 138

Turkey Run Hostas, 20
Uncle Will's Blackberry Farm, 81
U.S. Wellness Meats, 108
U-Pick Berry Patch, 94
Urban Farm—Columbia Center for Urban Agriculture, 26
Urban Roots, 52
URBAVORE Urban Farm (a Project of BADSEED), 45
Veggie Chicks, The, 15
Vesterbrook Farms, 20
Walk-About-Acres, 179
Walnut Haven Farm, 160
Weiler Dairy, 151
Wells Family Farm, 101
West Orchards, 66
Weston Red Barn Farm, 81
Willow Mountain Mushrooms, 53
Wilsdorf Berry Patch, 66
Wind Ridge Farm, 75
Windy Hill Farm, 38
WitnessTree Land and Livestock Farm, 118
Wood Mood Farm, 46
YellowTree Farm, 38